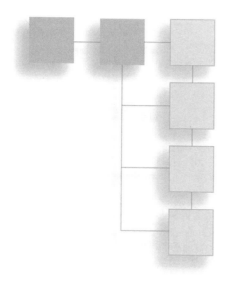

ARDUINO FOR TEENS

ROBERT W. PATTERSON
AND
KATHLEEN M. PATTERSON

Cengage Learning PTR

CENGAGE
Learning·

Professional • Technical • Reference

Australia • Brazil • Japan • Korea • Mexico • Singapore • Spain • United Kingdom • United States

CENGAGE
Learning®

Professional • Technical • Reference

Arduino for Teens
Robert W. Patterson and
Kathleen M. Patterson

Publisher and General Manager,
Cengage Learning PTR: Stacy L. Hiquet

Associate Director of Marketing:
Sarah Panella

Manager of Editorial Services:
Heather Talbot

Senior Marketing Manager:
Mark Hughes

Senior Acquisitions Editor: Emi Smith

Project Editor/Copy Editor:
Gill Editorial Services

Teen Reviewer:
Robert W. Patterson II

Interior Layout Tech: MPS Limited

Cover Designer: Luke Fletcher

Illustrator: Mike Tanamachi

Indexer: Kelly Talbot Editing Services

Proofreader: Gene Redding

For product information and technology assistance, contact us at
Cengage Learning Customer & Sales Support, 1-800-354-9706

For permission to use material from this text or product, submit all requests online at **cengage.com/permissions**

Further permissions questions can be emailed to
permissionrequest@cengage.com

Library of Congress Control Number: 2013948713

ISBN-13: 978-1-285-42089-9

ISBN-10: 1-285-42089-6

Cengage Learning PTR

20 Channel Center Street

Boston, MA 02210

USA

Cengage Learning is a leading provider of customized learning solutions with office locations around the globe, including Singapore, the United Kingdom, Australia, Mexico, Brazil, and Japan. Locate your local office at: **international.cengage.com/region**.

Cengage Learning products are represented in Canada by Nelson Education, Ltd.

For your lifelong learning solutions, visit **cengageptr.com**.

Visit our corporate website at **cengage.com**.

Printed in the United States of America
1 2 3 4 5 6 7 15 14 13

This book is dedicated to our various inspirations: the curious teen minds participating in the DELVE program, our son with his favorite letter "Y," and our former bosses who provided sufficient "free time" to explore the Arduino.

Acknowledgments

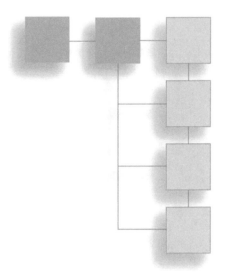

We'd like to acknowledge everyone who has made our Arduino experience a fun one:

- Ethan Brown of Firefly Fencing for providing information that led to our first Arduino design of extension lights interfacing with his scoring machines;

- Our fencing club members who endured our designs and experiments as unwitting testers;

- Arduino forum members who answered questions as the authors jumped into C++ programming;

- Our son who, with great patience, acted as teen reviewer as this book was written;

- Nick Gammon who supplied information on using an Arduino as a programmer for another Arduino;

- And, of course, our moms and dads, without whom we would not be here.

ABOUT THE AUTHORS

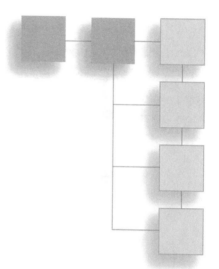

Robert W. Patterson is an electrical engineer who has been practicing hardware design and testing since the early 1980s. His first paid taste of engineering was as a co-op student testing high-speed Emitter Coupled Logic (ECL) with Digital Equipment Corporation (DEC). Later, he spent a summer with Teradyne Corporation writing "test vectors" for automated testing of Medium Scale Integration (MSI) and Large Scale Integration (LSI) logic devices.

He completed his Bachelor of Science in Electrical Engineering (BSEE) from Rensselaer Polytechnic Institute (RPI) while working a work-study job designing and building hardware control boxes for professors. Upon graduation, he designed and integrated high-speed memory cards and memory systems for Raytheon Company.

Along the way, there was also lots of dabbling in home projects—various digital clocks, analog guitar effects, and analog to digital converters and digital to analog converters as part of an audio delay effects box.

Since the summer of 2010, Robert has been active in the Arduino community, creating designs around Arduino cards, designing Arduino variations, and writing lots of code.

Kathy M. Patterson is an electrical engineer who has been practicing hardware and occasional software design since the mid-1980s. Her first paid taste of engineering was as a co-op student with Teradyne Corporation writing "checker" software.

Upon graduating from RPI with a BSEE she worked at Raytheon Company on various military communication systems. A later stint at Motorola Codex led her into data networking. Most recently, she worked as a high-level system engineer with ChipCom (later 3Com), duplicating and solving complex customer problems.

Along the way, Kathy earned a Master of Science in Electrical Engineering (MSEE) at Worcester Polytechnic Institute (WPI). Since the summer of 2010, Kathy has helped Robert work out hardware issues and software problems with Arduino-related designs.

Kathy did most of the writing for this book, while Robert supplied the drawings, most of the coding examples, and Arduino-related technical insights.

CONTENTS

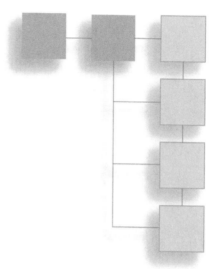

INTRODUCTION

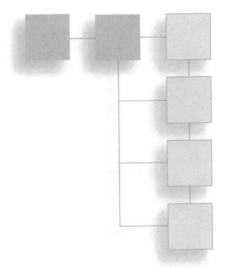

Welcome to Arduino! Arduino is a small, inexpensive microcontroller intended to be easy to use for artists, students, and other nontechnical people. Perhaps you fit into one or more of these categories.

This book introduces you to your Arduino and helps ease you into the world of micro-controllers. These little electronic brains are small enough and cheap enough to be found in many modern devices like alarm clocks, light displays, remote controls, art exhibits, drones, and robots!

You can use your Arduino to build or control these devices and more. You are limited only by imagination and motivation.

WHAT YOU'LL FIND IN THIS BOOK

You will find all the basics you need as a newcomer to buy and begin using an Arduino, including

- A survey of Arduino models
- Tools for using an Arduino and documenting your design
- Suggestions for translating your idea into a buildable project
- Microcontroller resource descriptions and what they're used for
- A discussion of other information sources
- Suggestions for extracting information from data sheets
- Directions and example circuits for connecting your Arduino to other devices

- Directions for using the IDE and downloading programs into your Arduino
- Code examples for controlling lights, motors, and other devices
- Debug guidelines and suggestions
- Suggestions for using forums for bragging and requests for help
- A discussion of shields
- Project suggestions

WHO THIS BOOK IS FOR

This book is for teens and young (or not so young) adults who wish to learn about microcontroller electronics in general and the Arduino in particular. It's meant for the intelligent beginner. Each chapter covers a topic that may or may not be new to you.

Although some programming or hardware experience is helpful, it's not required. As much as possible, tips and advice for the beginner are included. Proper names and jargon are presented, so you can look up more detail when you need it.

HOW THIS BOOK IS ORGANIZED

This book is organized into 14 mostly independent chapters. You can read them in any order you like or (temporarily) skip one that's not immediately relevant. When part of another chapter is needed first, we'll say so. Use the index when you need a specific piece of information.

Chapter 1 introduces the Arduino family. It describes the various Arduino models currently available and some of the advantages and drawbacks of each.

Chapter 2 discusses the tools you may want to have on hand when you get your first Arduino.

Chapter 3 talks about how to transform a good idea into a project you can build. It's a guide to thinking through what you would like to do in logical steps, starting with a general statement and then adding detail.

Chapter 4 provides a guided tour of your Arduino. The last section talks about the microcontroller chip in more detail and can wait until you need to understand its data sheet.

Chapter 5 discusses cookbooks, books, and other sources of information. Tips for making best use of these sources are included.

Chapter 6 is about reading data sheets. You need to do this when you move from reading cookbooks and copying designs to making your own.

Chapter 7 discusses Input/Output (I/O). It talks about how to connect your Arduino to the outside world without damaging it or anything else.

Chapter 8 covers the IDE and how to download your programs into your Arduino.

Chapter 9 talks about the programming techniques and provides example programs you can adapt.

Chapter 10 includes just enough C to start writing simple programs. Use this chapter with the examples from Chapter 9 if you are having difficulty getting started.

Chapter 11 talks about debugging your project and making it work.

Chapter 12 introduces forums and discusses how to select one and use it for showing off or requesting help.

Chapter 13 covers shields. Shields provide plug-in hardware that expands your Uno's capabilities and could make your project much simpler to build. Sometimes other Arduino models can use them, too.

Chapter 14 discusses some popular Arduino projects and their suitability as a first project. Your imagination is the only limit, but look here if you need a little inspiration to get started.

COMPANION WEBSITE DOWNLOADS

You may download the companion website files from www.cengageptr.com/downloads. It's where you'll find this book's example programs and other goodies.

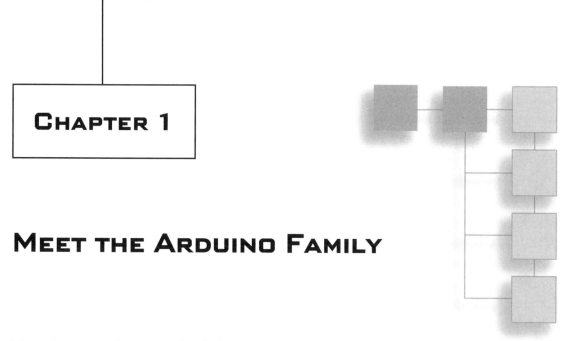

CHAPTER 1

MEET THE ARDUINO FAMILY

This chapter will answer the following questions:

- What is a microcontroller?
- What is an Arduino?
- What can you do with an Arduino?
- Why is Arduino so popular?
- What does open-source mean?
- What versions of the Arduino hardware are available?

MICROCONTROLLERS

An Arduino is a microcontroller, but what's a microcontroller? A *microcontroller* is an Integrated Circuit (IC), with supporting hardware, that executes instructions to monitor and control processes and physical devices. That was a lot of big words! You can think of the microcontroller as a small electronic brain.

Your electronic brain typically performs one specific job using switches, sensors, lights, motors, and other things. That one job may be a complex task such as driving a robot around the house without falling down the stairs or running over the cat. In other cases, the task may be really, really simple and boring, such as waiting for an animal to arrive at the bird feeder and then taking a picture of it.

Your microcontroller can't learn and must rely entirely on your instructions. It's very dedicated and will execute your instructions over and over and over until you stop it.

It isn't smart and will do what you tell it to, even when that's not really what you want.

Unlike a computer, a microcontroller typically controls a specific process or set of devices. Your microcontroller can run only one program at a time. A computer is general purpose and may run multiple programs at the same time. You could use your computer to do the same sorts of things as a microcontroller, but a microcontroller costs much less. You would probably be less heartbroken if you accidentally destroyed your microcontroller than if you destroyed your computer.

Microcontrollers are not new. Various IC manufacturers such as Motorola, Intel, and AMD have produced famous families of microcontrollers for decades. There is probably one inside your computer now. The innovation is selling some microcontroller families, such as the Arduino, to the hobbyist. To support the hobbyist, low-cost or free tools are available to work with these microcontrollers.

With so many microcontrollers available, why pick one over another? Consider the ease of use, cost, availability as circuit card (rather than individual components), available tools (including software development tools) and their cost, and the dedicated fan base. Some features such as clock speed and bus width, while important to engineers, won't make much difference to you, especially not at first.

Designed specifically for student use, the Arduino rates highly in all these important areas and is an excellent choice. In addition, the Arduino hardware, software programs, and software tools are open source. *Open source* means that all the information about the design and software is available via the Internet and free of charge.

Due to its low cost, ease of use, and open-source design, the Arduino has expanded to a wider audience. Its open-source nature in particular encourages users to share both their hardware and their software designs. You will find an active community of Arduino fans online.

The Need for Speed

Don't be fooled into thinking that a faster clock speed is always better. A slower clock speed draws less power and is still very fast by human standards. An eye blink takes about 400 milliseconds, while a single clock cycle at 8 megahertz takes 0.125 microseconds (.000125 milliseconds). That's 3,200,000 clock cycles per eye blink.

Many of the Arduino instructions execute in a single clock cycle, but some take more than one clock cycle. Sometimes the processor has to wait for other things, like data access to other ICs. For these reasons, clock rate doesn't translate directly to instruction rate.

Using a very conservative average of 10 clock cycles per instruction, there are 800,000 instructions per second, or about 320,000 instructions in the blink of an eye. Keep in mind that your average will depend on what your Arduino is doing and how efficient your program is.

Most likely, your Arduino will be controlling some physical device like an LED or motor. Your Arduino can turn an LED on and off much faster than you can blink. To you, the LED may seem to never light or be dim if the on-off cycle is repeated. Motors are even slower than a blink, so a motor turned on and off with sequential commands probably won't move your robot at all.

To make an LED visible or a motor move, some time must pass between when you turn it on and when you turn it off. Your Arduino could be doing other things while this time passes, or it could simply wait.

Unless you're doing some heavy-duty data processing calculations, your Arduino will probably spend most of its time doing nothing. That's normal and rarely a problem. Since most of the processor's time will be spent doing nothing, a faster processor isn't usually an advantage.

THE ARDUINO MICROCONTROLLER

A group of Italian engineers designed the Arduino to be an inexpensive, easy-to-use microcontroller for student use. Their driving motivation was to make a device easy enough that nonengineers could use it while keeping the cost very low. Students who know nothing about circuit design should be able to take an Arduino out of the box, plug it into their computer, and make something with it.

Since the Arduino is a learning tool, the design team wanted an open-source license to encourage people to use and expand upon their ideas. They licensed the circuitry design under a Creative Commons Share-Alike license, which allows anyone to study, copy, modify, and sell circuit designs based upon their original design. The only conditions are that they credit the Arduino team and release their designs under the same license.

The name Arduino is reserved for official boards. The sale of official boards is approved by and contributes to the support of the Arduino team. Sale of unofficial boards is permitted under the open-source license, but without the Arduino name.

A microcontroller circuit board is only half the picture. You need a way to program an Arduino, or nothing happens. An all-in-one programming tool, the Integrated Development Environment (IDE), provides a simplified way to program the Arduino. The IDE is also open source (under GNU General Public License, or GPL), as are the C/C++ libraries (under GNU Lesser General Public License, or LGPL). Chapter 8, "The IDE," is dedicated to the IDE.

THE ARDUINO FAMILY

The Arduino hardware is an open-source microcontroller design based around the Atmel ATMEGA processor family. The Arduino family of microcontrollers consists of a variety of official circuit cards and third-party devices. Only the official cards bear the Arduino name.

Since the design is open source, anyone—including you—can build and sell an Arduino as long as he names it something else. A staggering assortment of third-party devices has been created.

Like any family, the members of the Arduino family share some characteristics. They all have an Atmel processor, memory, Universal Serial Bus (USB) port, power regulator, Serial Peripheral Interface (SPI), and "headers" for connection to shields and other devices.

The family members also have their individual differences. The sizes of the boards, memory size, clock speeds, processor model, and other details vary. Some members have quirks, such as no power connector or USB port, sacrificed for compactness.

Regardless of which Arduino you select, it is programmed and used in more or less the same way using the IDE.

Making Sense of the Numbers

Comparisons of electronic devices seem to be all about the numbers. A number alone is not enough information to understand what you're buying. So before giving you a bunch to look at in the next section, let's look at what the numbers mean.

Memory Sizes

The Arduino memory is part of the processor. Any Arduino with one particular processor model will have the same memory sizes. There are three types of memory: SRAM, flash, and EEPROM. Static Random Access Memory (SRAM) is used for storing information such as variables while the program is executing. This information is lost when power is removed. Flash memory and Electrically Erasable Programmable Read Only Memory (EEPROM) are used for storing programs and information that needs to be kept even when power is removed.

You may be accustomed to memory sizes measured in megabytes or gigabytes, especially with your computer. These memory sizes, measured in kilobytes, may seem very small. Keep in mind that much of your computer memory is consumed by the operating system. The Arduino is not burdened by an operating system and uses the memory differently. This memory is sufficient for many applications.

Menu-driven programs may need additional flash memory to store the menu lines to be displayed. Data-processing–intensive programs may need additional SRAM for variable storage. If the onboard memory is inadequate, you can add memory external to the processor via a shield.

Shields are plug-in, stackable expansion modules. In addition to memory shields, you'll find motor drivers, GPS receivers, display drivers, serial interfaces, and many other shields. When you need a bit of hardware, there's probably a shield for that. Shields are covered in more detail in Chapter 13, "Expanding Your Horizons with Shields."

Memory on a shield will have slower access times than on-chip memory and consume Input/Output (I/O) pins. When you're certain that you'll need larger memory sizes, select an Arduino family member that has larger onboard memory.

Input/Output Pins

Much of the Arduino microcontroller's functionality is built in to the processor chip. The downside to this highly integrated approach is that the number of I/O pins is limited by the package of the chip. The number of pins varies depending on the processor model and its package.

Although the number of I/O pins is limited, the number of pins is not the limit of how many things you can monitor or control. While the simplest method is to connect one input or output signal to a single pin, this is not the only option. You can add a MUX (multiplexer) or a DEMUX (demultiplexer) to control or monitor many lines with only a few I/O pins. Yes, there's a shield for that.

Is it an input or an output? You must tell the Arduino how you are using each pin. The Arduino is very flexible, but there are limits. Digital pins can be inputs or outputs, but not both at the same time. Analog pins are only inputs but can be used as digital pins and then are inputs or outputs. Output analog levels can be generated using a Digital-to-Analog Converter (DAC) connected to digital pins.

A few, a specific few, of the digital pins can be used for Pulse Width Modulation (PWM). PWM is particularly useful for DC motor control, since it allows the speed of rotation to be controlled without the loss of torque (turning power). Analog waveforms, such as sine waves or triangle waves, can be generated from PWM signals and a bit of circuitry.

I/O of the Arduino is complicated enough that Chapter 7, "Input and Output," is dedicated to the topic.

Pulse Width Modulation (PWM)

Pulse Width Modulation sounds more complicated than it is. Modulation means changing something. That wasn't too bad. Now, what are we changing? From the name, we are changing the "pulse width." So far, that's not really helpful.

First, imagine a square wave signal. A square wave signal has a length of time high followed by a length of time low. This is one cycle. Now, if we change the length of time the signal is high to be longer and shorten the time the signal is low by the same amount, we have changed the width of the pulse, but not the cycle time.

Changing the amount of time the signal is high to be longer or shorter while keeping the cycle time the same is all there is to it. Figure 1.1 shows a pulse width modulated square wave. (If we change the cycle time instead, that's frequency modulation.)

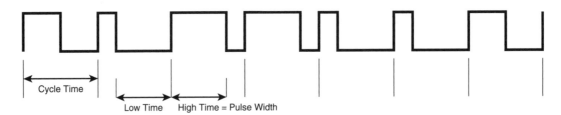

Figure 1.1
PWM.
© 2014 Cengage Learning®

Serial Interfaces

Serial interfaces allow the transfer of information one bit at a time, minimizing the number of wires and pins required. USB, Ethernet, Bluetooth, and Musical Instrument Digital Interface (MIDI) are all serial interfaces. Less familiarly, SPI, 2-wire interface (aka I2C), and In-Circuit System Programming (ICSP) are also serial interfaces.

Like all interfaces, data must be buffered and synchronized between the communicating devices, or data errors result. A special-purpose device called a Universal Asynchronous Receiver Transmitter (UART) performs this function. The UART also handles parallel-to-serial and serial-to-parallel conversion.

All Arduino boards have at least one UART built in. This UART is usually used for downloading programs, but you can reassign it for other purposes. If possible, reserve the hardware UART pins for program download to avoid download initialization issues.

As an alternative, regular I/O pins and some software can provide the UART functions. A software UART operates at a slightly slower rate and uses a bit more processor time.

SPI and I2C bus interfaces are provided in the Arduino design. These buses are used by the shields for control. They are available for other uses but require an understanding of how buses work.

FAMILY PORTRAITS

In this section, we'll look at some family photos. Here is a selection of some of the more popular official Arduino circuit boards, but note that new boards are being developed all the time, so there will be others by the time you read this. You can find the current product collection online at www.arduino.cc under the Products tab. Click on an image for more detail.

Official Arduino Products

There are more than a dozen officially recognized Arduino boards in the family. Included in this category are boards manufactured by SmartProjects for Arduino.

Also included are boards that are manufactured by other companies but tested for software compatibility and quality and licensed by Arduino. Arduino uses license fees for these boards to fund future development.

The Arduino Uno and the Arduino Mega 2560 are designed and built in Italy by SmartProjects. The LilyPad is designed and built by SparkFun, a U.S. company. Some versions of the Pro Mini are built by Arduino and others by SparkFun. The Nano is built by Gravitech, also a U.S. company.

Arduino Uno

The Uno, meaning *one* in Italian, is a good place to start. The Uno, shown in Figure 1.2, provides a reasonable number of I/O pins and enough memory for many applications. If you don't know what you are going to do with your Arduino, the Uno is a good choice. Table 1.1 summarizes some of the features of the Uno.

Figure 1.2
The Arduino Uno.
© 2014 Cengage Learning®

Table 1.1 Arduino Uno Feature Summary

Feature	Details
Microcontroller model	ATMega328P
Operating voltage	5 V
Digital I/O pins	14 (6 can be used as PWM outputs)
Analog Input pins	6 (may instead be used as digital I/O pins)
Flash memory	32 K
SRAM	2 K
EEPROM	1 K
Clock speed	16 MHZ
Connectors	3 headers for digital and analog, USB, power jack, ICSP header
Hardware UARTs	1
SPI	1
I2C	1

© 2014 Cengage Learning®

You can add features to the Uno by adding a shield. Shields provide circuitry to add functions, such as motor drivers, without the need to solder or to build custom circuitry. Shields are stackable so that you can use more than one at a time. Refer to Chapter 13 for more information on shields.

Arduino Mega 2560

The Mega 2560, shown in Figure 1.3, has much more memory than the Uno. It has 256 KB of flash memory and 8 KB of SRAM. The Mega 2560 may be more suitable for memory-intensive applications than the Uno.

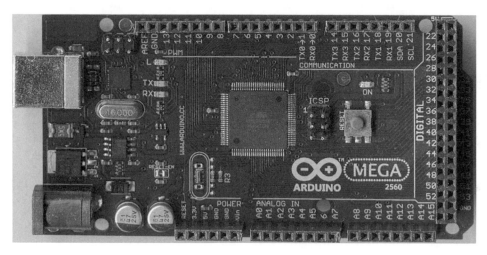

Figure 1.3
The Arduino Mega 2560.
© 2014 Cengage Learning®

The Mega 2560 provides more I/O pins than the Uno. It also has more serial ports. If you plan to connect your Arduino to the outside world through several serial ports, you might want to consider the Mega 2560.

Not all Uno shields will work with the Mega 2560. The SPI pins are typically incompatible due to their placement on the Mega 2560. Be sure that the shield is compatible before you try to use it.

Table 1.2 summarizes some of the features of the Mega 2560.

Table 1.2 Arduino Mega 2560 Feature Summary

Feature	Details
Microcontroller model	ATmega2560
Operating voltage	5 V
Digital I/O pins	54 (14 can be used as PWM outputs)
Analog input pins	16 (may instead be used as digital I/O pins)
Flash memory	256 K
SRAM	8 K
EEPROM	4 K
Clock speed	16 MHZ
Connectors	6 headers for digital and analog, USB, power jack, ICSP header
Hardware UARTs	4
SPI	1
I2C	1

© 2014 Cengage Learning®

Arduino LilyPad

The LilyPad was designed for the wearable processing market. It can be sewn into clothing and even washed. Components, such as switches and accelerometers, can be connected to the LilyPad via conductive thread to build more complex circuitry. Figure 1.4 shows the ProtoSnap version.

Figure 1.4
The Arduino LilyPad ProtoSnap.
© 2014 Cengage Learning®

Caution

Never wash a battery! Wait for textiles to be thoroughly dry before powering them up.

The LilyPad requires a USB-to-serial adapter board for program loading. During operation, a separate power supply is required. You only need one USB-to-serial adapter board. You need one power source for each LilyPad.

Although this model was designed to be worn, please don't wear this to an airport or train station! Wearable artwork has been mistaken for threatening devices. Save your artwork for a more appreciative audience.

Distributers are currently selling two versions of the LilyPad: one with the ATmega-168V and one with the ATmega328V. The "V" ending to the part number means that the processor can run at either 3.3 V or 5 V. Running with 3.3 volts makes the LilyPad especially suited to battery-powered operation.

The ATmega328V has the same details as the Uno, except that it can operate at 3.3 V or 5 V. The summary provided in Table 1.3 is specific to the version with the ATmega168V and can be considered the minimum provided.

Table 1.3 LilyPad Feature Summary

Feature	Details
Microcontroller model	ATmega168V or ATmega328V (see Uno)
Operating voltage	3 V or 5 V
Digital I/O pins	14 (6 can be used as PWM outputs)
Analog input pins	6 (may instead be used as digital I/O pins)
Flash memory	16 K
SRAM	1 K
EEPROM	512 bytes
Clock speed	8 MHZ
Connectors	USB-to-serial header
Hardware UARTs	1
SPI	1
I2C	1

© 2014 Cengage Learning®

Unlike the other types of Arduino circuit cards, the LilyPad does not have headers and cannot use shields.

Other Official Arduino Boards of Note

Two Arduino boards too cute to ignore are the Arduino Nano and the Arduino Pro Mini (see Figure 1.5). Both are very small and useful when space is at a premium. The Pro Mini does not provide a USB interface. You can use the Nano when you need a USB interface. Several versions are available, so be sure to check which processor model has been installed.

Figure 1.5
The Arduino Pro Mini.
© 2014 Cengage Learning®

Third-Party Arduino-Like Microcontrollers

The Arduino concept is open-source design. You, along with anyone else, can download schematics and copy the design. You can even build and sell designs copied from the Arduino. You should not, however, use the Arduino brand name.

Many Arduino-like designs have been modified slightly to add some specific feature or to support a particular application. Often these boards have names that are suggestive of their application or named after their designer. Since the designers vary widely, the designs vary widely, too. You might find that one of these designs suits your intended purpose perfectly.

Some of these unofficial boards are listed at http://arduino.cc/playground/Main/SimilarBoards. Even if you don't plan to buy one of these boards, browsing the list might give you some good ideas. You can also use your favorite search engine to find more Arduino clones.

Carefully read the information on a product you are interested in. Some are bare circuit cards without any components. Others are kits that require assembly, including soldering. Some are completely assembled and ready to use. Some are preprogrammed with a bootloader, while others are not. Know what you are getting before you order.

Search for a review of a particular device you are interested in. Reviews of many products appear on the web. Like anything your find on the web, consider the source of the information before you make your final decision.

Order your Arduino clone only from a reputable distributor. If your clone does not work, your distributor might be the only one who can help you.

Build Your Own

The schematics, design files, and tools are ready and waiting for you. The Arduino design is open source, and you can download all the files you need from www.arduino.cc.

Building your own Arduino encompasses a wide array of choices. You could build an Arduino on a solderless protoboard or as part of a custom circuit board design. You could assemble a ready-made kit or buy a bare board and components separately.

Before you undertake this option, investigate what you are getting yourself into. At a minimum, you need to know how to read schematics, data sheets, and part numbers. You need to be able to identify pin one on an IC and polarity of capacitors, diodes, and LEDs.

If you plan to build your own custom circuit card design, you need additional skills. You must use tools for schematic entry and mechanical layout. You need to make or have made a circuit card. You also need to order parts and assemble the board. Finally, you need to debug the design and fix any problems you find.

If you plan to use shields, be careful in your mechanical layout, or the shields might not fit.

Online Auctions

It may be tempting to buy the cheapest Arduino clone you can find from an online auction site. Be wary of counterfeit products stamped with the Arduino name but made in China or elsewhere. They might work, but they might not.

Table 1.4 summarizes the advantages and disadvantages of some of the various Arduino models available. If you know what you need, use it as a guide to select the most suitable version. If you don't know what you need, select the Uno because it is the most compatible with shields. Don't forget to check for new versions before making your purchase.

Table 1.4 Arduino Advantages and Disadvantages

Model	Advantages	Disadvantages
Uno	Low cost	Less memory
	Works with shields	Fewer I/O pins
	USB connection	1 UART
	Flexible power sourcing	
Mega 2560	More memory	More cost
	Works with some shields	Does not work with all shields
	USB connection	Larger physical size
	Flexible power sourcing	
	More I/O pins	
	4 UARTs	
LilyPad	Can be sewn together!	Requires tools to program and use
	Available sew-ins	Limited I/O
	Battery-powered operation	Can't use shields
		Components are pricey
Clones	Lowest cost	Buyer beware!
	Special-purpose built-ins	May require assembly
	Some work with shields	May require tools to program

© 2014 Cengage Learning®

KITS AND SUCH

Some official and unofficial Arduino boards are sold as part of a getting started or experimentation kit, with connecting wires and components. You might want to consider a kit if this is your first electronics project.

Read Chapter 2, "Tools of the Trade," and understand what tools you may want in a kit before ordering. Available kits vary wildly from one vender to the next, so shop around.

Another interesting option is a kit built onto a single PCB. The Arduino Mini, FTDI breakout board, LED, push button, buzzer, and light sensor are built as a single board so that it is already wired and ready to program. The pieces can be snapped apart later for use in other projects. A similar LilyPad version is also available and is shown in Figure 1.4. Since this idea is very attractive, I expect other vendors will copy the concept.

Which Arduino board should you buy? I would rather not give you the least useful answer by saying that it depends on what you want to do. I would recommend a kit with an official Arduino Uno purchased from a reputable dealer.

A kit should contain at least the following items. You could also create your own kit by simply buying these items.

- Arduino Uno (or official clone)
- USB cable
- Solderless protoboard (also called solderless breadboard)
- LEDs (more colors are more fun)
- Resistors (10 K ohm, 1 K ohm, and 220 ohm)
- Push button or toggle switch
- Buzzer or speaker
- Jumper wires

Arduino projects are addictive. Just one Arduino may not be enough. If you later decide that the Uno doesn't exactly fit your project, you can expand it with a shield or use it later in a different project. You might also want an Arduino separate from your project to experiment with while continuing to use your project.

Note

The Arduino by design is expandable with shields. Shields are plug-in, stackable boards that add functionality to the Arduino without the need to solder. Refer to Chapter 13 for more information on shields.

Before you go shopping for your Arduino, you might want to take a look at Chapter 2. Chapter 2 describes the tools of the trade, some of which you might also need to purchase.

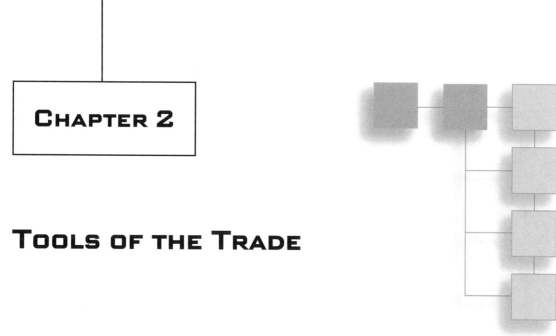

CHAPTER 2

TOOLS OF THE TRADE

This chapter will answer the following questions:

- What tools do you need to use an Arduino?
- What tools are available, and how do you use them?

If you are planning to skip this chapter, please read the sidebar, "Static Electricity: The Zap That Frustrates."

Static Electricity: The Zap That Frustrates

If you have ever walked across a carpet and zapped yourself on a doorknob, you have experienced static electricity. Dry air, synthetic clothing or carpeting, and motion combine to rub electrons off of their atoms. The charge keeps building until—zap—the electrons jump back home.

Electronic devices and Integrated Circuits (ICs) can be damaged or destroyed by Electro-Static Discharge (ESD)—the proper name for a static electricity zap. Some components, like Complementary Metal-Oxide-Semiconductor (CMOS) devices, are more delicate than others. Even though an assembled card, like an Uno, is less sensitive than a component, a static discharge can still damage it.

A zap too small for you to feel can damage your ICs. Worse, it may damage them in invisible ways that cause them to mysteriously stop working some time later.

Don't let this happen to you! Humidify the air, wear cotton clothing, and touch a large metal object, giving the electrons a new home, before touching your components.

The proper way to control static electricity requires a static mat, grounding wrist strap, ionized air generator, and connection to earth ground. Search for "ESD Control" for more information.

THE ABSOLUTE NECESSITIES

You absolutely must have a computer with an Internet connection to best use your Arduino. You will access the Integrated Development Environment (IDE), programming libraries, tutorials, video demonstrations, and online community of users through your computer via the Internet.

Here is a list of things you absolutely must have.

- Computer
- Internet
- Universal Serial Bus (USB) cable
- Nonconductive work surface
- USB adapter (for LilyPad and other models without a USB connector)

If you don't have a connection to the Internet in your home, your local library probably has a public network you can use. Although you can take a laptop computer to the library with you, it isn't necessary. You can download the IDE and programming libraries to a CD, DVD, or memory stick. You will probably need your librarian's help to do this for security reasons.

Install the IDE onto your computer at home from the CD. You don't need an Internet connection to run the IDE. Once installed, you will have access to the IDE's built-in libraries and tutorials without the need for an Internet connection.

The make and model of your computer doesn't matter so long as it's reasonably modern. Available versions of the IDE include Windows, Linux, and MAC. If you have any doubts about the suitability of your computer, check the current computer requirements for the IDE at www.arduino.cc under the Download tab. A USB cable and at least one USB port on your computer are the minimum.

Some versions of the Arduino, such as LilyPad, do not have a USB connector. For these, you also need a USB serial port adapter board. This board, shown in Figure 2.1, plugs onto pins on the Arduino and has a USB connector to attach it to your computer.

Figure 2.1
USB serial adapter.
© 2014 Cengage Learning®

You need a nonconductive work surface to place your Arduino on while working with it. A metal or conductive surface shorts the connections on the back side of the board, and that's never a good thing. Damage to you or your Arduino may result. Don't know if your surface is conductive? Use your multimeter to test it.

PAPER TOOLS

Tools are things that help you do something. Paper or its virtual equivalent might not at first seem to qualify as a tool. But consider the difficulty of beating that last level in your favorite game without looking up a cheat or walk-through. (Of course, you don't do that! It's an example.) If someone hadn't bothered to write it down, you wouldn't be able to do that. You wouldn't have the tool.

Data sheets, block diagrams, schematics, timing diagrams, and notebooks are the most common paper tools that engineers use. Each has its own special-purpose use. Since these paper tools were created with engineers in mind, they may seem a bit mysterious at first. Let's look at each of them in turn.

Data Sheets

Data sheets, aka specification sheets, provide all the information you need to use an IC or other component. They are typically available on the website of the device manufacturer and are referred to by the part number of the device. They vary in length depending on the complexity of the component. A complex device such as the Atmel microcontroller has a data sheet several hundred pages long. A simple device such as a resistor or a Light-Emitting Diode (LED) has a data sheet a few pages long.

Most IC manufacturers won't sell devices directly to you in reasonable quantities. You will need to go through a distributer such as Digi-Key, Newark, or Mouser Electronics. All of these distributers have device selection tools and include links to the manufacturer's data sheet.

The data sheet includes more precise technical information than you knew existed. You will probably not need all the information included in the data sheet, but it's there if you do. Refer to Chapter 6, "How to Read Specification Sheets," for help on extracting the little bit of data you need from the vast amounts available.

Of particular interest is packaging information. Look for through-hole packages. Dual In-line Package (DIP) devices are good for the hobbyist, since they can be inserted directly into solderless breadboards and easily soldered to solder-type breadboards. Beware: not all devices are available in through-hole packages.

Identification of pin 1 on a DIP is usually indicated by a dot or a notch in the pin 1 end of the device. The exact identification of pin 1 will be included in the data sheet. Make sure you can correctly find pin 1. If you plug in a DIP backward and power up your circuit, you will destroy the device.

Caution

A device plugged in backward gets very hot. Don't touch it! Remove the power supply and let it cool down.

Be careful with part numbers. For the information on the data sheet to match your device, make sure you match the part number exactly. Table 2.1 shows an example part number and what its pieces mean.

Table 2.1   The Anatomy of Part Number SN74ALS74AN

Code	Meaning
SN	Manufacturer code (Texas Instruments)
74	Series code (the first 74 indicates 7400 series)
ALS	Family code (Advanced Low-power Schottky)
74	Device identifier (Dual D-type Flip-Flop)
A	Revision (die revision; don't worry about this one)
N	Package (14-pin plastic 300 mil DIP)

© 2014 Cengage Learning®

TTL, CMOS, and ECL Logic

Small-Scale Integrated (SSI) circuits are commonly called *logic*. AND, NOR, and NAND gates, together with Flip-Flops, are the most common SSI devices. Medium-Scale Integrated (MSI) devices include adders, counters, shift-registers, and multiplexers (MUX).

The most common logic devices are available in a variety of technologies. Transistor-Transistor Logic (TTL), Emitter Coupled Logic (ECL), and Complementary Metal-Oxide-Semiconductor (CMOS) are just three of the technologies for sale. These technologies are generally not compatible with each other.

Each of these technologies has its own advantages and disadvantages. ECL is the fastest but consumes the most power. It isn't compatible with TTL or CMOS, and it requires a negative supply voltage. In general, ECL is a poor choice for the hobbyist (and many professionals).

Invented in the 1960s, TTL is the oldest technology and was once considered the standard logic family. Technology is constantly evolving, and now there are many families of TTL devices. Each family is a little different and in some way an improvement of the previous one. While new technologies are introduced regularly, older and less popular devices of a particular technology become obsolete and are discontinued.

These families, including standard TTL, are all currently in use, sometimes in the same circuit. Table 2.2 list some of the many TTL families. Although these devices are compatible, some care must be used when mixing them because propagation delay and hold times vary.

Table 2.2 Some of the TTL Families

Code	Meaning
H	High Speed
L	Low Power
LS	Low Power High Speed Schottky
ALS	Advanced Low Power Schottky

© 2014 Cengage Learning®

CMOS is faster than TTL but more static sensitive. CMOS draws very little power when signals aren't changing, but more power is drawn every time the signals switch state. Calculation of power draw is more complicated since it depends on how often your signals are changing.

CMOS is becoming the standard logic family. While some CMOS families are designed to be compatible with TTL and using TTL input (voltage) levels, others are not. You can use CMOS and TTL together, but you need to pay attention to interfacing them. Table 2.3 shows some of the CMOS logic families and whether you can use them with TTL.

Table 2.3 Some of the CMOS Families

Code	Meaning	TTL Compatible
AC	Advanced CMOS	No
ACT	Advanced CMOS with TTL-level input	Yes
HC	High Speed CMOS	No
HCT	High Speed CMOS with TTL-level input	Yes

© 2014 Cengage Learning®

You can operate CMOS devices with a wider power supply voltage range and with lower voltages than TTL devices. Lower voltages combined with lower power draw make CMOS ideal for battery powered circuits.

General information about the technology (TTL, ELC, and CMOS) is *not* included in the data sheet. Neither is general information about the families. In the old days when data sheets were printed as a book, this information was included in a section of the book. Now this information is in a separate reference document.

Unfortunately, there doesn't seem to be any standard name for a document with general information. Look on the manufacturer's website first for "logic" and then for "technology families" or "family characteristics" for general information. Including a family name, like ALS, in the search box will help. The information is available, so be persistent in hunting it down. Call or email technical support. They're paid to help you.

Very Large Scale Integration (VLSI) chips like microprocessors and microcontrollers are built using CMOS technology. Using the part number for the microcontroller on the Arduino you have or ATmega328P, go ahead and look up the data sheet. (I'll wait.) Wow! It's more than 500 pages! Save an electronic copy and print only a page or two when you need to.

Chapter 6 covers reading a data sheet in detail.

Schematic Diagrams

Schematic diagrams represent an electrical circuit in picture format. Figure 2.2 shows a minimal Arduino design. The Atmel microcontroller, a complex device, is shown as a box with pin numbers and signal names. Signals are sometimes grouped by relationship rather than sequential pin numbers. Sometime they are shown numerically with no relationship. Simple components such as capacitors and resistors are shown with special symbols.

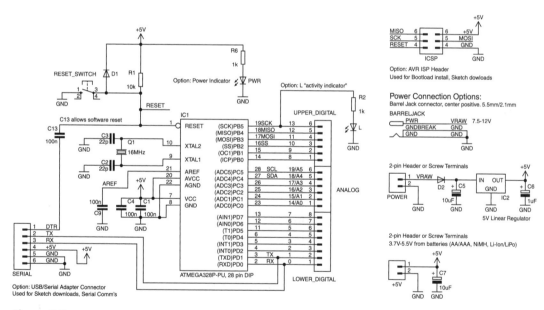

Figure 2.2
Minimal Arduino schematic.
© 2014 Cengage Learning®

The purpose of a schematic is to show where all the interdevice connections are made. Each individual wire and pin is represented. Every pin is shown, even when it remains unconnected (sometimes labeled N/C). For example, pins 2 and 4 of the reset switch are unused, but they're shown anyway.

Sometimes signals are connected by name with no line shown. This is common when signals cross page boundaries. In Figure 2.2, the ICSP connector has signals connected by name only.

Critical component values are shown; for example, C2 and C3 are 22 picofarad (aka 22 puff) capacitors. Less critical components, like the "L" and "PWR" LEDs, are shown by symbol only. LEDs are polarized—they have a positive and negative side—and the symbol shows that. Other details, like the color or exact part number, don't matter so much and are omitted.

The power connection is labeled +5V, although a note indicates that the actual range for power is 3.7 Volts to 5.5 Volts. Power is an input you must supply.

Using a simple box shape for the microcontroller hides the functionality of the device. Even when all the components are simple devices that are shown with understandable symbols instead of a box, it is not always apparent what the circuit actually does. Showing what the circuitry does is the job of the block diagram.

The schematic diagram is more than just a pretty picture. It's the document that starts the Printed Circuit Board (PCB) design process. Other tools use the data from the schematic to create the PCB layout and routing design.

Block Diagram

The block diagram shows functions and interconnection but not necessarily the number of wires. A group of related signals, like a data bus, may be represented by a single line. Its purpose is to explain what the sections of the circuit do and how they relate to each other. The amount of detail shown in a block diagram will vary, depending on what is being described.

Each block might be further broken down into smaller blocks to show additional detail. For example, a block labeled memory may be further broken down into three blocks that show three types of memory.

You will usually find a written description of the circuit's function with every block diagram, starting with an overview and working down to the details. It isn't necessary to understand every little detail, but reading the overview will give you an idea of what the designer intended.

Take a look at the Atmel microcontroller data sheet you saved previously. (You did save a copy, didn't you?) It shows a high-level block diagram near the beginning and a detailed block diagram for each major function in its own separate section.

Figure 2.3 shows a simplified block diagram for the ATmega328P. Drawn at the top and slightly larger than the rest of the blocks, the CPU is the star of the show. Note that multiple types of memory are shown as a single block. Some functions, like the watchdog timer, are omitted entirely.

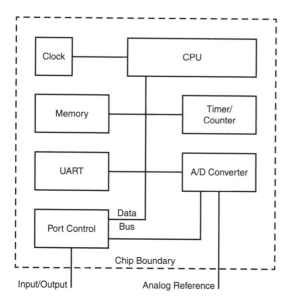

Figure 2.3
Simplified ATmega328P block diagram.
© 2014 Cengage Learning®

Bus connections are shown as a single line. Input/Output (I/O) connections are similarly grouped as a single line. But, from the block diagram you can easily see that all I/O must go through the port control function to reach the CPU.

Although the I/O port control block does not stand out as special, all your signals will come through this section. Everything you do will involve getting signals into and out of the microcontroller. Chapter 7, "Input and Output," will cover this critical function in more detail.

Timing Diagram

Timing diagrams show the timing relationship between signals. Although that seems obvious, there's a little more to it. Take a look at Figure 2.4. The little circuit shown at the top is labeled with four inputs on the left and one output on the right. Signals between gates are shown to clarify the timing relationships.

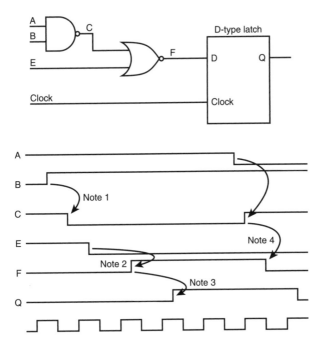

Notes:
1. Signal C will change sometime between the min and max propagation time for the NAND gate.
2. Signal F will change between min and max propagation time for the NOR gate after signal C changes.
3. Signal Q will change after signal F changes and after the rising edge of the clock signal.
4. Signal F will change after the NAND plus NOR prop. delay.

Figure 2.4
Timing diagram.
© 2014 Cengage Learning®

The propagation delay times in nanoseconds are shown in Table 2.4 for three types of NAND devices. Note that the delay L-H (low to high) is different from the delay H-L (high to low).

Table 2.4 NAND (7400) Gate Propagation Delay (ns)				
Family	**L-H Min**	**L-H Max**	**H-L Min**	**H-L Max**
ALS	3	11	2	8
AS	1	4.5	1	4
F	1.6	6	1	5.3

© 2014 Cengage Learning®

Reading the timing diagram from left to right, the change in signal C occurs one NAND gate propagation delay after the change in input signal B. Since signal C is going high to low, the change will occur anytime between 2 ns to 8 ns later for the ALS family. It could happen anytime in that range.

Similarly, the change in signal F caused by the change in input signal E occurs one NOR propagation delay later. NOR propagation delays are shown in Table 2.5. Note that the delay times within a particular family, like ALS, are similar.

Table 2.5 NOR (74) GateP Delay (ns)				
Family	L-H Min	L-H Max	H-L Min	H-L Max
ALS	1	12	1	10
AS	1	4.5	1	4.5
F	1.7	6.5	1	5.3

© 2014 Cengage Learning®

On the right side of Figure 2.4, the transition of signal F from high to low caused by input signal A will occur one NAND delay plus one NOR delay later. For each gate the signal goes through, the delay (and the time range the delay will fall within) increases.

The Flip-Flop has a different set of critical timing parameters. The signal presented at D must be stable for a setup time before the clock signal goes high to latch it. The signal has to remain stable for a hold time to guarantee the result at the output. Then the output signal Q will change after a propagation delay.

What happens if the signal doesn't meet the setup or hold times? You can't predict the result, and the output could be high or low. If the signal remains stable, the next clock cycle will latch it.

All the critical timing parameters will be included in the data sheet. Often a timing diagram illustrates the parameters that might be labeled symbolically. The high to low propagation delay might be labeled with a lowercase T and subscripted uppercase PHL (t^{PHL}). A table then lists the minimum and maximum values.

Multiple families (like S, AS, and ALS) may be combined into a single data sheet. Some families' parameters change with power supply voltage. The tables can be confusing, so check the supply voltage you are using and the part number of your device against the heading for the table. You might want to print a page and use a highlighter to mark your device or record the information in a notebook.

Once these devices are put together as a circuit, it is up to you to verify that the timing will work. Even if you don't care how long a signal takes to arrive at its destination, you probably don't want it to change multiple times unintentionally.

Inputs to the microcontroller on the Arduino are latched and synchronized with the microcontroller clock. Outputs are (obviously) synchronized with the clock. Refer to Chapter 7 for more details.

Notebook

We can't overemphasize the value of writing things down. Write down anything you don't want to forget. Maybe you can remember now, but will you remember next month which one of the 10 things you tried that finally worked? Do you really want to try them all again?

Perhaps you have a great memory. There are still reasons to write things down. Maybe you will invent something that will make you fabulously wealthy. Writing things down in a notebook will help document your invention. If there is a dispute with another inventor, at least you will have a written record you can use to prove you thought of it first. Don't forget to record the date (including year) along with your notes.

Sometimes a picture is the best answer, and it's hard to type a picture. Remember that this is a tool for you. Use whatever you want to record your information. Crayons or iPad? It doesn't matter as long as it does the job.

Useful Tools

In addition to the paperwork and absolute necessities, there are a variety of tools that will make things easier. You could probably get by without them, but their cost is reasonably modest. Some of these tools will make your project go much smoother, and many have uses beyond a simple electronics project.

Multimeter

A multimeter, as the name implies, measures an assortment of things, including DC voltage, AC voltage, and resistance. Fancier models measure additional things such as frequency and capacitance or have additional features such as diode test and range hold.

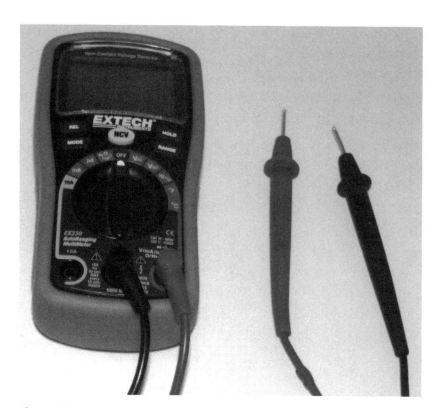

Figure 2.5
Multimeter.
© 2014 Cengage Learning®

A basic model that measures voltages and resistance is a good investment. The best answer to the question "Is it on?" is "I'll check." Always set your meter to measure voltage before trying to measure with it. Don't attach it first and then turn it on, or costly meter-destroying results may follow. Don't do this intentionally, or I'll tell your mother!

Caution

To avoid damage to your multimeter, turn it on and set it up for the measurement before connecting it.

A multimeter is a much faster way to find a resistor value than trying to read and decode the color code. Under some light conditions or if you are color blind, a multimeter may be essential. Is that band blue or violet? Is that one a reddish orange or an orangey-red?

Measuring the resistance across power and ground of an unpowered, newly proto-typed circuit might save you from powering up a design with your chips in back-ward. Buzzing out a circuit might help you find wiring mistakes.

There is no substitute for a multimeter for finding solder shorts and opens. Your meter can find things you can't see, like a solder short underneath a device.

A multimeter is a tool that's useful beyond electronics projects. Anytime you need to verify that the power has been removed, there's no better tool.

Protoboard and Jumpers

A solderless breadboard (aka protoboard) is handy when you're ready to move beyond making the built-in LED flash. The breadboard provides a quick and easy way to build up some temporary circuitry to play with. More permanent designs can be built and debugged with the protoboard before committing to soldered connections.

These breadboards vary in design and construction. Typically, ICs in DIP (Dual In-line Package) or similar form plug in directly, straddling the midline. Connections between the ICs and other devices are made with jumpers. Devices that can't plug into the breadboard directly, like motors, can have reasonably long wires soldered on that then plug in.

To make connections between components on the protoboard, you can use jumpers or solid-core wire. An assortment of colors will simplify the wiring and debug process. Observing some conventions will also help. For example, use black wire for ground connections and red wire for +5 Volts.

The internal wiring of a protoboard takes a bit of explanation. Figure 2.6 shows a protoboard. Each row is numbered and is divided into two halves. Each column is lettered. Within a row, holes in the columns labeled A through E are electrically connected to each other and are not connected to anything else. Holes in columns labeled F through J are similarly electrically connected to each other.

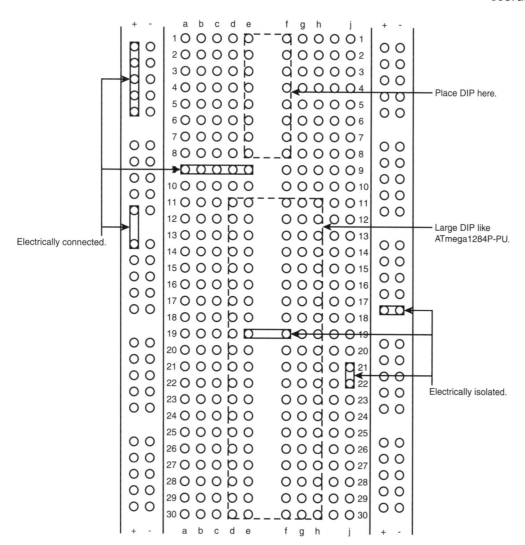

Figure 2.6
Solderless breadboard.
© 2014 Cengage Learning®

A typical DIP package straddles the gap between columns E and F, with the DIP leads plugging into columns E and F. Four more holes, in columns A through D, remain available for connection to other components via jumpers.

A wider DIP package must still straddle the gap between columns E and F. The leads will plug into other columns, leaving fewer holes for connections. If additional connections are required, a jumper to an unused row will provide four additional holes for connections.

Thin bus strips run the length of the breadboard, with the internal connections running lengthwise down the strip. These bus strips are intended to provide power and ground connections and are typically labeled + and –. Often, colored guidelines illustrate these connections.

It's up to you to make the actual connection to the power source, between the bus strips, and between the bus strips and the IC pins. You can plug component leads, such as a resistor, capacitor, and LED leads, directly into the protoboard.

Less-typical protoboards may have no bus strips or single bus strips. Bus strips might run across the board in rows rather than down it in columns. Some longer boards divide the bus strips into sections.

If you have any doubt or confusion about how the internal connections are made, you can quickly solve the mystery with your multimeter.

Figure 2.7 shows the minimal Arduino shown in the schematic in Figure 2.2 built on a solderless breadboard. The card mounted vertically in the right side of the picture is an FTDI breakout board.

Figure 2.7
Minimal Arduino built on protoboard.
© 2014 Cengage Learning®

Jumper wires with alligator clips may be useful for prototyping LilyPad circuitry. Alligator clips have some drawbacks. They tend to pop off what they are connected to. Unless they are equipped with protective boots, they tend to short together. A layer of craft foam on the underside of the LilyPad components might assist by providing the alligator clips something to bite on. Use your multimeter to make sure the craft foam is not conductive.

Power Adapter

At some point, you'll want to cut your Arduino loose from your computer. Two power options are an AC/DC power adaptor and batteries. If you're going mobile, you'll want batteries. If you're staying in one spot, you'll want an AC/DC adapter (aka power brick or wall wart). Refer to Chapter 7 for a discussion of battery-powered operation.

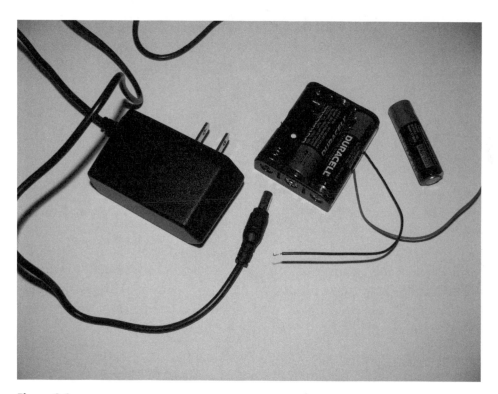

Figure 2.8
Power options.
© 2014 Cengage Learning®

Small Hand Tools

An assortment of hand tools will be useful both with electronics projects and generally around the house. Small pliers, cutters, wire strippers, screw drivers, and tweezers are the most helpful. You probably won't need a hammer very often.

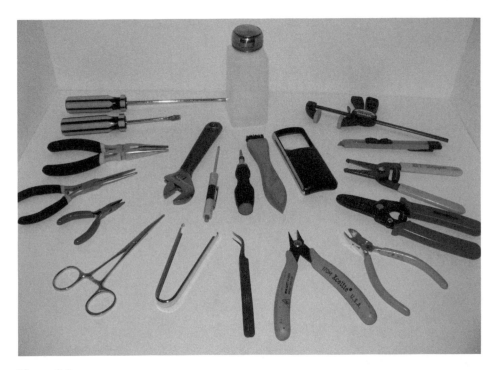

Figure 2.9
Hand tools.
© 2014 Cengage Learning®

An IC puller will assist in the removal of chips that are in sockets, hopefully without mangling the leads. Some practice is needed to do a clean job of IC removal, especially as the pin count increases. Slowly! Gently! Try to remove the IC level with the socket and without tipping it up on one end.

If you do damage the leads, you might be able to straighten them with small pliers. Try not to bend them around more than absolutely necessary. Even if you do this well, a repeat attempt will usually break the lead off and ruin the device. Save the damaged device to practice with, but keep it away from your working components.

OPTIONAL TOOLS

A variety of other tools are useful for special situations. You may or may not need some of these, depending on what you are building.

Soldering Tools

A roll of solder, a soldering iron, and a solder sucker (or solder wick) are the basic tools for soldering. Use a damp (not wet) sponge or brass shavings to clean excess solder and flux from a hot iron. Keep in mind that you are melting metal, so these things will be hot. You will need pliers or tweezers to hold hot parts.

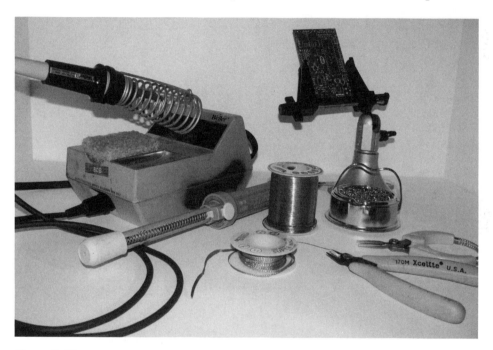

Figure 2.10
Soldering tools.
© 2014 Cengage Learning®

If you are new to soldering, you can find a variety of tutorial videos on the Internet. Be sure to heat the component lead and not the solder directly. A good solder connection starts with good mechanical contact and will be shiny when completed.

Wire Wrap Tools

Wire wrap is an alternative to soldered connections. Components are mounted in special sockets that have long pins. Connections are made by wrapping small gauge (30 AWG) wire around the pins with a special wire wrap tool.

Make power and ground connections first. Then build your circuit using the schematic as a guide. Highlight each connection on the schematic as you make it to avoid missing one. Double-check your work with a multimeter before populating your board with ICs. Don't forget to check for a short between power and ground.

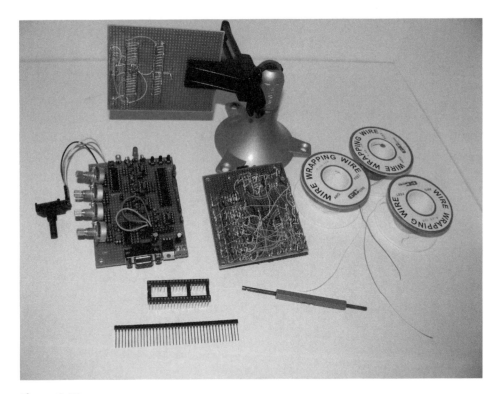

Figure 2.11
Wire wrap tools.
© 2014 Cengage Learning®

Oscilloscope

An oscilloscope (aka O-scope or scope) makes electronic waveforms visible. A scope can examine everything from static DC levels to small AC signals. It's especially useful for examining clock signals and modulated signals. A storage scope can capture one-time signals for detailed examination.

Figure 2.12
Analog oscilloscope.
© 2014 Cengage Learning®

An oscilloscope is on the pricy side, but you can rent it. Low-cost tools that attach to a computer can approximate the function of an oscilloscope for much less money. Search for USB oscilloscope.

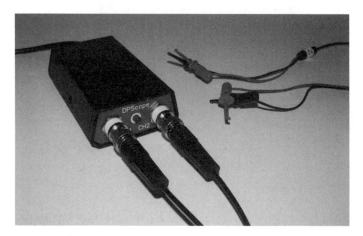

Figure 2.13
USB digital oscilloscope.
© 2014 Cengage Learning®

Surface Mounting Tools

Surface Mount Technology (SMT) provides components in very small packages. Resistors, capacitors, and LEDs are tiny. ICs come in a variety of SMT package styles. More complex devices are available in relatively small packages with many very thin leads. Mounting these devices with standard soldering tools is impossible.

Small Surface Mount Devices (SMDs) require specialized tools and handling. A special reflow solder, reflow oven (modified toaster oven), and hot-air rework station are the basic tools. Stencils and high-temperature tape are also useful.

Although not beyond the scope of a hobbyist, working with SMT devices requires practice and persistence. Through-hole packages are much easier to work with, especially for a beginner.

Figure 2.14
SMT tools.
© 2014 Cengage Learning®

You can mount SMT parts on adapter boards or breakout boards, which have through-hole pins. This allows you to use parts that are only available in SMT packages in the same way as through-hole parts. Figure 2.15 shows a variety of SMD to through-hole adapters.

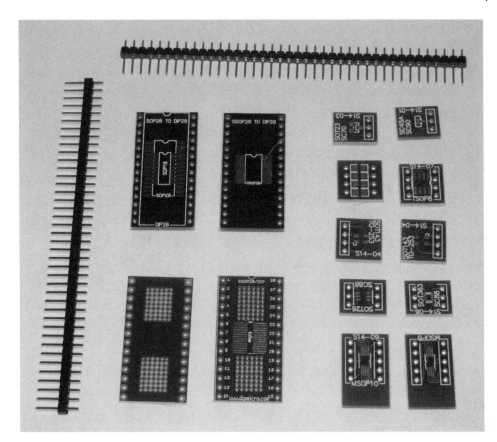

Figure 2.15
SMD to through-hole adapters.
© 2014 Cengage Learning®

LilyPad Tools

The LilyPad is a special case. Instead of solder, conductive thread is used to sew together circuits. For this you will need cloth, conductive thread, and sewing needles.

As the name implies, conductive thread is conductive. To separate connections, you need to maintain physical spacing between the threads, since the thread is not insulated. The thread doesn't conduct electricity as well as a wire, and the natural resistance may be important in some cases.

Some fabrics will conduct electricity. Test your fabric with a multimeter to make sure you won't have issues before you sew your circuit together. Wet fabrics also conduct electricity. Be careful not to short-circuit your battery by touching threads together or getting your project wet.

If you don't like the idea of sewing or are uncomfortable with exposed connections, you can use wire instead of conductive thread.

As mentioned in "The Absolute Necessities" section, you will also need a USB serial port adapter board. This board, shown in Figure 2.1, plugs onto pins on the Arduino and has a USB connector to attach it to your computer.

Other Tools

Logic analyzers and protocol analyzers are special-purpose tools for more complex circuits. Logic analyzers examine multiple signals and show their timing relationships. This tool is useful for parallel data buses. If you need to be sure your data bus is stable before the clock signal arrives, this is the tool you need.

Protocol analyzers examine and parse a serial data stream into meaningful messages while looking for errors. There are analyzers for every protocol, and you probably won't need one of these unless you are creating a serial messaging interface from scratch.

The Serial Monitor tool in the IDE is a form of protocol analyzer, allowing the Arduino to send serial messages via the USB interface and display them for you. This can be a handy debugging tool and is discussed more in Chapter 11, "Debugging."

Many other engineering tools exist, but they are probably not useful to the nonengineer.

Some other tools are completely optional but make working with an Arduino more enjoyable (see Table 2.6). Lights, a magnifier, a dedicated workbench with a nonconductive work surface, and a storage area are all nice things to have.

Table 2.6 Tools Checklist

Tool	Desirability	Use
Computer	Must have	Programming Arduino
Internet	Must have	Finding information and downloading tools
USB cable	Must have	Connecting Arduino to a computer
Nonmetal work surface	Must have	Avoiding short circuits and shocks
USB serial adapter	Variable	Required for connecting the LilyPad; optionally used for connecting other models

(continues)

Table 2.6 Tools Checklist (*continued*)

Tool	Desirability	Use
Multimeter	High	Measuring voltages, resistance, current
Protoboard	High	Debugging circuits before committing to solder
Jumper wires	High	Connecting prototype circuits on solderless breadboard. Select the alligator version for connecting prototype circuits using LilyPad components
Paper tools	High	Recording and retrieving vital information
AC power adapter	Nice	Powering up the circuit without computer attached
Oscilloscope	Nice	Converting waveforms to visible images; debugging
Pliers	Nice	Bending leads; holding hot components
IC puller	Nice	Removing ICs from protoboard without destroying leads
Wire cutters	Nice	Cutting wires and making them shorter
Screwdriver	Nice	Manipulating screws
Wire strippers	Nice	Stripping the insulation off wires
Soldering iron	Nice	Soldering
Solder sucker	Nice	Removing solder
Magnifier	Nice	Reading part numbers, checking solder connections
SMT hot air rework station	Optional	Removing/installing SMT ICs
SMT (toaster) oven	Optional	Reflowing solder
Logic analyzer	Optional	Examining timing relationships
Protocol analyzer	Optional	Debugging message-based protocols

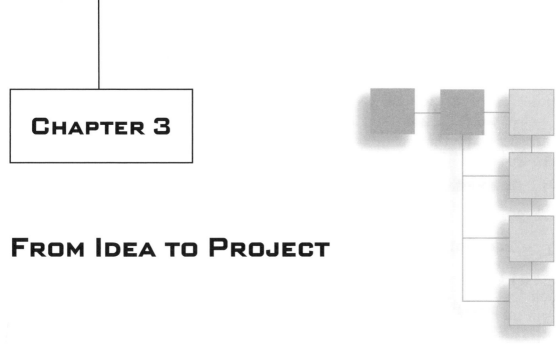

CHAPTER 3

FROM IDEA TO PROJECT

This chapter will answer the following questions:

- How do you make a good idea into a project?
- What do you do if you don't have an idea?
- Where do you start?
- What do you do if you're stuck?

TOP-DOWN OR BOTTOM-UP

Key to success for all but the simplest projects is organization. This chapter suggests a method for organization starting with a simple statement about what you would like to build and ending with physical pin assignments. This is not the only approach, but it's a good place to start, especially with a first project.

There are two main approaches to designing a project or system. You might start with the big picture and add detail as you go. This approach is called *top-down* and might feel more comfortable if you like to envision the finished project before getting caught up in the details.

The top-down approach is particularly useful for complex projects. Dividing the project into manageable chunks will keep you from feeling overwhelmed and allow you to work one simpler problem at a time.

Alternatively, you might start with fussy little details and expand them as you go. This approach is called *bottom-up* and might feel more comfortable if you like to tinker with little pieces before combining them into something bigger.

The bottom-up approach is particularly useful when you already have little pieces working and want to combine them into something more complicated.

It does not matter which approach you use. In practice, you will probably use some combination of the two. You could start at both ends and meet in the middle. If you get stuck on your project, try working from the other end for a while. Regardless of how you get there, in the end you will have a complete project.

The following sections present a top-down approach, if you read them in order. If you read from the last section to the first, the approach is bottom-up.

THE BIG PICTURE

What do you want to do, make, or prove? Don't get bogged down by the details at this point. Just think of a three- or four-word description: Make a Robot, Build a Theremin, Animate a Fountain, Build a Camera Trap, Draw Laser Patterns on the Ceiling.

Try to avoid being too vague. Make a Thing to Do Something is definitely too vague. If you type the description into a search engine, it should come up with at least an approximation of what you have in mind. If a search engine can't find it, you probably need a better description.

Conversely, being too specific might set you up for disappointment. Build a Scale Model Bellagio Fountain might be too specific. Build a Small-Scale Dancing Fountain might be better, since it allows some wiggle room. Certainly, use the famous fountains as inspiration, but make it your own, too.

At this point it might help to draw a picture* or pictures to help explain what you have in mind. The drawing does not have to be realistic or artistic. It is just a tool to help you capture your vision. Your vision of a robot might be a stationary arm to manipulate objects with a pincer-claw, or it might be a machine to roll into the kitchen to fetch a cold root beer. Your vision is uniquely your own.

It is not necessary for you to be completely original. You might want to clone a project from a book or a website for your first project. Your three-word description may be Build Project #2 (from a *Monstrous Mastermind* book—a fictitious name). If you are borrowing ideas from books or other projects, write down what they are and where they came from.

You might choose to keep your pictures private or share them. Sharing allows you to get good ideas from other people, but it also exposes you to criticism. Choose who you share with carefully.

---

*I have avoided the word "sketch" here because Arduino programs are called sketches.

Adding Detail

A picture by itself may not capture all you would like your project to be. Some concepts are just too complex or hard to draw. Now is the time to add some words or additional pictures to fill in detail. Write things down as you think of them.

Ask yourself questions. How will someone use this thing? Do you want the user to push buttons or turn dials to make things happen? Is it radio controlled? How many lights will it have? Does it have a speaker or a buzzer? Does it connect to the Internet?

Even if you are shy about your artwork, it might be helpful to describe your project to a friend. Your friend just might ask some thought-provoking questions. If you're asked a good question, write it down, even if you don't have an answer right now.

Describing your project to your pet might work, too. Just forming the description into words will help you collect your thoughts. Some things that look like a good idea on paper don't sound as good when you say them out loud. Other times they sound even better.

You might want to search the Internet or books for projects similar to your own idea. Be careful that you don't get sidetracked or confused about what you would like. Skip this step if it's more distraction than help. This project is your own and not (necessarily) a clone of something else.

Let the ideas bounce around in your brain until they settle down to a firm idea. Taking some time with this step can save you aggravation later. Sometimes adding a feature later really doesn't take much effort, but sometimes it requires you to nearly start over.

After you are reasonably certain of what you want, write it down. Even if you have jotted down notes as you were going along, write down what you have decided to make. Again, this is a tool for your own use. It does not need to win awards for great prose, nor is it cast in stone. You have my permission to change your mind as long as you write down what you finally decide.

Divide and Conquer

It's time to break your project idea into manageable chunks. The goal is to partition the project into pieces that you can deal with separately. It makes sense to separate an LCD display from a radio control and from a motor. Although each piece will eventually work together, the Arduino will be doing the coordination, and the pieces don't directly connect to each other.

Most Arduino projects have a group of unrelated pieces connecting directly to the Arduino and to nothing else. Although this is typical for Arduino projects, there are obviously exceptions. One exception might be a radio-controlled kill switch for a robot gone wild. The kill switch would control the power directly just in case the Arduino program didn't work as expected.

Some components can be directly connected to the Arduino, whereas other devices need some interface circuitry. You can determine later if you need interface circuitry or not. Right now, just capture all the main pieces by functional description.

Remember the block diagram from Chapter 2, "Tools of the Trade"? It might make sense to draw one for your project. Your diagram probably looks like Figure 3.1. (You can make a copy of Figure 3.1 rather than drawing your own if you prefer.)

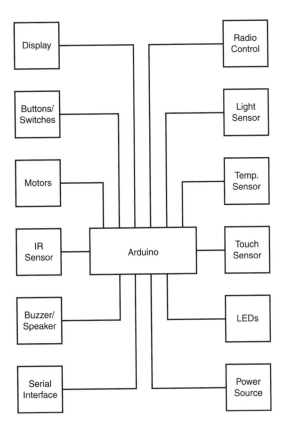

Figure 3.1
General-purpose block diagram.
© 2014 Cengage Learning®

Once the pieces are properly partitioned, you can work on each piece separately. You can follow the remaining steps in the design process, focusing your attention on one piece at a time as you go through them. Alternatively, you can follow the remaining steps in the design process all the way through for one piece and then continue on to the other pieces.

OF PARTS...

Regardless of the project, you are making a physical contraption. You need materials, supplies, and tools. Eventually, you must go shopping (or its virtual equivalent) for the things you don't already have.

Materials include things like motors, detectors, buttons, switches, lights, and displays, as well as resistors, capacitors, and Integrated Circuits (ICs). You might need a box or some sort of enclosure to mount your project in or material to build one with. You need stand-offs and screws to hold things together. You may need a power supply or a power cord.

You need supplies like wire, glue, electrical tape, and solder. You may need tools like protoboard, jumpers, pliers, cutters, and a soldering iron.

For a simple project, you might need only your Arduino and a Light-Emitting Diode (LED) or two. For a complex project, the list of ingredients is a lot longer.

For each section of your design, make a general list of what you need. It's okay if you don't know exactly what you need right now. You might put a generic description like "display" on your list for now. Try to be as specific as you can. A "4-line LCD display" or "7-segment display" is a better starting point in the search for parts.

After you have made a general list of materials for your project, you need to convert that to something more specific so that you can shop for it. If this is your first project, you may find that this step takes more time than you expected. It may be a bit confusing and even a little scary.

Even something as seemingly simple as a pushbutton switch comes in thousands of variations. Motors also come in a staggering diversity. One specific IC may be offered in six different package types. Who knew there were so many types of LEDs?

Don't panic. There are tools to help you find what you need. Distributors offer online device selection tools. Manufacturers publish specification sheets for every gadget they make, from nuts and bolts to aircraft. Most manufacturers also put out a device selection guide of some sort and application notes telling you how to use their devices. Your favorite search engine can help you find these tools.

Helpful Tool	What	Where
Selection Tool	Part search engine for all manufacturers	Website of distributor
Selection Tool	Part search engine for a single manufacturer	Website of manufacturer
Selection Guide	Device selection advice	Website of manufacturer
Spec. Sheet	Data or specification sheet	Website of manufacturer or link from distributor
Application Note	How to use instructions	Website of manufacturer

© 2014 Cengage Learning®

Unfortunately (for you), these tools were developed with an engineer in mind. Don't feel too bad. Every engineer started out just where you are now.

Each type of device has a special set of words used to describe them. Yes, I mean jargon. Most tools assume you already know the jargon for the devices. For example, switch selection guides use the terms "poles," "throws," and "normally open" without defining them anywhere.

Different manufacturers of the same type of device use the same words, and some are shared with related devices. For example, switches and relays use mostly the same jargon. Once you get comfortable with the jargon, it won't be so confusing.

Don't worry if you are feeling a little lost right now. Chapter 7, "Input and Output," shows examples of connecting various devices to the Arduino. Feel free to borrow them for your own purposes. You can find other examples on the Arduino playground and in cookbooks. Chapter 6, "How to Read Specification Sheets," offers examples on extracting information from data sheets.

Like most things, the first time going through the process is the worst. After you have done it a few times, you will have a small set of favorite devices that you will use often. Having extras of these favorite parts will make your next projects go much faster.

It certainly is possible to build anything you want from scratch, but sometimes you don't need to. There is a shield for nearly any function a beginning/intermediate user could need. Shields are designed specifically for the Uno and may (or may not) work with other models. They simply plug in to the Uno and can be stacked up, although not without limits. Sorry to say, but you will pay for this convenience. Shields are not the most economical way to go. Refer to Chapter 13, "Expanding Your Horizons with Shields."

Once it's time to go shopping, where do you go? While there are local retail distributers of electronic components, you can find a wider selection at national online distributors. Three well-known U.S. national distributors are Digi-Key Corporation, Mouser Electronics, and Newark. Use your favorite search engine to find "electronic component distributors." Smaller distributors are sometimes better for beginners; their smaller selection of basic items makes it easier to choose parts. Example are www.Dipmicro.com and www.taydaelectronics.com.

Distributors who carry electronic components usually sell a wide range of devices. You can probably shop for all of your component needs in one place to save on shipping costs.

...AND PINS

Now that you have all the parts or at least have them on order, it's time to think about connecting them to your Arduino. You need to wire your physical parts to the Arduino's physical pins.

Working on one piece of your design at a time, list the major electrical components by type. Give each piece a name, called a *reference designation* (ref des). Reference designations are used because they are quicker to write or say. (Although the term "reference designation" is a mouthful.)

Perhaps motor M1 controls the left wheel of a robot and motor M2 controls the right wheel. M1 is a lot faster to write than "the motor that controls the left wheel." The two circuits might be identical, differing only in ref des and Arduino pin numbers.

The table that follows shows typical reference abbreviations that engineers use. You can use anything meaningful to you, but using standard abbreviations allows you to share your design. These designations are also used on the schematic diagram.

Component	Reference Designation
Motor	M
Capacitor	C
Resistor	R
Variable resistor	VR (also known as a potentiometer)
Diode	D
LED	D (Light Emitting Diode; it's a special diode, but it's still a diode)
Integrated Circuit	U or IC

(continues)

(*continued*) Component	Reference Designation
Switch	SW
Button	SW (buttons are switches, too)
Inductor	L
Connector	J
Socket	X
Crystal	Q or X
Fuse	F
Transistor	T or Q

© 2014 Cengage Learning®

Any electrical device has the connections numbered (pin numbers) or named. Note the number of pins on your list. Every pin can then be referenced uniquely by the combination of ref des and pin number. For example, U10-1 means IC U10 pin 1.

Add a description next to the designation for major components. It doesn't help to give every component a short name if you can't remember what it means. If you have two or more identical components like motors, you don't want to get them confused later. When you get your parts, you can label the larger parts with a marker or stick-on label, using the ref des as a nickname.

Smaller components like 10 K ohm resistors have unique R numbers but are interchangeable. It doesn't matter which 10 K resistor you pick when you build the circuit. You obviously don't want to mix in other value resistors.

Different types of components need different types of connections. A motor might use a PWM (Pulse Width Modulation) output pin, while a button uses a digital input. Ground connections are usually made to a common pin and don't need a separate ground pin for each device.

Some ICs might take an 8-bit word. They need a group of pins and need to be selected from a single port. (Don't worry about what *port* means now; all will become clear in Chapter 7.)

Shields also need pins that can't be used for anything else. Some shields use a lot of pins, while others use only a few. This varies depending entirely on the shield you select. If you choose to use shields, you need to assign these pins first since they can't typically be changed without difficulty (usually requiring cutting, wiring, and soldering). Although physically stackable, not all shields are compatible electrically with each other. Chapter 13 covers using shields in more detail.

Input/Output (I/O) is such an important topic that Chapter 7 is dedicated to it. You can read that chapter now or later, but match your I/O needs to the Arduino pins. As long as they are the correct type, that's enough for now. If you don't have a straight-forward match, you might need to read the whole I/O chapter now.

Write down your I/O-to-pin mapping. Include reference designation, pin number, pin type (analog or digital), input or output, drive requirements, and anything special about the signal. Dog-ear the page in your notebook. When you are wiring your project or programming the Arduino, don't guess about pin numbers. Check them against your map.

If you have more than one Arduino type, be sure to note which one you are using with your pin map. The pins available vary with the specific model of Arduino you have.

Be aware that pins aren't generally used as both input and output while your Arduino is running. Although this is technically possible, it is not useful at beginner/inter-mediate levels. Refer to Chapter 7 for further details.

If you have been designing from the bottom up, pay careful attention to making sure you have not used the same pin for more than one purpose.

Top down or bottom up, ensure you have enough pins and, if possible, reserve the serial pins, 0 and 1, for programming (sketch downloads), and leave a couple as spares.

There are two related ways to capture your physical connections. A *wire list* is a list by signal name of all the places a signal goes by ref des and pin number. All parts, including 2-pin components, are listed by ref des and pin number. For a resistor, it doesn't matter which is pin 1 and which is pin 2. For a capacitor, it might make a big difference since some are polarized devices.

A schematic contains the same information in visual form with the connections drawn as lines. You don't need special tools to draw schematics. You can use a rectangle shape, pin number, and ref des instead of fancy symbols.

The block diagram can be the starting point for your schematic. Take your block diagram and add one line for each connection. Add the detail of the ref des and pin number at each end. Fill in the detail within each block, and you have a schematic.

Follow some confusion prevention conventions when drawing lines to show connections on your schematic. Show connections as a T-shape or a dot on 4-way intersections. Figure 3.2 provides examples.

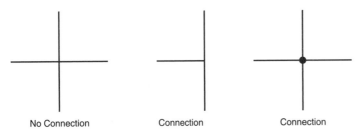

Figure 3.2
Schematic connections.
© 2014 Cengage Learning®

You're on a Budget

There are a number of ways you can supply power to your Arduino circuit. Low-power circuits (under 500 mA) may be powered via the USB port of your computer. Circuits with greater power needs, like those with motors, require an external (non-USB) power source. Your power source sets your power limit. Examine the label on your power supply for its voltage and current rating.

It's good practice to hold some power in reserve, especially since you are using Complementary Metal-Oxide-Semiconductor (CMOS) devices. (Yes, you are! The microprocessor chip is CMOS, and its power draw increases as signals switch.)

Regardless of the method you use, there is a limit. You need to add up the power requirements of your pieces and see if you are over your power budget. Power is an input and is covered in more detail in Chapter 7.

Didn't do the math? Check your supply voltage with your multimeter. If the level is lower than it should be, you may be over budget. On the other hand, you might have a short circuit. In any case, don't leave a circuit with an unexpectedly low supply voltage powered up.

Remove the power and disconnect one or two of your more power-hungry pieces. If the voltage returns to the proper level, you're definitely over budget. If not, there may be a short circuit. Refer to Chapter 11, "Debugging," for help.

Wiring It Up

As discussed in Chapter 2, there are a number of ways to build a circuit. For a new design, you might want to use a protoboard since it's the fastest to connect and the easiest to change.

Once you have written the Arduino program and tried out both the hardware and the software, you might want to build your circuit in a more permanent way.

As with the previous steps, you can consider each major piece of the design separately until the software needs multiple pieces at the same time. You want your button push to make something happen!

GOING WITH THE FLOW

Arduino programs, called *sketches*, are sequential instructions. Before you can start writing code, you need to translate your idea into a series of step-by-step directions. If you omit this step, you could end up with the hardest of all possible problems to find: the logic bug.

It is up to you to translate your idea into a set of instructions that make your project work. To assist with this translation, it is often helpful to think of how you might instruct a person to do the job.

The person you should imagine is literal in his understanding. He is slavish in following all the steps in order, never skipping one or changing the order. He does exactly what you say to do regardless of what you mean to say. He can only do one thing at a time but is really, really fast.

Don't worry for the moment about how you would write the code for your set of instructions. Don't make the mistake of trying to write the code without thinking through the logic. The idea at this stage is to get a set of ordered steps that do what you want.

Some projects have a natural sequence to them. Listing the steps or adding numbers to the picture (or pictures) to show the order of events is sufficient. Keep in mind that the main program executes as a loop. The last step is always to return to the first step.

It may be helpful to draw a diagram that shows the directions executed in a sequence indicated by arrows. The name for this type of diagram is a *flowchart*. You don't need anything really formal. This is a tool. If you don't find it helpful, a sequential list of steps is just as good.

Some projects do not have a step-by-step nature, and even if they do, two things may happen at once. Many projects such as robots, musical instruments, and toys have a random nature. There may be times when two notes are played simultaneously. How do you handle cases when two things happen at once?

The Arduino executes instructions very fast in human terms. To the Arduino, people are really, really slow. Your Arduino can turn an LED on and off so quickly that you never see it lit. Instructions to light a series of LEDs one at a time seem to a person as if they were all turned on at the same time.

Usually when two things need to happen at the same time, the requirement can be satisfied by those two things happening in rapid succession. People cannot tell the difference.

Less visible to you, but no different, is the case when two notes are played at the same time on a musical instrument. The Arduino can check each key (or button) one at a time in rapid succession. This method is called *monitoring*.

On the other hand, if you want people to notice that LEDs are being turned on one at a time in series, you need to let some time pass between each one. The same is true to make a motor move. Some time must pass between when it is turned on and when it is turned off.

Just because time is passing doesn't mean that the Arduino is doing nothing. While time passes, it can be running a monitoring loop, servicing interrupts, or performing calculations.

It does all things in rapid succession. Regardless of what it is doing, it is only doing one thing at a time.

Excuse me! Please stand by while we process this important, time-critical data. Thank you for your patience. We now return to our regular program, already in progress.

Interrupts or *exceptions* are special input signals that cause the processor to save what it is doing now and execute an Interrupt Service Routine (ISR). Then the processor returns to what it was doing at the point where it left off. ISRs are like a weather update in the middle of your favorite TV show.

You don't have control over when interrupts occur or know what the Arduino will be doing when one arrives. Like a text message, an interrupt could arrive at an awkward moment.

Situations like keeping your robot from running over the cat require immediate processor intervention. They need interrupts.

Like trying to do your homework while someone is pestering you, there are drawbacks to interrupts. Interrupts that are too frequent, take too long to handle, or happen at a bad time keep you from getting your work done. Try to reserve interrupts for truly exceptional situations.

Refer to Chapter 9, "Writing the Code," for information on sequential programs, monitoring loops, and interrupts.

I Don't Know What to Make!

The Arduino playground idea area (http://arduino.cc/playground/Projects/Ideas) and exhibition area (http://playground.arduino.cc/Projects/ArduinoUsers) are excellent places to look for information. Books, cookbooks, and magazines have an editor who (allegedly) sanity checks them.

Many other projects are available on the web; however, the quality of Internet content varies widely. Check to be sure enough information is available before you pick something to make. A half-finished example is not what you want.

You don't need to limit your search to projects using only the Arduino microcontroller. Nearly any project built with a microcontroller can be built with an Arduino. Some projects without a microcontroller can be automated with an Arduino.

Pick a project that will be fun to use when you are done. The motivation for building anything isn't really the challenge of doing the work. The real prize is playing with it when you're done.

EXAMPLES

Arduino sketches (programs) have two sections: setup and loop. The setup section is used to configure the I/O and initialize the system to a known state. The loop section repeats endlessly until the Arduino is reset or power is removed.

The following examples start with setup and initialize. This is good programming practice, so make it a habit. The remaining steps form the loop section, with the last step returning to the beginning of the loop.

Traffic Light Example (Part I)

The traffic light is a popular example since it needs only a few parts and assembles quickly. Programming is also relatively straightforward but is reserved for Chapter 9. This example shows the logical flow that underlies the program.

Figure 3.3 shows the inner workings of a traffic light made with three LEDs and an Arduino Uno. The lights cycle through the colors automatically on a 3-minute cycle. The 3-minute cycle is red for 90 seconds, green for 75 seconds, and yellow for 15 seconds. When a pedestrian pushes the button during the green light, the light cycles to yellow immediately and subsequently red.

The LEDs are about the right size for a model railroad traffic light. If you want a traffic light for your bedroom, add a case and high-power lights or LED arrays. Real traffic lights are big; they are 3–4 feet tall with Frisbee-sized (8–12 inch) lights. For home use, build a miniature version.

Figure 3.3
Traffic light controller.
© 2014 Cengage Learning®

Sequential logic makes this an excellent example. A simple list of steps, shown next, is really all that you need to get the majority of the program flow. It has the added thrill of a button to push.

1. The setup section initializes three pins as digital output and one as digital input.

2. The loop section turns on the yellow LED, and the other two turn off.

3. A timer times 15 seconds.

4. The red LED turns on, and the other two turn off.

5. A timer times 90 seconds.

6. The green LED turns on, and the other two turns off.

7. A timer times 75 seconds.

8. Repeat loop. (Go to step 2.)

These steps certainly make the normal cycle work fine. But how do we handle the excitement of the button?

Step 7 needs to monitor the push button to see if anyone has pushed it. If someone has, the program continues to step 8 without waiting for the timer to expire. Step 8 loops back to step 2 and lights the yellow LED, giving the desired behavior.

Figure 3.4 shows the sequential steps listed as a flowchart. Figure 3.5 shows the detail of step 7 as modified to monitor both the switch and the timer.

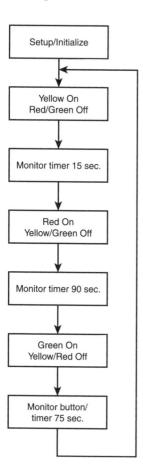

Figure 3.4
Traffic light flowchart.
© 2014 Cengage Learning®

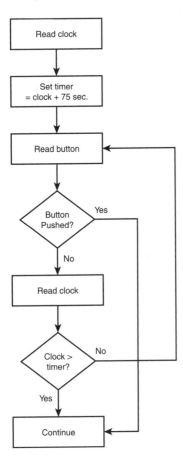

Figure 3.5
Monitor flowchart.
© 2014 Cengage Learning®

The actual coding for this example is in Chapter 9. Here's a materials list and schematics just in case you want to try this for yourself.

Description	Manufacturer	Part Number	Reference Designation
Momentary switch	APED Components	MJTP1230	SW
Red LED	Vishay Semiconductor	TLHK5800	D1
Green LED	Vishay Semiconductor	TLHY5200	D2
Yellow LED	Vishay Semiconductor	TLHG6405	D3
220 ohm resistor	Vishay BC	#SRF2500002200FR500	R
Microcontroller	Arduino	Uno	U1

© 2014 Cengage Learning®

Any Arduino can be substituted for the Uno. You have probably noticed that the Uno connections are numbered. These numbers match the labels that are silkscreened onto the PCB next to the header connectors.

LilyPad has limited I/O, and you need to change the pins used to ones that are available. Use the silkscreen on the LilyPad as a guide. Any digital pin will do.

You can substitute any resistor from 220 ohm to 1K ohm and 1/8 watt or bigger. The resistor's function is to limit the current through the LED. Just about any LED should work for this circuit.

Any switch should work, as should touching a jumper from pin 2 to ground. A momentary switch is preferred, or the switch must be returned to the open position for the light to turn green. Figure 3.6 shows the traffic light schematic.

Use the USB port on your computer to power the circuit. To work without your computer attached, you can use three AA batteries wired in series.

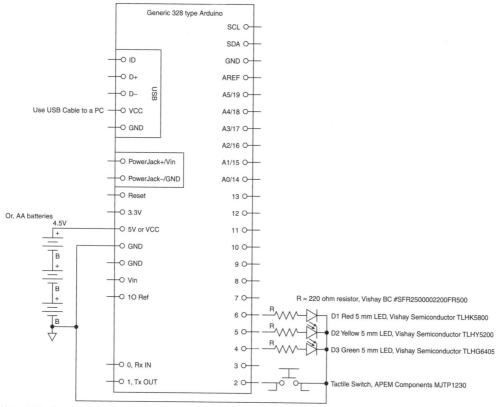

Figure 3.6
Traffic light schematic.
© 2014 Cengage Learning®

Although this example seems trivial, it does cover all the steps in the design process. You can modify this example for use in any project that requires timers, buttons, and LED lights.

If you plan to use the buttons, refer to Chapter 9 for information on debouncing a switch. This example only needs to see the button change once to continue with the program. It doesn't matter if the button changes multiple times; only the first time matters.

Puppet Show Example (Part I)

Figure 3.7 shows a picture of an animated puppet show. The three-word description gives a pretty good idea of what the project is, but a picture provides a much better idea. Remember, a picture is a tool for you. An ugly drawing on the back of a crumpled napkin is adequate.

Figure 3.7
Animated puppet show.
© 2014 Cengage Learning®

As you probably noticed, I'm not an artist. Go ahead and snicker now. Feel better? You might be amused by my lack of artistry, but now you have a good idea of what I had in mind.

You might have questions. Why bears and not kittens? What song are they playing? Is there more than one song? Is this show coin operated? Some of these questions might raise issues or offer new ideas.

This is meant to be a show. The marquee shows a countdown to the next show, then "Now appearing," and then "The Three Bears." The curtain opens, and a spotlight lights up. The music starts. The bears dance and sing. The music ends. The spotlight goes dark, and the curtain closes. The marquee shows a countdown to the next show.

For the Arduino to do the work, this description must be converted to a step-by-step process. The following list shows the steps for the show.

1. Initialize: define pins, close curtain, turn music off, turn spotlight off, turn motors off, blank marquee.

2. Update marquee with "Next show — 5:00 minutes."

3. Count down time to 0, updating marquee every second.

4. Update marquee to read "Now appearing…."

5. Wait 5 seconds.

6. Update marquee to read "The Three Bears."

7. Open curtain.

8. Turn on spotlight.

9. Play music and move bears around.

10. Stop music.

11. Turn off spotlight.

12. Close curtain.

13. Return to step 2.

This example has a natural sequence to it. Step 3 implies some additional substeps. We need to keep track of time and test it to see when we should do something. Sound familiar?

Parts of this example are similar to the previous one. The biggest differences are the speaker and the motors. A less obvious difference is the use of a spotlight instead of an LED. The speaker, motors, and spotlight might need driver circuits controlled by the Arduino pins.

The materials you need for the puppet show include four motors (three for puppets, one for curtain), dot-matrix display, curtain, spotlight, speaker, and (of course) an Arduino. The additional nonelectronic materials you need include three stuffed bears, curtain, curtain rod, box to use as a stage, zip ties, and some screws.

Chapter 7 considers driver circuits. Let's leave this example here for now. We'll discuss it more in Chapter 9.

Pinball Machine Example (Part I)

Figure 3.8 shows the basic features of a pinball machine. Why build one? Because it's a fun, old-school toy! Pinball machines run the range from purely mechanical devices to purely virtual devices. This one has a combination of mechanical, electrical, and electronic pieces.

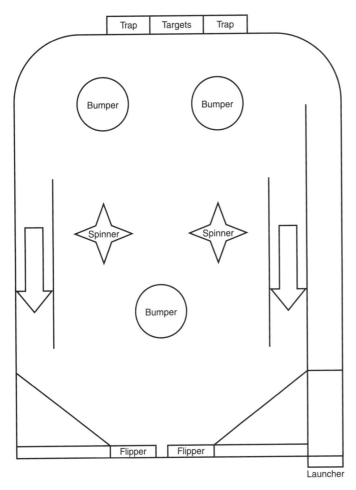

Figure 3.8
Basic pinball machine framework.
© 2014 Cengage Learning®

For the pinball example, the description necessarily has less sequence to it and more feature description. After the ball is launched, you don't really know what's going to happen. That's part of the fun.

Most pinball machines have a basic collection of features as shown in the figure. Special features are layered on top of these. A painted background, artwork theme, and music tie the whole package together.

Pinball machines usually have some sort of theme to them. A better theme provides a more memorable game. A horror movie, a cartoon, a fairy tale, a TV game show, a book, or even a video game might provide inspiration. Selecting a classic that's been around forever is a good choice.

A theme that's too trendy might be passé by the time the machine is done. A theme that's too simple won't be fun to play more than once or twice. A theme that's too seasonal might only be fun sometimes. Will Halloween still be fun in February?

Picking a theme now, in the early stages, rather than later suggests features not otherwise obvious. For example, picking the theme "Road Trip" suggests a police siren and lights as well as "Speed Trap" and "Tourist Trap" hazards and "Rest Stop" bonus area.

Unlike the two previous examples, this example lends itself to a bottom-up approach. Starting with just the basic features, the machine needs a ball launcher, flippers, and bumpers. Once these basic features are working, you can add theme-specific targets, spinners, ball traps, lights, a bell, music, magnets, and some sort of bonus area. Some things are mechanical or electrical, while others are electronically controlled by an Arduino.

Play the machine while working on it. That way you'll see where the ball tends to end up and where you need more excitement.

The Arduino's program involves a monitoring loop to check all the sensors. The loop also handles flashing the lights and updating the score. Since anything can happen at any time, there is no way to predict where the action will be at any time.

Whoa! Wait a minute. There is a lot going on at the same time. You know that the Arduino can do only one thing at a time. How do you do more than that? The short answer is you don't. The long answer is that you do all these things one at a time, sequentially, doing a small portion of each one, but very fast, so that it appears each is happening together.

The following list of steps shows how your Arduino can control a pinball machine with a monitor loop. Step 1 is, as always, an initialization and setup step.

1. Initialize Arduino pins and pinball machine.
2. Release ball to shooter.
3. Read tilt sensor.
4. Read scoring pads.
5. Read spinning targets.
6. Read traps.

7. Update score.

8. Check for fallen ball.

9. If ball falls, go to step 2.

10. Otherwise, go to step 3.

As with the other examples, we'll leave the programming for Chapter 9.

CHAPTER 4

A GUIDED TOUR OF YOUR NEW ARDUINO

This chapter will answer the following questions:

- What parts does an Arduino have?
- Do you really need to know this?
- What resources does an Arduino provide?
- How do you use these resources?

ARDUINO PARTS

The Arduino is a physical device built out of Integrated Circuits (ICs) mounted on a Printed Circuit Board (PCB). The location and function of each of these ICs is a relatively small part of the story. Even so, it's worth knowing how to identify the pieces and understand what they do.

Figure 4.1 shows a picture of the Arduino Uno with the various physical pieces identified. The exact appearance of your Arduino depends on the model and the revision (indicated by an R number). The model name and revision are silkscreened onto the bottom of the PCB.

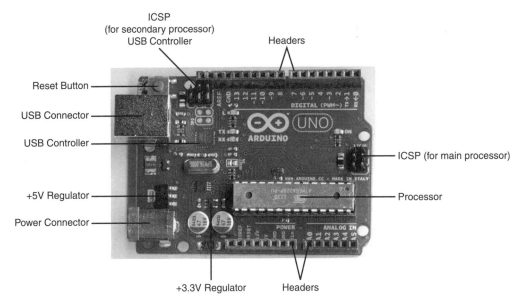

Figure 4.1
The Arduino Uno's parts.
© 2014 Cengage Learning®

Figure 4.2 shows a picture of the LilyPad Protosnap with the various pieces identified. The exact appearance of your Arduino LilyPad depends on the model and revision. Unfortunately, while there are many versions of LilyPad, the version and revision are not marked anywhere on the device. The Arduino LilyPad Simple Board is the version of LilyPad built into the Protosnap pictured in Figure 4.2.

Figure 4.2
The Arduino LilyPad's parts.
© 2014 Cengage Learning®

The Microcontroller

Your Arduino has an Atmel microcontroller IC. This IC is the large one located on the board. Sometimes this IC is a through-hole part mounted in a socket, and sometimes it's a Surface Mount Technology (SMT) device soldered to the PCB. The Atmel logo and part number appear on the device, along with the manufacturing code (lot number/date code). Most new (circa 2010) Arduino boards have an ATmega328P microcontroller.

The model number of the microcontroller, not the package style, determines the resources that the IC provides. *Resource* is the collective name engineers use for the things inside the device. Memory, registers, CPU, timers, Input/Output (I/O) ports, Analog/Digital (A/D) comparator, A/D converter, clock generator, and power management are the typical resources that an Atmel processor provides.

Resources will be discussed in more detail later in this chapter. Some of the resource details will matter to you. These are discussed in Chapter 7, "Input and Output." A more detailed discussion is included later in this chapter for the interested reader.

There may be a second, smaller Atmel microcontroller (ATmega16u2) on the board used as a Universal Serial Bus (USB)-to-serial converter. Older models use an FTDI IC for this function.

Reset Button

The reset button is the only button on the Arduino. This button is used to reset the processor (hence the name).

On reset, the Arduino either starts the bootloader or starts your sketch (program). If your Arduino has a bootloader installed, the bootloader checks for download of a new sketch. If no download is initiated, your previously loaded sketch starts after a few seconds.

If no bootloader is present, your sketch starts immediately. If you have no sketch and no bootloader, nothing happens.

Refer to Chapter 8, "The IDE," for more information on downloading your program and reset behavior.

USB Connector

The USB connector provides a means to connect to your computer. It is not the only means, but it is the most convenient. This connection provides both data transfer and power. Although the amount of current that the USB port can supply is limited to 500mA, it is adequate for most uses. Motors, relays, servos, solenoids, or more than about 25 LEDs need a separate power source.

A second, smaller Atmel microcontroller device (or an FTDI device on older boards) forms a USB endpoint for data transfers. Your computer functions as the USB host.

The practical consequence is that you can't use the USB port to connect two Arduino boards. You don't need USB for this, because the serial ports do the job. See the example at the end of Chapter 9, "Writing the Code."

A USB host shield permits an Arduino to act as a USB host for some types of devices, like game controllers. Refer to the shield's information for compatibility listings.

The LilyPad does not have a USB connector and associated parts. Connection is via a USB-to-serial interface board.

Power Regulators

When power is supplied via the barrel jack connector or via the Vin pin on the power header, the +5 Volt power regulator takes the input power and adjusts and conditions it to 5 Volts for the board.

In all cases, the specification sheet for your Arduino model details a minimum and maximum input voltage. Do not exceed this range. Do not apply a voltage greater than the maximum, or permanent damage to your Arduino may result. If the incoming voltage is too low (below approximately 7.5 V) the 5 V regulator may not work correctly. (It won't be damaged; it just won't generate a useable 5 V output.)

Caution

Do not exceed the maximum input voltage level specified for your model Arduino. Permanent damage to your Arduino might result.

If the input voltage is at the higher end of the allowable range (12 Volts) and the current draw is heavy, the regulator becomes hot. Don't touch a regulator you think might be hot, or you'll get burned. If the regulator gets too hot, a thermal shutdown may be triggered, and power to the board will be suspended.

Caution

Once again, the power regulator might be hot. Don't touch it!

A thermal shutdown protects your Arduino from permanent damage. If a shutdown occurs, remove the power and allow it to cool down. Lower the supply voltage or lighten the current draw to prevent a repeat shutdown.

Newer boards have an automatic power selection circuit. The +5 Volt power regulator is selected when Vin/2 is greater than 3.3 V. USB power from the USB connector is selected if Vin/2 is less than 3.3 V.

On some older models, a jumper is used to connect the power source.

On newer Arduino models, a second +3.3 Volt regulator provides 3.3 Volts to a pin on the headers. Older models supply this pin from the FTDI chip.

The LilyPad is supplied with power by a battery or indirectly via the serial USB breakout board connected to a USB port. It doesn't have regulators.

In-Circuit System Programming Header

You can use the In-Circuit System Programming (ICSP) header to download a bootloader or to download a sketch. An AVR ISP programmer is required to use this feature. Refer to Chapter 8 for further information.

Some LilyPads have holes where an In-Circuit System Programming (ICSP) header can be installed to use this feature. You need to solder pins into these holes to use this feature. Not all LilyPads provide these holes.

If your Arduino has a second Atmel processor on it, there will be a second ICSP header. You can use this header to change the second processor's program to provide different functionality. Don't do this unless you understand what you're doing because you might lose the USB port functionality. Don't panic; you can restore it.

Headers

Headers are connectors formed by a strip of sockets. These headers provide connections to the processor pins and act as standoffs for shields. The majority of connections you make to your Arduino are via these headers.

Take a good look at your board, and you will see that the pins are labeled on the silkscreen next to each pin. Pins are roughly divided into four groups: analog, digital, power, and ungrouped.

The analog group is marked "analog in" as a reminder that these pins are analog input only and not analog output. Analog pin names start with the letter "A" followed by a number. You can also use analog pins as digital (input or output) pins.

Digital pins are programmed as either input or output. Those digital pins capable of Pulse Width Modulation (PWM) are indicated by a tilde symbol (~) next to the signal name. Digital pin names have a number only.

The power group of pins includes the power outputs and ground connections. You can also use Vin as an input if the barrel jack connector is not used. The other (ungrouped) pins include special-purpose pins like RESET and AREF. Refer to Chapter 7 for more details.

By design, the signal names and pin names are the same and can be used interchangeably without confusion. For your convenience, you might want to call the signals something else. For example, you might want pin 6 to control motor 1 and call the signal "motor1" to be more meaningful to you.

Although you could relabel the pins on your Arduino, it is easier to make a map. Obviously, a good place to keep your map is in your notebook. When you write your program for the Arduino, this mapping is part of the initialization portion of your sketch. You can then use your signal names for the rest of the sketch.

Not all Arduino models have headers. Some of the physically smaller models have holes that may have wires, pins, or sockets soldered into them. The silkscreen next to these holes indicates the signal names. These smaller models are not plug-in compatible with shields because of their smaller size.

The LilyPad doesn't have headers. Instead, it is ringed by pads with a hole in the middle. The LilyPad may be connected by wrapping (sewing) conductive thread around the pad and through the hole. If you prefer to use wire, you can solder to the pad. Some LilyPad models have snaps for connection. In any case, the silkscreen next to the pad indicates the pin name.

The LilyPad keeps the Arduino naming convention. Analog inputs are labeled with the letter "A" followed by a number. Digital pins have a number only. PWM pins are not specifically labeled. The number of pins on the LilyPad may be limited. Depending on the model of LilyPad, the pin names (and numbers) may not be sequential.

LEDs

Four LEDs provide information on the state of the board. "ON" or "P" indicates that power has been supplied to the board. "RX" and "TX" indicate information flow over the USB connection. "L" can be used to indicate anything. Most bootloaders use the "L" LED to indicate that they are working.

LilyPads vary in the number and location of indicator LEDs.

THIS IS NOT ON THE TEST

You don't need to understand how the Arduino microcontroller works to use it. Like your computer, you can use your Arduino without knowing much about it beyond how to turn it on.

There are only a few things you really need to know. You need to know how to connect it to your computer. You also need to find the reset button. If required, you need to plug in a power supply. Knowing what the LEDs on the board indicate is helpful.

You need to understand how to use the I/O; see Chapter 7. Your Arduino needs to connect through the I/O pins to make something exciting happen.

If you are interested in microcontrollers (or microprocessors), the Arduino has a full-fledged high-performance 8-bit RISC processor capable of 20 MIPS (million instructions per second) with a 20 MHz clock. Your clock runs at 16 MHz or 8 MHz, so your performance is scaled down proportionally. You can even program it in assembly-level language and manipulate registers directly if you're really enthralled.

At this point, you have learned all you need to know from this chapter. If you are interested in more detail, read on. If not, you can safely skip the rest of this chapter, confident that you know what you need to.

Microcontroller Versus Microprocessor

A microcontroller is a standalone microcomputer on a chip. Memory, clock, and I/O ports are integrated into a single device with the processor core, which includes the Arithmetic Logic Unit (ALU) and associated registers. They are intended for dedicated applications. Your coffee maker, toaster oven, and alarm clock have a microcontroller inside.

Microprocessors maximize I/O pins and use external memory and support devices. You can certainly embed a microprocessor into a design. You can also use it as a more general-purpose device. Your computer has a microprocessor (or two) inside.

ARDUINO RESOURCES

More interesting than what the Arduino microcontroller has in terms of components is the resources that can be used to do anything you want. Most of these resources are provided by the microcontroller IC, and this puppy can do a lot.

The model number of the microcontroller, not the package style, determines the resources that the IC provides. Resource is the collective name engineers use for the things inside the device. Memory, registers, CPU, timers, I/O ports, A/D converter, clock generator, and power management are the typical resources that an Atmel processor provides. Figure 4.3 shows the top-level block diagram for the Atmel ATmega328P, used on the Arduino Uno. Each resource is represented as a block with lines showing how they are interconnected.

Using the microcontroller resources efficiently is the key to getting the best performance from your Arduino. For a lot of projects, you probably don't need the horsepower, but when you do, you need to understand how to best use what's available.

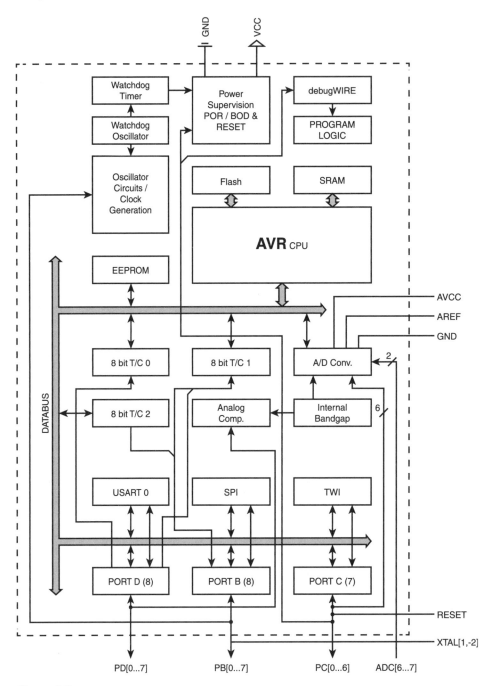

Figure 4.3
Atmel microcontroller block diagram.
© 2013 Atmel Corporation

How to Count Like an Engineer

When numbering registers or counting bits, engineers start with 0 instead of 1. That's because we're really counting in binary. Microcontrollers, microprocessors, computers, and calculators all use *binary*, the number system based on two.

Registers, in the register file, are named using their binary address to prevent confusion. Register 0 is accessed by B00000 (B indicates binary) on the control lines. The last register, register 31, is accessed by B11111. In total, there are 32 registers.

Hexadecimal (the number system based on 16) numbers compactly represent binary numbers. One hex digit is equivalent to four binary digits. Hex numbers start with 0x, so register 31 is at address 0x1F.

The next address, 0x20, isn't register 32; it's a totally unrelated register. Remember that the last register's name and address are one less than the total number of registers. (Pronounce the address as *two-zero*, not *twenty*, to avoid decimal/hexadecimal confusion.)

Memory sizes are based on binary as well, so that a memory size is a power of 2. One K of memory is 1024 bytes, numbered 0 to 1023, not 1000 bytes. Like registers, count the first memory location as zero and the last as one less than the total size.

The CPU Core

The thinking part of the microcontroller is the CPU core, which is composed of various sections working together. The major pieces are the Arithmetic Logic Unit (ALU), Program Counter (PC), Instruction Register (IR), decoding functions, Status Register (SR), and 32 general-purpose registers (known collectively as the *register file*).

Registers are small byte or word width memories whose contents are quickly available to the ALU. In the case of the Arduino, they are 8 bits wide. You can use six of the registers as three 16-bit registers (named X, Y, and Z). The PC, SR, and IR are also registers.

The PC, SR, and IR have special purposes. The PC keeps track of where the instruction that the CPU is currently executing is stored in memory. Manipulating the PC allows jumps in program execution.

The IR holds the current instruction that is decoded and operates the control lines for the register file and the ALU.

The SR holds information about the last executed operation. You can use the contents of the SR to make decisions. Each bit of the SR has a special meaning. For example, bit 1 indicates that the result of the last operation was zero. Other bits indicate conditions like overflow and underflow.

The ALU performs the actual arithmetic, logical bit-wise operations, and comparisons. The operands typically come from registers, and results are stored to a register.

Decisions are made based on the outcome of these operations or the results stored in the SR.

The details of using the ALU, register file, PC, SR, and IR are hidden below lines of C code. This is a good thing! Although you can write assembly-level instructions to directly manipulate the ALU and these registers, it's not necessary.

In real life, even engineers rarely write in assembly-level code or look at programming from the register level. That's the job of a compiler.

Professional programmers can produce 10 lines of debugged code per day on average. It doesn't matter if the code is written in assembly language or in a high-level language like C. Either way, it's 10 lines. A lot more can be done in 10 lines of C than in 10 lines of assembly-level language.

Like a professional programmer, you will write code in C. Your IDE will translate your code to instructions the CPU core can understand without any help from you.

When you need bit-level manipulation, C provides that. The Arduino's I/O pins correspond to individual bits in registers. You use individual bits to control individual signals. Don't worry about this now. Chapter 9 tells you everything you need to know, and the hard part is done for you by functions.

The instructions that the CPU can understand are collectively called the *instruction set*. If you are interested, you can look up the instruction set of the Atmel microcontroller in the data sheet. These assembly-level instructions are available for use, but you will be happier if you stick with C. No one is likely to help you with assembly-level programming when you run into difficulty.

In addition to the ALU, registers, and memories, the CPU core has some special-purpose control units: I/O modules, clock distribution, power management, system control/reset including watchdog timer, interrupt unit, timer/counters, Serial Peripheral Interface (SPI) unit, USART, 2-wire interface, analog comparator, and A/D converter.

Flash Memory

Flash memory is a type of Electrically Erasable Programmable Read Only Memory (EEPROM). The main difference is the size of the block that can be erased and rewritten. The block size is larger for flash memory than other types of EEPROM, allowing faster erase and rewrite operations.

The flash memory stores the program for the CPU. This memory is nonvolatile, which means that it is not erased by removing the power. There are two configurations for the flash memory: with bootloader and without.

When a bootloader is used, the highest sector of the flash memory stores the bootloader program. The rest of the flash contains your sketch (aka program or application code).

The Arduino is usually preprogrammed with a bootloader when you buy it. If not, you can find a bootloader file on the Arduino website. Refer to Chapter 8 for details.

You can erase and rewrite this memory 10,000 times. Although this is a very large number, it is finite. To put this into perspective, you can erase and rewrite a sketch an average of 3 times per day for 10 years or 10 times per day for 3 years.

SRAM

The CPU uses Static Random Access Memory (SRAM) to store information (data) from your sketch. In addition to general-purpose storage, the SRAM contains the register file and I/O registers.

SRAM is volatile memory. It will lose its contents whenever power is removed.

EEPROM

EEPROM memory is nonvolatile memory that can be used to store any information you want to keep through a reset or power cycle. This is the only nonvolatile memory that you can write to under sketch control.

You can erase and rewrite this memory 100,000 times. This is a big number, but it is finite. You can erase and rewrite a block an average of 30 times per day for 10 years. That's 10 times more than flash memory.

I/O Modules

The names of the input/output modules—port B, port C, and port D—may seem a little odd. The letter names are consistent with other members of Atmel's AVR IC family. You don't really need to worry about this. Just call them by their names: port B, port C, and port D.

I/O ports are where your microcontroller meets the real world. Behind each header pin is a microcontroller pin. A set of three registers controls each microcontroller pin.

How do pin names silkscreened onto the Arduino map to the port and pin numbers? The mapping is shown in Table 4.1 for the ATmega168 and 328. These are software pin names and not physical device pin numbers!

The data sheet and the remaining tables in this chapter use hardware ports. Use Table 4.1 to translate ports to Arduino pin names.

Table 4.1   ATmega168/328 Hardware Port to Software Pin Mapping

Port	Pin	Port	Pin	Port	Pin
PB0	8	PC0	A0 (14)	PD0	0 (RX)
PB1	9	PC1	A1 (15)	PD1	1 (TX)
PB2	10	PC2	A2 (16)	PD2	2
PB3	11	PC3	A3 (17)	PD3	3
PB4	12	PC4	A4 (18)	PD4	4
PB5	13	PC5	A5 (19)	PD5	5
PB6	crystal	PC6	reset	PD6	6
PB7	crystal			PD7	7

© 2014 Cengage Learning®

Digital pin names are just numbers. Analog pin names start with the letter "A" and have a number. You can use all of these pins as digital inputs or outputs. They are individually programmable. If inputs, they can have pull-up resistors. These pins are tristated (high impedance) during reset and default to inputs.

Unused input pins should not be left floating. Use the internal pull-up resistors to guarantee the state of the pins. You can use external pull-up (or pull-down) resistors instead. It is not recommended that you connect unused pins directly to power or ground.

Use caution when changing pins between input and output or output and input during program execution. Read the data sheet to understand the issues involved before attempting this.

Most port pins have alternate functions. Obviously, you give up the normal function of the pin when you use these. Alternate uses are discussed in the section that describes the related function.

Chapter 7 covers use of input and output pins in detail.

Clock Generation, Power Management, and Sleep Modes

Clock generation provides, well, the clock. Although this is more complex than it sounds, you don't usually need to worry about this.

One exception is if you have a new IC that has never been programmed with a bootloader. The IC default setting is the internal RC clock divided down to 1.0 MHz. The bootloader sets the clock to the external crystal oscillator running at 8.0 MHz (3.3 V powered cards) or 16.0 MHz (5 V powered cards). Once it's set, the clock source remains the external crystal oscillator.

The external crystal attaches to pins PB6 and PB7 of the Arduino, as shown in Table 4.2. Because these pins are always in use, their other functions also listed in the table are never available. Similarly, PC6 is committed for the reset function.

Table 4.2 Clock Port and Pin Mapping

Port and Pin	Function	Signal Name
PB0	Divided system clock output	CLKO
PB6	Chip clock oscillator pin 1	XTAL1
PB6	Timer oscillator pin 1	TOSC1
PB7	Chip clock oscillator pin 2	XTAL2
PB7	Timer oscillator pin 2	TOSC2

The Arduino has a crystal connected to PB6 and PB7.

© 2014 Cengage Learning®

Power management allows unused circuitry to be shut down when it's not in use to save power. Because CMOS devices consume the most power when they are changing state, halting the internal clocks reduces the power consumption.

Six sleep states shut down various combinations of clock domains. Each sleep mode offers a variety of wake-up sources.

If you're using sleep modes, you need to pay attention to the internal clock distribution. The clock distribution and sleep modes are detailed in the data sheet.

Active Low Signals

Most of the time, signals are considered active if they are a logic high. A logic high might also be referred to as "true." A logic low might also be referred to as "false."

Sometimes we want signals that are active low signals—signals take effect if they are low. This is referred to as *negative logic*. To indicate that an active low signal is "true," the signal name has a bar (a line) over it.

RESET, pronounced "reset bar," is an active low signal. Normally this signal is pulled high (+ 5 V) with a pull-up resistor and is inactive (aka "false"). To reset the microcontroller, RESET is pulled low (0 V). The RESET signal causes action when it's low ("true"). You might also see active low signals indicated in datasheets as RESET/, RESET-, or RESET*.

System Control and Reset

Reset can be internally or externally triggered. Internal reset can be generated from Power-On Reset, Brown-Out Reset, and Watchdog Reset. The reset button on the Arduino applies an external reset. Table 4.3 shows the external reset port mapping.

Power management and reset circuitry are used together to initiate program download, as described earlier in this chapter.

Table 4.3   Reset Port and Pin Mapping

Port and Pin	Function	Signal Name
PC6	Reset Pin	$\overline{\text{RESET}}$

© 2014 Cengage Learning®

Watchdog Timer

The Watchdog is a special timer that is periodically reinitialized as a fail-safe to program execution. For large complex programs, programming errors might cause the processor to behave in unexpected ways.

Even the most complex program will have quiet periods when not much is happening. During these quiet times, low-priority or housekeeping tasks are done. If there are no quiet times, the processor is overloaded or inefficiently programmed.

Low-priority tasks might include monitoring the input voltage, checking for serial communications, or storing status information. Another of these tasks is reinitializing the Watchdog timer, sometimes referred to as *petting the dog*.

The Watchdog timer generates a reset (or an interrupt, or both an interrupt followed by a reset) if the periodic reinitialization fails to happen. The Watchdog is not needed for simple programs. Only complex programs that might run away need this protection.

Interrupt Unit

Interrupts, also called exceptions, are special signals that cause the processor to interrupt normal operation and handle a special situation, an exception. The interrupt handling unit controls and prioritizes all the interrupt sources.

There are 26 possible interrupt sources, many of which are internally connected. External interrupt sources include the external and pin change interrupt sources that are listed in Table 4.4.

Table 4.4   Interrupt Port and Pin Mapping

Port and Pin	Interrupt	Signal Name
PB0	Pin Change Interrupt 0	PCINT0
PB1	Pin Change Interrupt 1	PCINT1
PB2	Pin Change Interrupt 2	PCINT2
PB3	Pin Change Interrupt 3	PCINT3
PB4	Pin Change Interrupt 4	PCINT4
PB5	Pin Change Interrupt 5	PCINT5
PB6	Pin Change Interrupt 6	PCINT6
PB7	Pin Change Interrupt 7	PCINT7
PC0	Pin Change Interrupt 8	PCINT8
PC1	Pin Change Interrupt 9	PCINT9
PC2	Pin Change Interrupt 10	PCINT10
PC3	Pin Change Interrupt 11	PCINT11
PC4	Pin Change Interrupt 12	PCINT12
PC5	Pin Change Interrupt 13	PCINT13
PC6	Pin Change Interrupt 14	PCINT14
PD0	Pin Change Interrupt 16	PCINT16
PD1	Pin Change Interrupt 17	PCINT17
PD2	Pin Change Interrupt 18	PCINT18
PD2	External Interrupt 0 Input	INT0
PD3	Pin Change Interrupt 19	PCINT19
PD3	External Interrupt 1 Input	INT1
PD4	Pin Change Interrupt 20	PCINT20
PD5	Pin Change Interrupt 21	PCINT21
PD6	Pin Change Interrupt 22	PCINT22
PD7	Pin Change Interrupt 23	PCINT23

There is no PCINT15.

When an interrupt occurs, a special piece of software called an Interrupt Service Routine (ISR) stores the CPU's current state. The interrupt is processed, and the CPU's state is restored. You must keep ISRs short to avoid interfering with normal program flow and to avoid overflowing the stack.

Timer/Counters

There are three timer/counter modules: one 16-bit module and two 8-bit modules. These modules allow the processor to accurately time events using the system clock or to count events presented at the input pins. These modules also generate PWM waveforms.

On the Arduino, timer/counter 0 and timer/counter 1 can be used to count external events using the input capture inputs. You can use all of the timer/counter modules for PWM and timing with the internal clock.

Table 4.5 shows the timer/counter and PWM pins. The name PWM doesn't appear in the table because the official function name is *output compare match*. The name is descriptive of how the signals are generated, but PWM is easier to remember.

Table 4.5   Timer/Counter Port and Pin Mapping

Port and Pin	Function	Signal Name
PB0	Timer/Counter 1 Input Capture Input	ICP1
PB1	Timer/Counter 1 Output Compare Match A Output	OC1A
PB2	Timer/Counter 1 Output Compare Match B Output	OC1B
PB3	Timer/Counter 2 Output Compare Match A Output	OC2A
PD3	Timer/Counter 2 Output Compare Match B Output	OC2B
PD4	Timer/Counter 0 External Counter Input	T0
PD5*	Timer/Counter 0 Output Compare Match B Output	OC0B
PD5	Timer/Counter 1 External Counter Input	T1
PD6	Timer/Counter 0 Output Compare Match A Output	OC0A

*PD5 has two functions; only one can be used at a time.

© 2014 Cengage Learning®

SPI Unit

The SPI unit provides communication capability using a master-slave serial protocol. You will also use the SPI pins for bootloader or sketch downloads. Don't worry; the IDE does the hard work for you.

In addition, you can use the SPI for fast (up to 8 MHz) data transfers between Arduino boards and other SPI-compatible devices.

Table 4.6 shows the SPI pins. Any time the SPI is used, all the pins are used, and you can't use them for anything else. PB2 ($\overline{SS}$) must be set as an output for the master; if you set it as an input and bring it low, the SPI functions as a slave device.

When more than one slave select is needed, any unused pin can be used for each additional slave select. In addition, the ground signal for all SPI devices must be connected.

Table 4.6 SPI Port and Pin Mapping

Pin and Port	SPI Function	Signal Name
PB2	SPI Bus Master Slave Select	$\overline{SS}$
PB3	SPI Bus Master Output/Slave Input	MOSI
PB4	SPI Bus Master Input/Slave Output	MISO
PB5	SPI Bus Master Clock Input	SCK

© 2014 Cengage Learning®

Universal Synchronous/Asynchronous Receiver Transmitter (USART)

A USART is a flexible serial communications device that allows two devices to talk to each other. Communication is full duplex, meaning that each device can send and receive data at the same time.

The USART is special because it allows devices with vastly different clock speeds to communicate. It buffers and synchronizes signals so that data is not lost.

Table 4.7 shows the USART pins. Many applications use only RXD and TXD, leaving PD4 available for other purposes.

Table 4.7 USART Port and Pin Mapping

Port and Pin	Function	Signal Name
PD0	USART Input Pin	RXD
PD1	USART Output Pin	TXD
PD4	USART External Clock Input/Output	XCK

© 2014 Cengage Learning®

Two-Wire Interface

The Two-Wire Interface (TWI) provides a means to interconnect up to 128 devices with standard speeds of 100 KHz and 400 KHz. This is a two-wire bus protocol in which one device becomes the bus master for the length of a transfer. All other devices act as slaves for the transfer. This interface is a good choice when connecting multiple Arduino boards. This interface goes by a variety of names, including two-wire interface, TWI, and I2C. It is compatible with Philips' I^2C protocol. Table 4.8 shows the TWI pins, which you need to use for this interface. In addition, the connected devices must share a ground connection. A ground is required for all serial communication, usually supplied by a separate wire that isn't mentioned in the interface description.

Table 4.8 Two-Wire Port and Pin Mapping

Port and Pin	Function	Signal Name
PC4	Two-Wire Serial Bus Data Input/Output Line	SDA
PC5	Two-Wire Serial Bus Clock Line	SCL

© 2014 Cengage Learning®

A/D Conversion

The A/D conversion module allows the microcontroller to monitor analog signal levels. The A/D converter translates an analog input voltage to a 10-bit digital value through successive approximation. This conversion takes about 100 microseconds.

Only one pin is connected to the A/D converter at a time. Monitoring multiple pins requires the converter to be time shared among the pins. Table 4.9 shows the analog pins.

Table 4.9 A/D Port and Pin Mapping

Port and Pin	Interrupt	Signal Name
PC0	ADC Input Channel 0	ADC0
PC1	ADC Input Channel 1	ADC1
PC2	ADC Input Channel 2	ADC2
PC3	ADC Input Channel 3	ADC3
PC4	ADC Input Channel 4	ADC4
PC5	ADC Input Channel 5	ADC5

© 2014 Cengage Learning®

The analog conversion needs a reference voltage. You can select the level present at AREF or one of two internal references. A decoupling capacitor at the AREF pin is recommended; your Arduino board already has one.

Analog Comparator

The analog comparator compares analog inputs present on AIN0 (positive input) and AIN1 (negative input). The comparator's output is high when the positive input pin has a higher voltage than the negative input. It's low when the negative input exceeds the positive input. Table 4.10 shows the external inputs to the analog comparator.

The comparator's output will set a register bit, and it can trigger timer/counter 1. In addition, the comparator can trigger an interrupt.

Any of the analog input signals can be internally connected to the negative input. You use the ADC multiplexer to select the analog input pin. Consequently, you must disable the ADC to utilize this feature.

Table 4.10 Analog Comparator Port and Pin Mapping

Port and Pin	Function	Signal Name
PD6	Analog Comparator Positive Input	AIN0
PD7	Analog Comparator Negative Input	AIN1
PC0–PC7	Analog Input 0 to 7	AIN1 (internal connection)

© 2014 Cengage Learning®

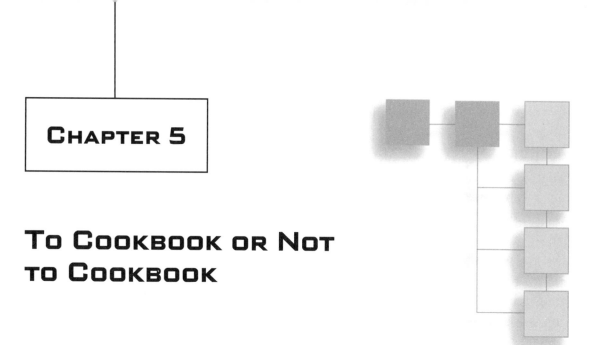

CHAPTER 5

To Cookbook or Not to Cookbook

This chapter will answer the following questions:

- Where can I learn how to use my Arduino?
- What is a cookbook?
- Why is a cookbook good?
- Why is a cookbook limiting?
- Are online projects good?
- What other books are available?
- What's the best place to find information?

INFORMATION SOURCES

You can learn nearly all you need to know about the Arduino by reading the data sheet for the Atmel microcontroller and experimenting with it on your own. As satisfying as that is, it's time consuming. And unless you're careful, you could destroy your Arduino.

Fortunately, you don't have to learn on your own because there are many information sources to choose from. Books, online tutorials, web pages, forums, and more make high-quality information readily available.

You may not be familiar with some of the information sources or even know that they exist. This chapter presents and discusses the most practical ones.

THE ARDUINO TUTORIALS AND IDE

The Arduino was invented for the very purpose of teaching nontechnical people how to build useful things with it in a simple, easy-to-use way. To support that goal, the official Arduino website contains a wealth of information organized into sections.

The Learning portion provides a text with diagram tutorial section. Many example programs are included, with explanations of what they do and how to use them. To make things even easier, the example programs from the tutorials are built into the IDE (under the File tab). You don't even need to download them or type them!

The first example is flashing the built-in "L" LED! No surprise here. In addition to providing a usage example, this simple program provides a quick way to verify that you have everything installed and connected correctly. It is especially useful because it needs no external components. (It's also a quick check for when things suddenly stop working.)

Drivers Are Difficult

When using the Integrated Development Environment (IDE), you must select your Arduino model from the IDE's Tools>Board drop-down menu. In addition, you must have the correct driver installed on your computer.

Finding and installing the correct version of driver for your Arduino model is the most challenging part of using one. If you are having difficulty communicating with your Arduino, see Chapter 8, "The IDE," for assistance.

Although the examples are divided into numbered sections, this order may not be the best sequence for you. Start with the basics and let your interests guide you from there. Some of these examples require components you won't have on hand. Follow some of the links provided for more information. Don't follow them all, or you'll start to feel like you're Alice chasing a white rabbit. Eventually you'll end up back where you started.

Note that the website and IDE present these examples in different orders. The website provides a grouping of sorts, whereas the IDE presents them alphabetically. It's not as silly as it might seem. The alphabetical ordering of the IDE files makes them easier to find.

It may seem that some topics are missing. For example, there isn't a basic motor example in the Learning section. These "missing" topics are more advanced in terms of the additional circuitry required; driving a basic motor requires more current than an Input/Output (I/O) pin can handle. Unless you are putting an engineering degree to work, consider using a shield as a quick and reliable way to add the necessary circuitry. If you want to try it without a shield, consult the Playground section.

Refer to Chapter 13, "Expanding Your Horizons with Shields," for more information on shields and how to use them. Shield makers supply directions and usage examples for their products. Usually, a library of functions accompanies the shield so that a simple function call is all you need to control the shield.

These tutorial examples aren't complete projects. "Not good enough!" you say. They don't "do" anything. For those who want real projects that actually do something, there is another option: the cookbook. We will discuss cookbooks in the next section.

The biggest drawback of the Arduino website is that it's missing a C/C++ language tutorial. For those who already know C/C++, the language reference provides a convenient refresher. It's too abbreviated for those new to programming and just sufficient for those with experience with other languages.

Cookbooks

Arduino and electronics cookbooks are much like cookbooks about food. They all have a collection of recipes and directions for preparation. Also, like food cookbooks, electronics cookbooks vary considerably in content. Some focus on a particular topic, like motion or sensors or programming. Other cookbooks include a taste of many different things.

Some cookbooks are written with the absolute beginner in mind. A good beginner cookbook will spell out everything you need to do. Although these books are limited in the number of recipes they present, they include detailed step-by-step directions. Often, pictures and illustrations accompany the projects.

Frequently these books start with a simple project like flashing an LED. Each subsequent project then builds on the previous one to end with one exciting project at the end of the book.

Most beginner cookbooks attempt to teach you programming or electronics while you are enjoying your Arduino. Some key concept may be explained with each project. To get the best use from these books, you need to start at the beginning and work your way through the projects. You may not necessarily build each project, but read through the directions and software example to be sure you understand it.

Jumping to a project in the middle of the book could be difficult. If you skipped a project that explained a programming or electronics concept you don't understand, you may be left feeling very confused. Finding what you missed might be more difficult than you think. It's hard to find something in an index if you don't know what it's called. (It's hard to find it with a search engine, too.)

Other cookbooks assume you already know how to cook and are looking to make something unusual or really special. These books may include terms like "braise" or "spurious signals" without explanation. An engineer would use these books more like a reference book. When you need something special, you look it up. Otherwise, you cook on your own.

Like food cookbooks, most of these books include an ingredients list and recommended sources for hard-to-find items. They may or may not have a section on substitution of ingredients for when you don't have a particular item on hand and want to build it today.

Software is a big part of a successful project. Software excerpts or full-length software examples accompany each project, and a cookbook would be incomplete without them. Most cookbooks include complete software examples, but at some point you'll need to modify or combine them to suit your own purposes. Modifying or combining software examples, like cooking, takes a bit of practice.

If you follow the recipes to the letter, they produce a functioning project. Wiring must be precise. Programs must be copied exactly, and the gaps in excerpts must be filled. But if done accurately, the project should work.

A Comment About Comments

Comments are written for one purpose and one purpose only: for people to better understand what the code is intended to do. Because the compiler strips all comments from your code before compiling it, comments don't use any of the Arduino's memory. The good news is that you can use all the comments you want. The bad news is that to be helpful, your comments must match the code in intent and execution. A comment that indicates one thing while your code does another is less helpful than no comment. Is the comment right, or the code right? It's up to you to keep your comments up to date.

Comments are a type of documentation. Make a habit of including comments to record your intentions so your code is easier to debug later. If you need help, comments are essential, because most people decline to debug code if it doesn't have them. Examples in books and online should have comments, too.

Cookbooks Are Good

A beginner-level cookbook teaches you a variety of things with a series of projects. Each project provides a complete, functioning device for you to play with—a toy. You will be learning things, but you mostly get to play. Don't underrate play.

A toddler with a bucket of water and a funnel is studying hydrodynamics. But to him, it's just fun.

Your Arduino should be fun, too. A cookbook is probably the fastest way to build (and program) something to play with. Although the first few projects probably seem less than thrilling, you have to start somewhere. These are less about the project than they are about going through the steps to build and program one.

It's tempting to jump right to the last exciting project, but exercise a little patience. You will get the most from these books by starting at the beginning and working your way through the projects. While you are having fun, you will also be learning electronics and programming. Each recipe you follow increases your knowledge base without having to do a bunch of boring reading.

Basic cookbooks often include information on making measurements, soldering, reading schematics, and other important topics. These topics are not covered in depth, but they are enough to get started with.

Cookbooks intended for the experienced user can help when a particular problem comes up. Because these books are more sophisticated in their approach, you may need to hunt around to find what you need. Knowing the name of what you are after will help considerably but is not a guarantee. Some information is hard to find even when you know it's in there. These books are great for the experienced user and horrible for the beginner.

Cookbooks Are Limiting

You need to make a lot of recipes before you learn how to cook. One of the biggest drawbacks of cookbooks is their incompleteness. Building every project in a variety of cookbooks will create a working knowledge base you can move forward with. There is certainly nothing wrong with that, but you may never find a cookbook with exactly what you want to make in it. Can you adapt a recipe to your needs or cook without one? Can you change a project or build one not supplied in a book?

Cookbooks can be habit forming. It may be difficult to move beyond the comfort of step-by-step directions to strike out on your own. Even if you have all the knowledge you need, you might not know where to start. (Lucky you! Start with Chapter 3, "From Idea to Project.")

Although you can learn a lot about electronics and programming from a cookbook, what you learn will be limited to the things the projects require. The techniques used, especially programming techniques, may not be best practice. This becomes especially apparent when the microcontroller controls/monitors more than one thing at a time. Cookbooks don't usually cover this common situation well.

Troubleshooting may be hard if you don't understand the concepts behind a project. To make things worse, one of the best-kept secrets in publishing is that mistakes happen. Just because you read something in print doesn't make it true.

A publisher lists omissions, errors, mistakes, and other boo-boos in a document called an *errata sheet*, often available online. Authors also list mistakes found in their books online. It's a good idea to look for an errata sheet before embarking on a project. Some mistakes are also listed online by users/reviewers of a book, independently from the publisher and author, although these user lists aren't as complete.

Every Arduino book ever published includes a section on installing the IDE. (Yes, this book has one, too.) Because you only install the IDE once, assuming all goes well, at least one chapter of every book is wasted space. In addition, the first few projects may be nearly identical. Is it worth buying yet another cookbook for the one thrilling project at the end?

Reading a cookbook recipe, magazine article, or technical paper takes a serious amount of effort. Don't think a cookbook is going to do all the hard work for you. It's not enough to let your eyes travel over the words. They have to sink in and be understood.

Thinking takes time. Depending on what you already know, reading just four pages may take a week. Stop and research what you don't understand as you go. Work through the example calculations. Check your device data sheet for yourself.

Eventually, you'll want to make a project that's all your own. If you have been heavily dependent on cookbooks, take some time to wean yourself away from them. Start by modifying or combining projects. The last step from cookbook to independence can be a big one.

ONLINE PROJECTS

There are a million exciting Arduino projects on the Internet. Okay, that's an exaggeration. But there really are a lot of them, even after you eliminate duplicates.

Most of these projects sound more exciting than flashing an LED, although LED projects can be fun, too. Read the background on some of the more interesting projects, and you may be surprised to find that years of work have gone into them. Don't plan on building a copy of one in a weekend.

LED Fun?

Blinking LED projects can be fun. Don't believe me? Check out "persistence of vision" projects. Strobe lights, color-shifting mood lights, and crude video games are other possibilities.

Who doesn't love a flashing light? What TV explosion would be complete without a flashing LED duct taped to a car bumper in the previous scene? When it starts blinking faster, you know something exciting is going to happen.

Like anything on the Internet, the quality of online projects depends on the source of the information. The level of detail provided, like quality, varies greatly. Some projects have step-by-step directions, whereas others have very little actual implementation detail.

Many online projects don't attempt to teach the beginner. They don't provide enough detail for the beginner to clone or, worse, they are just advertisements to get you to buy the kit. Any project without software is incomplete. Consider these projects as inspiration rather than instruction.

Before you jump right in and start building something you found online, check to be sure that the project actually worked. Some online projects get to the debug phase and stall there permanently. All you will get out of copying them is experience.

You don't need to copy a project exactly. You will be better off building your own version of a project that you understand. It's easy to get caught up in the excitement and pick a project that is too complex. Build a simplified version first, and then expand it once it's working.

If you're brave, you don't need to limit yourself to Arduino projects. Any project for a microcontroller can be adapted for the Arduino. Microcontrollers are now commonly programmed in C, and translation is straightforward. You will need to pay attention to pin assignments and drive capabilities. You will also need to translate the hardware-specific part of the software.

ONLINE TUTORIALS

For the beginner, online tutorials are a better resource than online projects. Type "Arduino" and "tutorial" into your favorite search engine, and you will find dozens of tutorials. Tutorial format varies from text-only descriptions to videos to step-by-step directions with pictures. Some tutorials are a series of installments, whereas others are standalone, special-interest episodes.

Serial tutorials may be geared to work with a product or a kit a vendor is selling, whereas others are associated with a book or magazine. Knowing the source of the tutorial will let you consider the maker's intentions.

Yes, a distributor is trying to sell you parts, accessories, and kits. That's how it makes its money. A magazine or book is trying to get you to subscribe or buy the book. These sources are motivated to provide high-quality information. Unless a vendor's information is useful, you won't be successful and buy more stuff. Unless a book or magazine's information is helpful, you won't buy it or visit its website.

Access to tutorials is generally free, and you don't need to buy the kit to use the information. Depending on how the tutorial is structured, you may need to start at the beginning and work your way through the installments in order.

Tutorials are great because you can pause and repeat them. Watch them as much or as little as you like. Check out a tutorial from a different source if you get stuck or don't understand.

Using the model name of your Arduino should get your search engine to cough up better, more specific tutorials. For example, you can discover LilyPad tutorials by searching for the obvious "LilyPad" and "tutorial."

Special-purpose tutorials can help you handle specific but tricky situations. Many of these are created by individuals on their favorite topic (or gripe). Arduino and Arduino-related tutorials will probably be your primary interest.

Other useful special-purpose tutorials are not Arduino specific. Tutorials on soldering, making measurements with a multimeter, using a protoboard, and controlling a motor are just a few of those available. Look these up as you need them.

FORUMS

Forums are a public online meeting place for people with similar interests. They have a variety of uses, but let's consider them as a source for instructional information. Refer to Chapter 12, "Bragging Rights and Pleas for Help," for a more thorough discussion of forums. (Read Chapter 12 before you post anything.)

Caution

Forums are public places. Like any public place, keep yourself safe. Never post anything personally identifiable or agree to meet in person.

An official forum can be found at www.arduino.cc under the Forum tab. In addition to the official one, every reseller or vender has its own forum. Magazine websites also have forums. More Arduino forums seem to appear every day. Although this leads to a lot of duplication, it does give you more choices about where to find the information you need.

Forums have different membership requirements. Some you can browse, perhaps in a limited manner, without joining. Most require you to join for full access to materials or to post questions or comments.

Forums often have guides for the beginner. You are not the first beginner to have that exact problem. A resolution to your problem has likely been posted already. Read the beginner guide first, followed by the FAQ section.

Forums by their nature are fluid and change as people come and go. Some people are knowledgeable and helpful. Others are snarky and abusive. Moderators, people charged with keeping it clean, are sometimes professionals and sometimes volunteers.

The tolerance level for abuse depends on the moderator. Professional moderators, employed by commercial sites, are far less tolerant than volunteers. They have more at stake, because their job depends on it.

Every forum has occasional posts by agitators looking to stir up trouble or blow off steam. Ignore those people. It's the moderator's role to keep people in check, not yours. If these posts are more than occasional or you are uncomfortable with the attitude of a forum, use a different one. There are plenty to choose among.

OTHER BOOKS

In addition to cookbooks, there are a variety of other Arduino-specific books. These range from slim getting-started guides to thicker learn-by-doing courses. Because there is quite a bit of overlap in these books, it doesn't make sense to buy lots of them. Pick and choose the best.

In addition to Arduino-specific books, you will find a collection of other books helpful. You don't need to become an expert, but you will need some specific information on electronics and programming.

Yes, you could find information on electronics online, but only if you know what you're looking for. You can look up the "relationship between voltage and resistance," but only if you already know there is a relationship. If you don't know what to look up, search for "basic electronics."

Owning a library of books that covers the topics you need is a great resource. Some of the information you will use all the time. Other things you will want to look up once in a while. Looking something up in a book you are already familiar with is much faster than hunting a new source.

Programming is a little harder to look up online because you will get too many results. You don't really want to take a full course on C programming; you just need a few basic things. BASIC is also a programming language unrelated to C.

Carefully review any results from a search on "basic C programming" to be sure you really got what you wanted.

If you have a particular special interest, a book on that topic may be a good addition to your library. For example, a book on motor control, robotics, or automation might be a good choice if your interest is in building an autonomous bottle-fetching robot.

Visit your school or local public library to examine its collection for books that appeal to you. Don't limit yourself to the Arduino section. Check out the books on neighboring shelves, too. The best book to own is one you want to read.

C Programming

There are two big differences between Arduino C and standard C. The first difference is in structure, and the other is in execution.

In standard C, the main attraction (no pun intended) is the `void main()` function. `Main()` is where program execution starts, and simple programs often don't have any other functions.

In Arduino C, `void main()` is still there but has been hidden by the IDE. (You can look at `main.cpp` located in the Arduino Cores folder with a text editor, such as Notepad++.) Your code is placed in two required functions: `void setup()` and `void loop()`. `Setup()` executes once and only once. As the name implies, it's used to set up your Arduino and perform anything that needs to be done once up front.

After `setup()` has run, the function `loop()` is repeatedly called. This is different from standard C in that the program execution does not terminate. The name `loop` emphasizes that the Arduino code will continually loop until the power is removed or reset is applied.

In addition to the two required functions, you are free to write (and call) your own functions. Place these functions outside of `setup()` and `loop()` to ensure that they have global scope.

If you don't know C or you are a little rusty, a book on the C programming language intended for the beginner is a good addition to your library. That's not an error. I really do mean plain vanilla C and not C++.

It's true; C++ is a "newer" language. It's based on standard C and adds features to support structured programming. These features include overloading, inheritance, objects, and better standardization (portability). If you don't know what these mean, relax. You don't need them.

Because C++ is based on C, all of the C language is part of the C++ language. (There are a few minor differences around structures and their declaration.) All of the plain-vanilla C you need to program your Arduino will compile with a C++ compiler, like the IDE.

Although C and C++ have much in common, they differ in approach. C is a procedural (step-by-step) language, whereas C++ is an object-oriented (structured) one. Beginner books present the language from these different perspectives. (In reality, you can program with either approach in either language.)

At this point, it becomes a philosophical discussion. Unless you are already familiar with the object-oriented approach, C is arguably the better choice because your programs are likely to be procedural. Some hard-core programmers insist that C++ is just as good, if not better.

Okay, you could get a book on C++ instead. Look for one that uses the language first, structure second model. If the book starts with a description of objects and type definition statements, it's not the one you want.

You don't need to read the whole book cover to cover unless you want to. The topics you need to understand are (in no particular order) variables, constants, loops, decisions (`if` statements), functions (subroutine calls), reading/writing pins, some bit manipulations, `#including` libraries, and declarations. Additional nice-to-know topics are structures and pointers.

You don't get style points for writing fancy code. By keeping the code simple, it is easier to debug and reuse. Use the constructs you understand. Include enough comments so that someone else can understand your intentions. Six months from now, you will need these comments for yourself.

The official Arduino website (www.arduino.cc) has a reference section containing a language reference guide. For each construct listed, there is an explanation and an example. Unless you are already familiar with C, you might find the online guide a bit too brief.

General Electronics

Unless you have a cookbook that covers the topic, a book on general electronics is useful. Like programming books, electronics books intend to teach you everything there is to know. You don't need to be an expert, but you should understand the key concepts.

Key electronics concepts for the Arduino user include open/closed circuit, Ohm's law, power calculation, scientific/engineering units, voltage drop, open-collector and open-drain, pull-up resistors, and voltage dividers. Check your book's index for these terms.

As an alternative to a book, this information can be found on the Internet if you search for any of these terms. Online tutorials are also available.

Component identification is important for the hobbyist. Because you are likely to reuse your components, you need to know how to recognize them. Most components have a recognizable appearance and are marked with a code that identifies their value.

Full-color images of components, easily found on the Internet, provide a great way to identify your components. Search for images of "electronics components." Be careful of scale. Pictures make the components look much different in size than they actually are.

Local User's Groups and Clubs

Your school or local public library may have an Arduino club. (The usual warning to use caution in public places applies here, too.) The usefulness of these clubs will depend on the experience of the members and advisors.

Even if the clubs aren't truly useful, it can still be a lot of fun talking about what you would like to accomplish. Sometimes all you need to solve your own problem is to bounce ideas off of an attentive listener.

Don't expect other Arduino users to wire your circuit or program your Arduino for you. Even if you can find someone willing to do so, you won't learn if you deprive yourself of the opportunity. Get those who know to teach you. Let them describe the necessary steps, and then try it yourself.

No club at your school? Start one. In addition to getting help with your Arduino project, you get college application bonus points for starting a club. It looks good on a job application, too.

The Total Picture

No one information source can provide everything you want. Every source has its strengths and drawbacks. Books contain a lot of information but become dated and may contain errors. Basic information doesn't change, so that's not the issue. Arduino models do change, however, and the pictures in Chapter 1, "Meet the Arduino Family," will look old fashioned in time. As for errors, check the errata sheet for your edition and print or save a copy.

Cookbooks, while great for getting started, quickly become boring if the recipes aren't fun to make more than once. Like cookbooks, tutorials are good while you're learning but become boring later.

Forums are a great source for current information. Unlike other sources, they depend on the diligence of the moderator to keep the content relevant. Some forums become cluttered with commercial offers or inappropriate content. The posts need to be sorted or indexed to make the information easy to locate.

There are a lot of forums with nearly identical content, and it doesn't make sense to visit them all frequently. This abundance does provide options when your favorite forum has problems.

You will end up using information from a variety of sources. Your favorites will shift depending on what your current project is and what you find most helpful. Take notes as you go, and your notebook will become your best resource.

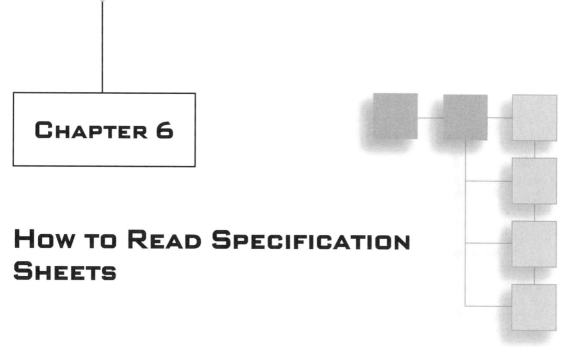

CHAPTER 6

HOW TO READ SPECIFICATION SHEETS

This chapter answers the following questions:

- What is a data sheet, aka specification sheet?
- When do I need to read the data sheet?
- Where do I get one?
- How do you read one of these things?
- How does the Atmel data sheet apply to an Arduino?

DATA SHEETS

When you need the most accurate technical information available on a component, the data sheet is where you find it. *Data sheets*, aka specification sheets, are documents written by a component manufacturer that supply all the technical information you might need to use their products.

Writers intend these documents for a technically savvy audience. They omit general information that's considered common knowledge. As a newbie, you may not have this "common knowledge." That's okay; you can find this information on the Internet once you know the terms you're looking for.

Although data sheets include a vast amount of information, you will only be interested in specific pieces. Extracting these pieces is an art form. Reading them becomes easier when you understand what you are and aren't interested in.

Let's look at a data sheet in general and then take a more detailed look at the data sheets for three devices: a shift register, a microcontroller, and a transistor. These aren't arbitrary choices. You are likely to use these components in your projects.

ANATOMY OF A DATA SHEET

Each company writes its own standards for the data sheets it produces. There is no industry-wide format for data sheets; however, they do contain the same information.

A data sheet contains the following:

- Title
- Feature summary
- Description
- Pinout
- Signal names and descriptions
- Logic diagram
- Truth table
- Maximum ratings
- Recommended operating conditions
- DC characteristics
- AC characteristics
- Timing diagrams/switching waveforms
- Mechanical information
- Ordering information
- Packaging information
- Limitations
- Version
- Errata

Title

At the top of the data sheet, you will find a title. The title varies but includes the device number (or numbers) and a descriptive name. Multiple similar devices may be included in a single data sheet. Make sure to match your part number exactly to one of those listed in the title.

Oddly, the word *data sheet* does not appear in the document title. Rather, it's a document type.

Feature Summary

A brief feature summary or a bulleted summary list of the device's key features appears at or near the top of the first page of the data sheet. Major features are listed at the top, with more minor features listed toward the end of the list.

Simple devices have simple descriptions. Complex devices may have feature lists that extend for a page and a half.

Some of these features or words used in the summary will be unfamiliar to you. Gradually, you will learn the jargon. Everyone has to start somewhere, so don't feel discouraged if you are looking up a lot at first.

Description

A description of the device's functions accompanies the summary list. This wordier narrative explains the device's normal functions and special properties. The expected audience for a data sheet is an engineer, so don't feel intimidated by the acronyms or jargon.

Simple devices have simple, short descriptions. Complex devices have extensive descriptions, sometimes divided into sections and indexed. The data sheet for an Atmel microcontroller, like the one on your Arduino, is hundreds of pages long.

Keep electronic copies of your data sheets, and don't attempt to memorize them. They're reference documents.

Pinout

The pinout, illustrated with a diagram, shows the assignment of signals to package pins. It isn't possible to use a device without this vital information.

A particular device is available in more than one package type. The number and arrangement of pins varies by package type, so the pin assignment will also vary.

Beware! Transistors do not have standard pinouts. You must look up the pinout for each one.

Signal Descriptions and Names

Signal names for simple devices, like transistors and logic gates, are standard. In the case of logic gates, signal functions are explained by a truth table. A number at the end of a signal name distinguishes each gate when a single package contains multiple gates.

For more complex devices, signal names and descriptions occupy their own section near the top of the data sheet. Read this section to get an understanding of how to connect and use the device.

The exact signal names vary by manufacturer but are consistent within a data sheet. There are some de facto standards; for instance, *clock* is often abbreviated as CLK and *reset* as RST. You will quickly become familiar with the ones used in your copy of the data sheet.

Signal names may be shown with a bar over them (or a slash after them) to indicate that they are active-low signals. Sometimes these signals are shown with no bar but are described as active low. RESET and OE (Output Enable) are often active low. See Chapter 4, "A Guided Tour of Your New Arduino," for a discussion on active-low signals.

Logic Diagram

The logic diagram shows the function of the device in equivalent "gates." This is not how the device is actually designed, but it's a model to help those familiar with standard logic to understand.

The logic diagram may take several forms, and a single data sheet may have more than one. They convey equivalent information, so pick the one that makes the most sense to you.

More complex devices have block diagrams instead of an equivalent logic diagram. A logic diagram would be too complicated to follow, or the manufacturer might consider it proprietary. Very complex devices, like a microcontroller, have multiple block diagrams that show various levels of detail.

Truth Table

For logic devices, the truth table or function table shows the outputs for every configuration of inputs. Symbols you might encounter while reading a truth table are usually explained nearby. If not, they are reasonably standard, and you can find them on the Internet.

Maximum Ratings

Maximum ratings are the maximum that the device can withstand without permanent damage. Ratings include voltage and current limits, power dissipation, and thermal limits. You must not operate a device above the maximum rating. Stay within the recommended conditions.

Recommended Conditions

You can operate a device indefinitely under the recommended conditions. The maximum supply voltage, maximum low input voltage, and minimum high input voltage are some of the conditions specified. Operating temperature range is also specified.

If you're going to operate in hot or cold environments, an industrial or automotive temperature range–rated part might be a good idea. For extreme environments, such as a high altitude balloon experiment or perhaps an amateur rocket flight, a military-rated part might be better. Table 6.1 shows typical temperature ranges for these ratings.

Table 6.1   Typical Temperature Ratings

Description	Min.	Max.	Application
Commercial	0°C	70°C	Household or indoor
Industrial	–40°C	85°C	Automotive or outdoor
Military	–50°C	125°C	High-altitude balloon or amateur rocket

Check the recommended operating conditions section of your device data sheet for temperature range.
Use temperatures specified as operating conditions.
Storage temperature refers to unpowered thermal exposure.

© 2014 Cengage Learning®

If not all the parts you plan to use are available (or affordable) for the wider temperature range, you may need a temperature-controlled environment. For short exposures, an insulated capsule (Styrofoam cooler) may be sufficient.

Check the data sheet for the recommended operating conditions. The *storage temperature range* refers to unpowered thermal exposure. The device needs to be warmed or cooled to the operating range before applying power. If it isn't, the device may be damaged and isn't guaranteed to work.

Arduino Temperature Range

Although the temperature range of the Atmel microcontroller IC is specified, the Arduino's temperature range is not. That means your Arduino isn't guaranteed to work at a particular temperature.

DC Electrical Characteristics

DC or *static characteristic* refers to the conditions that exist after inputs and outputs have stabilized. Input and output voltage levels and currents are specified.

The tables displaying this information are complex because they cover various Vcc (power) conditions and sometimes capacitive output loading. Read the headings for the tables carefully. If you get confused, print a page of the data sheet and highlight your device and conditions. Then keep the highlighted page in your notebook for future reference.

DC characteristics worth noting are the power supply range and the minimum high and maximum low signal levels specified with your supply voltage. Note the maximum power drawn by the device for use in your power budget.

You may need to calculate power indirectly from the maximum continuous rated current multiplied by the supply voltage.

Edge-Sensitive and Level-Sensitive

Edge-sensitive inputs respond to either the rising edge or the falling edge of the input signal. Clock inputs are often edge sensitive.

Level-sensitive inputs respond whenever the input voltage exceeds the thresholds. Level-sensitive signals are sometimes described as asynchronous because they do not have a definitive relationship with the clock.

Some devices, like the 74HC595, have a combination of edge-sensitive and level-sensitive signals.

AC Electrical Characteristics

AC, or *switching characteristics*, refers to the transient conditions created when inputs or outputs change state. The maximum operating frequency, rise and fall times, setup and hold times, propagation delays, and output disable times are among the many parameters (properties) specified.

Naming the parameters allows them to be referenced elsewhere in the data sheet without further explanation. Some of them may be used in timing diagrams, for example. All the important parameters listed will have a name.

Most parameters seem to start with *t* because they are times. A subscript indicates which time. For example, t_{SU} represents setup time.

Be sure to check the conditions specified with any table. Each table is a little different. If at first the tables seem identical, check the output loading conditions and supply voltage indicated especially for CMOS devices.

Minimums and maximums are guaranteed. Typical values are not guaranteed, so don't rely on them. Data sheets for newer devices often do not specify typical values for that reason.

Timing Diagrams and Switching Waveforms

Timing diagrams show the timing relationships between inputs and outputs. These signals are shown in a digital way with rise times and other AC characteristics ignored. Not all data sheets will include one. A typical shift register data sheet shows a logic "one" clocking through the shift register outputs.

Complex devices have a timing diagram for each section. CPU address and data on buses may be represented by one line with an indication of valid or invalid. Wide buses can be more compactly and readably depicted in this way.

Switching waveforms show the AC switching characteristics generated by the output drivers. Slew rates, rise times, fall times, and propagation delays may be depicted with switching waveforms.

Specific test conditions are used to measure these parameters, and your performance may vary. Real-life waveforms are never this neat. On the other hand, unless you are working with high frequencies, ugly waveforms are rarely a problem.

Mechanical Information

The data sheet includes mechanical information such as device body size, pin dimensions, pin one indication method, and lead-forming (how the leads are bend) parameters. You may be referred to a separate generalized document instead.

Mechanical information for Printed Circuit Board (PCB) layout may be included or referred to in another document. If you are designing your own board, you need this information. If you are using a solderless breadboard, any standard Dual In-line Package (DIP) package should work well.

Ordering Information

Ordering information includes both packaging information for the components and how the finished devices are prepared for delivery. The letter suffixes in the part number indicate the package type and the temperature range.

Finished devices might be delivered in tubes, on reels of tape, or in small boxes. The body types, temperature ranges, and packaging for shipping information are often presented as a table. Other information may also be shown, such as whether the device is "Green" or lead free.

Limitations

With the increased use of electronics in health care equipment, many manufacturers now include a warning not to use their devices without special approval. A more general limitation against use where lives may be at risk is now standard. Other limitations may be specified, such as prohibited use in explosive environments. Take these restrictions seriously.

Version

The data sheet has a version number or a letter. Toward the end of the data sheet, there may be a revision history. This version and history refer to the data sheet and not the device.

Errata

There may be an errata listing. Unlike book errata, these errors are in the device and not the documentation. Problems are documented as they're found, so it's a good idea to check the errata section of a new data sheet version.

Some device flaws have a workaround. A *workaround* is a method of compensating for a particular device defect, since a device can't be modified after manufacture. Sometimes there is no workaround, and a particular feature can't be used.

Examples

The next sections look at some real-life data sheets for three devices you are likely to use. Shift registers provide both drive and output expansion. Because you have an Arduino, you already have an Atmel microcontroller.

The transistor is a cheap, convenient switch for drive applications. A brief discussion of Ohm's Law and heat sinks is included because these concepts are needed to use transistors, and they aren't covered elsewhere.

The 74HC595 Data Sheet

Let's look at the data sheet for the 74HC595, an 8-bit shift register. (This choice isn't arbitrary. You will likely use this device or one like it.)

To locate a data sheet, use your favorite search engine with the terms *74HC595* and *data sheet*. Surprise! This device has more than one manufacturer.

Often, semiconductors devices are made by more than one company. These devices are "form, fit, and function" the same and can be used interchangeably. They are easily obtainable, and more than one source provides price competition, making them less expensive.

All the data sheets for the 74HC595 device contain the same information. Pick one and download an electronic copy. The sharp-eyed may notice there is a 74HC595 and a 74HC595A. The A version is a minor (does not impact form, fit, or function) improvement over the non-A version.

A long-established semiconductor manufacturer like Texas Instruments (www.ti.com under Products>Logic) or Fairchild Semiconductor (www.fairchildsemi.com under "logic") is an alternative to a search engine when you're looking for a data sheet. Semiconductor companies and divisions are bought and sold like any other business. In time, the names of the companies change.

As you may recall from Table 2.1 in Chapter 2, "Tools of the Trade," most part numbers start with two letters indicating the manufacturer. Texas Instruments produces the SN74HC595 and a high-power DMOS version, the TPIC6B595. ST Microelectronics makes the M74HC595 and a high-power DMOS version, the STPIC6D595. The two-letter code is unique to a manufacturer but might not be obvious.

The 74HC595's data sheet follows the general format. Whether you have one of these devices or not, look at the data sheet. You don't need to read every word, but identify the sections.

Part Number Shorthand

Try saying *SN74HC595* five times. It's not meant to be a tongue twister, but it is. All of these letters and numbers are meaningful, but most of the time all we really want to know is the device's main function.

The shorthand is the device's unique part number. In this case, 595 is the shorthand for any brand, any technology device with 595 in the part number.

In addition to standard output drivers, some component versions are available in tri-state, open-drain (or open-collector), output-enabled, high-power, and other flavors. These other flavors have different part numbers (and data sheets).

Let's compare the TPIC6B595 to the 74HC595. Both are 8-bit shift registers with output latches. The TPIC6B595 is an open-drain device that can pull an output low with 150 mA capability, but it can't drive an output high. A pullup resistor (or drive circuit) is needed. A typical use is controlling devices requiring more power or a voltage greater than Vcc, like banks of LEDs or relays. This is similar to the way low-side switching transistors are used.

By comparison, a 74HC595 is only able to pull an output low with 6–8 mA of current, but it can drive an output high with the same amount of current. (Excess current draw compromises the output voltage levels.) No pullup resistor is needed. The 74HC595 is limited to a total of 70 mA of current through all I/O pins. This is sufficient for many applications, such as driving single LEDs.

High-power versions of some components, including the 595, are available. These components typically have very different part numbers from the regular version and have different package sizes and number of pins.

A very good example is the TPIC6595 family, the high-power, open-drain version of the 74HC595. You can buy TPIC6595, TPIC6A595, TPIC6B595, TPIC6C595, and TPIC6D595, each with different current sink capabilities and package sizes ranging from 16 to 24 pins. www.avnet.com is a good source for the TPIC6x595.

Floating Pins

Generally speaking, it's okay to leave unused outputs unconnected. Input signals, particularly control signals, should not be left disconnected or "floating."

Floating CMOS device inputs change all by themselves from electricity in the air. They should be connected to Vcc or to ground either directly or with a resistor.

The data sheet specifies any pins that must be connected for proper operation. It's the definitive source for this information.

The Atmel ATmega328P Data Sheet

The Arduino family of microcontroller boards is based around the Atmel AVR microcontroller Integrated Circuit (IC) family. Most of the functionality of the Arduino comes from the Atmel microcontroller chip. Only power regulation and, on some models, the USB interface are provided by other ICs. Understanding the design details of the Arduino therefore depends on understanding the abilities of the microcontroller IC.

Atmel wants you to know what its microcontrollers can do, and it wants you to find using its devices easy and convenient. To assist you and other users, a page on Atmel's website (www.atmel.com/products/microcontrollers/avr/default.aspx) is devoted to the AVR family.

Information provided by Atmel includes data sheets, application notes, and user guides. Debuggers, emulators, and evaluation kits are offered for the engineer. An AVR software development suite is available, but it incorporates more tools than you likely need. (Because it includes fewer integrated tools, the Arduino IDE loads faster. Use the Arduino IDE until you outgrow it.)

Preliminaries

Before jumping straight into the data sheet, please read Chapter 4. Specifically, read the section "This Is Not on the Test" unless you have already done so. It gives you the background information you need to better understand the data sheet.

The techniques for reading a data sheet apply to all types of data sheets. After our practice with simpler devices, we're now ready for a challenge. Because the Arduino is the subject of this book, it makes sense to hone your skill on the data sheet for an Atmel microcontroller. Let's use the microcontroller on the Uno as an example for this section.

The data sheet provides the most detailed information available for a device. Once the device has been built into a product, the design engineer writes a manual or user guide. The manual should contain all the information you need and have implementation-specific information.

Each Arduino has a user information page located at www.arduino.cc on the Products page. Although it's not truly a manual, this page may contain all the information you need. Check the information page for your Arduino model to identify the microcontroller model used. When you need information about the microcontroller that's not included in the information page, you can find it in the data sheet.

The Correct Data Sheet

The first step in reading a data sheet is locating the correct one. Data sheets are written by the manufacturer and are available on the manufacturer's website, in this case Atmel. You can find a data sheet at www.atmel.com/products/microcontrollers/avr under the Documents tab. Use the search feature of the Atmel website if you have trouble finding the correct document. There is also a link to the correct data sheet on the Arduino web page for the Uno.

When the manufacturer's website is difficult to navigate, perhaps the fastest way to find a data sheet is to type the device number into a search engine together with the words *data sheet*. Give your search engine a try with the Uno's microprocessor model. If you don't have your Arduino Uno on hand, use *ATmega 328P data sheet*.

One of the returned results should be the data sheet (not the summary) from the Atmel website. (You can read the summary if you prefer, but we will be discussing the full version here.) Unfortunately, this search method also finds links to older versions of the data sheet. The URL that follows guides you to the latest data sheet and application notes is www.atmel.com/devices/atmega328p.aspx.

Once you have the data sheet, save an electronic copy to your local drive or CD-ROM. Because it is indexed and searchable, the electronic version is better than a printed copy. You can print a page or two later if you really need to. Don't blindly print the whole data sheet because it is hundreds of pages long.

The title on the relevant data sheet reads "Atmel 8-Bit Microcontroller with 4/8/16/32KBytes In-System Programmable Flash."

The first item to note is that these are all 8-bit microcontrollers. From the title, it is apparent that the main difference between these devices is the size of the built-in memory.

You should see the part number 328P listed along with a variety of others. Most data sheets cover more than one related part. Use the highlight text feature (of Adobe Reader) to mark your device if you find it confusing.

Also on the cover page, you will find a document number and a revision version letter. The current version for the 328P device is labeled 8271E–AVR–07/2012. 8271 is the document number, and E is the revision letter. The revision letter is the revision of the document, not the revision of the device. AVR is the family of microcontroller devices. 07/2012 is the month and year. Although the document number won't change, the revision letter and date may.

The 328 Data Sheet

The Atmel data sheet is in most ways a typical data sheet. All the expected sections are there; they are just longer. We'll talk about some of the highlights, but you can read the data sheet for details.

Unless you are building your own design around this device, the data sheet is a reference document. Read about a feature you are exploring, but don't read it cover to cover or try to memorize it.

Each section starts with an overview that explains how that feature works in more detail. If you are confused by the feature summary, check out the overview in the detailed section. Use the index to quickly locate that feature's section.

Pinout

The Uno uses the 28 PDIP package. If you examine the signal names associated with the pins, they will seem familiar. We've seen these names before. Take another look at Table 4.1 in Chapter 4. To this, we now add another layer of mapping for the package pin.

If you bought a fully assembled Arduino, you don't need to worry about physical package pins. If you are designing your own PCB or using a microcontroller chip with a solderless breadboard, you have to map the signal names to the correct package pin.

Rather than the more confusing software pin number, use the unambiguous signal name because this matches the Arduino documentation and software. Be sure to select the pinout that matches your package.

An explanation of the signal functions and meanings follows the pinout. Sometimes the signals are described individually, like AREF. Other times, as for Input/Output (I/O) ports, they are described collectively.

Overview and Block Diagram

The overview section provides a description of the major functions, whereas the block diagram shows how the functions relate to each other. Figure 4.3 in Chapter 4 shows the block diagram from the data sheet. Read the overview section and take a look at the block diagram to get a feel for how the pieces fit together.

From the overview, it is clear that the AVR CPU with associated memories is the central feature of the microcontroller. Both the CPU and the memories have detailed sections of their own in the data sheet.

Other blocks may or may not have an individually detailed section, depending on complexity. Some functions, like the interrupt controller, aren't shown on the top-level block diagram. Other blocks, like power supervision, are split between multiple sections. Use the index and table of contents to locate the sections covering your interest.

The AVR CPU

The AVR CPU section is worth studying. This architecture, the Harvard architecture, uses separate data and instruction buses. Instructions are pipelined and can, in theory, execute one instruction per clock cycle.

You need to be a skilled programmer to get close to this level of performance. Fortunately, you don't need to be an expert because the compiler does the hard work for you, and the typical project requires little computing power.

As an Arduino user, you will be using macros and function calls for most of your programming. Then it's up to the compiler to make the most efficient machine code possible.

You can write machine code in assembly language; the IDE supports it. But it's time consuming and error prone. Plus, it's difficult to beat the performance of modern compiler-generated machine code. Unless you have an interest in machine code, it's much more efficient to write C code and let the compiler do its job.

Take a look at the AVR CPU block diagram. There is some overlap between this block diagram and the top-level block diagram shown at the front of the data sheet. The memories shown in both block diagrams are the same memories. The CPU block diagram shows additional detail, including that the flash contains the program instructions and the SRAM contains data. The flash, SRAM, and EEPROM memories are discussed in the next section.

Take the time to explore this section of the data sheet; it's readable and contains a lot of information. Because it was written for the engineer, not all common engineering concepts are explained. For example, the stack, register file, pipelining, indirect addressing, and their uses are not explained. Don't worry about the gritty details; let the compiler do its job.

The Stack

The stack is simply a section of the SRAM used as a first in, last out (FILO) memory. A memory location or register keeps track of the top of the stack. Your microcontroller uses the stack as temporary storage for a variety of things, like local variables. The stack is most commonly used to service interrupts and for code jumps, as when functions are called.

Memories

The Harvard architecture has two memory spaces: one for instructions (flash), and one for data (SRAM). An additional memory (EEPROM) occupies part of the data memory space. The EEPROM provides nonvolatile memory for data storage that would otherwise be impossible; the instruction and data memories occupy separate paths in the Harvard architecture. The size of the memories varies with the model of the Atmel microprocessor.

You can set up the program memory (flash) in two ways. The typical Arduino uses a boot program called a *bootloader*. The name emphasizes its function of placing application code into the program sector.

A boot code section is not a requirement; the ATmega microcontroller and consequently the Arduino can be programmed with an in-circuit programmer instead. This frees up the boot sector for additional program space. An instruction memory map shows how the flash memory is used. There are two instruction memory maps in the data sheet: one with a boot sector and one without.

The data memory map, distinct and separate from the instruction memory map, shows the SRAM, register file, I/O registers, and extended I/O registers. Using the memory address space to control I/O is called *memory-mapped I/O*. In addition to I/O registers, control and status registers, as well as other peripherals like counters, are located in this space.

Although you could, you won't be manipulating memories directly. Macros and function calls from regular or special-purpose libraries do the hard part for you. More accurately, the person who wrote the functions has done the difficult bit for you. Then the compiler takes care of all the messy details for you. Trust the compiler.

Clock Distribution

For normal Arduino uses, the clock distribution is not something to be concerned about. The Arduino Uno uses an external 16.0 MHz crystal oscillator as the system clock. There's little reason to change it.

If you purchased a microcontroller chip with no bootloader on it, you need to select the crystal oscillator as the system clock. The easiest way to set the clock select fuse (and the other fuses) is to put a bootloader on the chip. You can remove the bootloader later (by overwriting it) if you want because the fuse to use the crystal oscillator will stay set.

Internally, the system clock is divided into separate domains, which allows unused sections of the microcontroller to be shut down when they're not needed. The clock domains are illustrated and described in the clock distribution section of the data sheet.

Power Management

Clock distribution becomes more important when you need to save power. CMOS devices consume the most power when they're actively switching. Slowing or stopping the clock dramatically reduces the power consumption.

Sleep modes can stop the clock for individual sections of the microcontroller. Sleep modes are particularly useful for extending battery life. The ADC, Analog Comparator, and other pieces can be disabled to save power. The data sheet contains a number of recommendations on minimizing power consumption.

Interrupts

You may find the interrupt section of the data sheet a bit confusing unless you are already familiar with the concept of interrupts. Think of an interrupt as having two pieces: the trigger for an action and the action itself.

The Interrupt Service Routine (ISR) performs the action. Usually two jumps are involved. The first jump is to a fixed (instruction) address called the *interrupt vector*. The interrupt vector in turn contains a jump to the start of the ISR. The ISR is a fancy name for a small piece of code. Refer to Chapter 9, "Writing the Code," for more on ISRs.

Each interrupt source has its own interrupt vector. Twenty-six interrupt vectors are provided and detailed in the data sheet. (Be sure to use the table for the 328P microcontroller.)

The interrupt trigger is the interrupt source. The microprocessor provides a plethora of interrupt sources, both internal and external. The internal interrupt sources include the timer/counters, Serial Peripheral Interface (SPI), Universal Asynchronous Receiver Transmitter (UART), Two-Wire Interface (TWI), Analog Digital Converter (ADC), watchdog, and memory-ready signals. External interrupts include reset, several dedicated interrupt pins, and 24-pin change interrupts bundled together into three groups (PCINT0-7, PCINT8-14, and PCINT16-23).

Many pin change interrupts become unavailable when the pins are used for something else. PCINT6 and 7 are not available when the clock comes from the external oscillator, which is always the case on the Uno. PCINT14 is not available because that pin is fused for reset. (Again, this refers specifically to the Uno.) PCINT15 is not brought out to a pin on the 328P.

Control registers provide individual and global interrupt control. Some interrupt sources are latched and some are not. Allowing another interrupt to occur while servicing the current interrupt is called *nested interrupts*. Nested interrupts are disabled by default.

You can use nested interrupts—with caution. They are notorious for causing stack overflows, which are a type of software crash.

I/O Ports

The digital I/O ports are configured and controlled by three registers. The Data Direction register bits (DDRB, DDRC, and DDRD) control whether the port bits are configured as input or output.

The Port register's function depends on the direction configured. This register controls the use of the internal pullup for pins configured as inputs. For outputs, this register controls the driver level for pins.

The Pin register contains the input value of the pins. Some functions are not obvious. Writing a "one" to a Pin register bit toggles the corresponding bit in the Port register.

Because pins are at a premium, most pins have alternate functions. When an alternate function is enabled, the pin can't be used as general I/O, and the I/O configuration registers don't have an effect on it. The remaining pins in the port are unaffected.

I/O pins are typically configured at the beginning of a program and then left alone. It is possible, but not recommended, to change the configuration during program execution. If you change the configuration during operation, the data sheet details some of the issues you need to address.

Use the Arduino function calls for I/O configuration because they are simple and convenient. You can accomplish configuration with direct register accesses, but there isn't really an advantage.

For reading and writing the pins, there may be an advantage to direct register accesses—typically speed! Direct port manipulation is fast, but you give up the configuration checking that the functions `digitalRead()`, `digitalWrite()`, and `analogRead()` perform.

Function calls require the CPU to do extra steps, so they are slower than direct accesses. Using direct register reads and writes is faster. Let's keep some perspective on speed here. Even a slow function is extremely fast by human standards. Speed becomes an issue for audio signals, accurate timekeeping, and fast display updates.

Refer to Chapter 7, "Input and Output," for a more extensive discussion on I/O and how to use it.

Timer/Counters

There are three timer/counters built in to the 328P. They provide the obvious counting and timing and the less obvious PWM, frequency generation, frequency measurement, and pulse width measurement. In addition, a variety of events can trigger interrupts, including count matches and rollover.

As an Arduino user, this section of the data sheet doesn't give you all the information you need. The use of the timers is integral to some of the time-related Arduino functions. Table 6.2 summarizes the common Arduino functions with the timers they employ.

Table 6.2   Arduino Function Timer Summary

Timer	Function	Use
0	millis()	Millisecond time measurement
0	micros()	Microsecond time measurement
0	delay()	Delay in milliseconds
0	delayMicros()	Delay in microseconds
0	analogWrite()	Sets up PWM on pins 5 (PD5) and 6 (PD6)
1	analogWrite()	Sets up PWM on pins 9 (PB1) and 10 (PB2)
2	analogWrite()	Sets up PWM on pins 3 (PD3) and 11 (PB3)

© 2014 Cengage Learning®

Multiple functions that depend on the same timer may interfere with each other. For example, the use of the `delay()` and `millis()` functions change the PWM signals on pins 5 and 6. Also, modifying the prescaler for a timer impacts the functions that depend on that timer.

Libraries beyond the default ones and their functions may use the timers to make measurements. You may see occasional interferences.

SPI

The SPI provides a means for two devices to communicate with each other in a master-slave configuration. The data sheet gives a good description of how the SPI interface is configured and used. Because this is a standard interface, you can find descriptions in other sources if the data sheet is unclear. Any peculiarities of the microcontroller implementation of the SPI are described in the data sheet.

For the Arduino user, there are SPI functions that can be used to set up and transfer data. The Arduino SPI library page provides commands for setting the SPI clock frequency and clock/data modes. The SPI master sends out a clock pulse for each bit transferred; it is not a free-running clock.

This interface is also used to download boot code with an in-circuit programmer. The programmer uses the reset pin to take control and program the flash memory. Any devices connected to the SPI pins should be designed not to interfere with the SPI Clock (SCK), Master In Slave Out (MISO), and Master Out Slave In (MOSI) pins when reset is asserted to avoid signal interference with the programmer.

The SPI standard defines how the data is formatted, sent, and received. It does not specify how the data is used. This is up to you, or it may conform to another protocol.

You can connect multiple SPI slaves; however, each slave needs a unique Slave Select signal. One typical use of SPI is to send data to a shift register, such as 74HC595, or to a device with multiple shift registers, such as MAX7219. Shift registers can be daisy-chained with the data passing through each device to the next in line. The entire chain shares the clock and Slave Select line.

For the Arduino user, the SPI hardware provides a good way to connect serial devices. The devices can be completely devoid of intelligence, like a shift register, or they can be smart, like a shield with a microcontroller on it. Or they can be a mix, because each is supplied with its own Slave Select.

Software can mimic the SPI interface; however, anything done in software is much slower than in hardware and requires more processing power. As a first choice, use the hardware! The Arduino libraries provide convenient functions both to control the SPI and to imitate it in software.

Usart or Uart

What's the difference between a USART (Universal Synchronous Asynchronous Receiver Transmitter) and a UART (Universal Asynchronous Receiver Transmitter)? The difference is the ability to operate synchronously—that is, with an external clock.

The advantages of an external clock include faster transmission speeds. The disadvantages include the need to carry an additional signal and a restriction on transmission distances unless external drivers/receivers are used to maintain signal integrity.

USART

The USART is one of the most flexible serial communication devices available. Asynchronous communication, buffering, error detection, interrupt generation, and configurable frame formats are its major advantages over the TWI and SPI.

The features of the USART can support an SPI interface. Unlike the other SPI interfaces, the USART provides hardware-supported frame generation, buffering, and error checking.

It's difficult to adequately sum up in just a couple of paragraphs a device as complex as a USART. But let's try anyway, at least for the most common case. There are three pieces of information needed to set up the USART: clock source, baud rate, and frame format.

Typically, you will use the USART (as a UART) asynchronously with no external clock line. The UART uses an internal clock set to the baud rate selected (such as 9600) to sample the incoming bits. The start bit synchronizes the receiver timing and locates the middle of the bit time.

The advantage is that the clock signal doesn't need to be brought over the connection, which saves a wire. It also gives the mode its name, *asynchronous*, meaning there isn't an external clock. This is used so often that it's typically called *normal mode*. The data sheet calls it *normal asynchronous mode*.

The next piece is frame format. Serial data is just a bunch of ones and zeros. To extract meaning, you need to organize the bits in a recognizable way. Frames are a group of bits with a particular organization. At the most rudimentary level, they have a start indicator, data, parity (or some sort of error detection), and an ending indicator.

The usual frame configuration for a UART is 1, 8, none, and 1, translating to one start bit, eight data bits, no parity bits, and one stop bit. With the addition of a "none" up front meaning no polarity, this is the typical configuration for a computer serial port. (For a computer, this is often called 8N1, with no reference being made to the start bit.)

Bits that are transmitted that have no use beyond the data transmission are called *overhead*. Start, stop, and parity bits fall into this category. All serial data streams have overhead, so your data transmission rate is less than the baud rate.

That brings us to our last piece of configuration: baud rate. *Baud rate* refers to symbols per second. This doesn't necessarily translate to bits per second because some symbols encode multiple bits. Other times, multiple symbols represent one bit. Our case is the simplest; our baud rate is our bit rate. (As mentioned earlier, bit rate is not the same as data rate.)

For example, a baud rate of 9600 bps with 8N1 requires 11 bits to be transmitted for each 8-bit data byte, yielding an approximate data rate of 6980 bps. For those keeping score, the 11 bits are one start bit, eight data bits, one stop bit, and one "space" bit, meaning one bit time period before the start bit can go active again.

The data sheet contains all the information you need to use the USART in all conceivable configurations and with many system clock speeds. You could easily go into information overload here. Divide and conquer by breaking it into the three basic elements: clock source, frame format, and baud rate. Disregard everything else that doesn't apply to your configuration.

As an Arduino user, you will most likely use functions to set up the USART. Specifically, you will use the function call `Serial.begin(9600);` which sets up the default 8N1 configuration with 9600 baud rate. Parameters for this function allow you to set other configurations. If you need a configuration that this function does not support, you may need to read the data sheet to figure out how to configure the USART.

For example, maybe you need nine data bits instead of eight. Clearly, this is a frame format issue, and you can skip directly to that section. You quickly discover that three bits in a register control the number of data bits in the frame. Reading the description provides the vital information that two register reads are required, and the register containing the high bit must be read first. Concatenation with the low register yields the 9-bit data word.

Communication with your computer uses the USART, both for download and during sketch execution for the serial monitor. You can use this connection for other purposes like sending data to your computer for storage or processing. You can use USART for connection to some device other than your computer. But you can only do one of these things at a time.

Pins D0 and D1 provide the connection to the USART via the USB port. Because the connection to your computer is so useful, make an effort to keep these pins free. If you must use them, avoid attaching drivers to these pins to prevent download issues. (Don't use them as inputs.)

TWI

Don't be confused by the name. TWI (Two-Wire Interface), 2-wire interface, and I^{2}C (Philip's brand name) are all names for the same interface.

The TWI provides a means for multiple devices to communicate with each other over a bus in a master-slave configuration. The protocol provides a master arbitration process, so multiple masters are possible. (Only one device will be master at a time.) This is a standard protocol.

The data sheet gives a good description of how the TWI interface is configured and used. Because this is a standard interface, you can find descriptions in other sources if the data sheet is unclear.

The peculiarities of the microcontroller implementation of the TWI are described in the data sheet. There is a note about the TWI in the revision E data sheet errata.

The TWI defines how the data is formatted, sent, and received. It does not specify how the data is used. That's up to you, or it may conform to another protocol.

Analog Comparator

The analog comparator, as the name implies, compares two signals with each other. The result is lower than or higher than, with no levels in between. It can't tell you how much higher or lower.

The ADC can always use the default signals AIN0 and AIN1. The comparator and ADC are not completely independent. When the ADC is disabled, the AIN1 signal can come from a variety of other sources. The result of the comparison can set a register bit, generate an interrupt, or be counted.

There is a note about the ACME bit described in this section in the revision E data sheet errata.

Analog to Digital Converter

The ADC operates much like a standalone ADC, using a technique called *successive approximation*. One bit at a time, from the MSB to LSB, is set and the result converted to an analog level. The converted level is compared with the original level. If the result is closer to the original, the bit stays set. If not, the bit is cleared and the next bit is set.

Successive approximation takes a fixed amount of time per bit, so more accurate results take longer. The ADC provides 10 bits of accuracy but can be used as an 8-bit ADC if less precision is required.

An analog multiplexer allows one of eight input signals, or several built-in sources, to be selected as the input to the ADC. (When used with the ADC, the MUX can't be used with the Analog Comparator.) Only one of the inputs can be converted at a time, so each must be monitored in turn.

The data sheet explains the function of the ADC in extensive detail, including register definitions, timing diagrams, and a Nyquist reference.

Bootloader

As an Arduino user, you don't need to concern yourself with this section. Just use a version of the bootloader from the Arduino site and remember to set your board type in the IDE to match. Label your Arduino with the bootloader version for future reference.

The bootloader has other functions, too. It sets the fuses to select various features, such as the crystal oscillator as the system clock. These fuses remain set, and you can remove the bootloader later by overwriting it.

If you purchased a microcontroller chip with no bootloader on it, you need an in-circuit programmer. Refer to Chapter 8, "The IDE."

Electrical Characteristics

Just as it does for simple devices, the electrical characteristics section of a data sheet specifies the maximum and minimum operating parameters. These values are guaranteed, unlike typical characteristics.

Tables specify DC electrical characteristics. Characteristics common to all devices are presented in some tables. Other tables cover only one device. Make sure to find the table for the 328P, which is different from the 328.

Operating voltage and temperature ranges are among the items specified. Current draw for CMOS devices depends on the supply voltage and the frequency of operation. The tables in this section reflect that. Among the AC characteristics specified are timing waveforms for the serial interfaces.

Register Summary

The register summary, like the memory map, shows the addresses of all the registers. In addition, it references the name of each bit and the data sheet page that describes the register. Two addresses are specified for some registers. The address to use depends on the assembly-level command used to make the access, as indicated in the table's notes.

The Arduino libraries contain macros defined as the register addresses and bit names. They allow you to refer to the registers and bits by name rather than address and bit number.

Instruction Set

For the interested reader, this section provides the complete instruction set for the microcontroller. Assembly-level mnemonics, operands, operation, description of the operation, relevant bits in the status register, and number of clock cycles required are indicated in a table.

The IDE supports using assembly-level instructions. You must understand the microcontroller's internal structure to use them effectively. If you don't, stick with C and let the compiler perform the translation.

Ordering Information

If you need to order a replacement microcontroller for your Uno, this section gives you the part number to order: ATmega328P-PU for a 28-pin DIP. You can also read the markings on the device. This part is specified to work over the temperature range of -40°C to +85°C. The ATmega328P-PN can run hotter, up to +105°C. (The other parts on the Arduino may or may not support that higher temperature.)

OHM'S LAW AND POWER CALCULATIONS

In the following sections, Ohm's Law describes the relationships between voltage, current, and resistance. These relationships are fundamental to physics and electronics. If you understand basic algebra, these values are easy to calculate. Web page calculators exist for those who are mathematically challenged.

You can calculate power from voltage and current. You can derive algebraic substitutions for voltage or current from Ohm's Law when one of those values isn't easily available. Here's Ohm's Law and the equation for power.

Ohm's Law	$V = IR$	Voltage = Current × Resistance
Power	$P = IV$	Power = Current × Voltage

Some components, like diodes, aren't characterized by Ohm's Law. Instead of a resistive value, they have a characteristic voltage drop. Don't be confused by the name. *Voltage drop* is the voltage difference from one side of the component to the other.

The voltage drop for diodes is typically 0.7 V (higher for LEDs) and is specified in the data sheet. Power for these devices is still calculated in the same way. In this case, the voltage is the voltage drop.

The Transistor

The discrete transistor is one of the most versatile semiconductors. It can be used as an oscillator, amplifier, current source, or switch. Every complex semiconductor is built out of collections of transistors. You can build anything out of them! But you will most likely use one as a switch.

The most confusing aspect of using a transistor is picking one; there are literally thousands to choose among. The data sheets for transistors don't follow the same general format but still contain all the information you need. Let's look at a little background information and then go on to the selection process.

There are two major families of transistors, distinguished from each other by the type of semiconductor technologies they are constructed with. Bipolar Junction Transistor (BJT) and Field Effect Transistor (FET) devices are the most common.

Both BJTs and FETs are produced in complementary device types. BJTs come in NPN and PNP flavors. FETs come in N-channel and P-channel flavors. The differences are inherent in the construction of the device and the type of the minority charge carrier. The practical implication is that the first flavor uses a positive control voltage to turn on, and the second uses a negative control voltage to turn on. See Table 6.3.

Table 6.3 Transistor Flavors

Flavor	Voltage Type
NPN BJT or N-channel FET	Positive control voltage
PNP BJT or P-channel FET	Negative control voltage

© 2014 Cengage Learning®

Some applications, like class AB audio amplifiers, require matched complementary transistor pairs. Most applications don't need these pricey matched pairs but do require the correct device.

Unfortunately, the length of this book doesn't allow in-depth analysis of these examples. You can find information on transistors online or in your basic electronics book. Look for BJT or FET transistors used as switches. Internet transistor calculators are also available.

BJT Transistors

BJT transistors have three pins: Base, Emitter, and Collector. See Figure 6.1 for the symbols and pin names. For the NPN device, a small current injected into the base induces a large current to flow from the collector to the emitter.

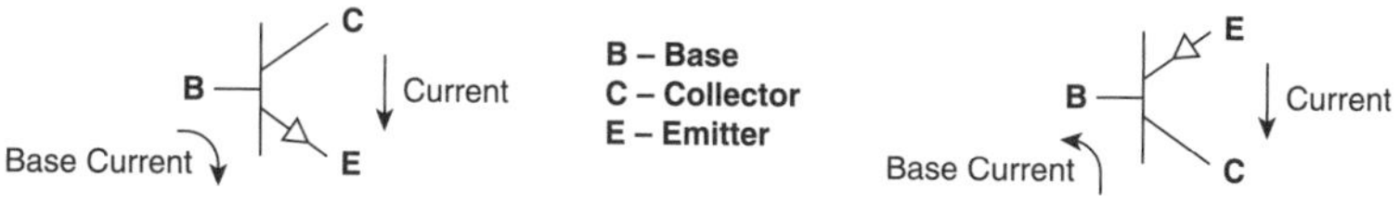

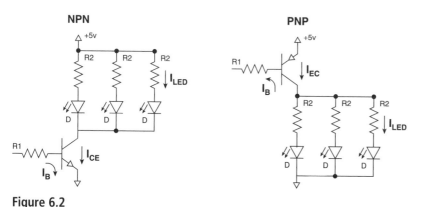

Figure 6.1

BJT transistors.

© 2014 Cengage Learning®

A base current flows when the voltage of the base is positive relative to the emitter voltage. When the base voltage is lower than that of the emitter, no current flows between the collector and the emitter. (There will be some small leakage current that you can usually ignore.)

For the PNP device, a small current drawn from the base induces a large current flow from the emitter to the collector. When the base voltage is negative relative to the emitter, the transistor is on. When the voltage is positive, the transistor is off.

Figure 6.1 shows the direction of current flow through the NPN and PNP BJT transistors. The current through the base is usually much smaller than the collector-emitter current.

The data sheet parameters to look for in BJT transistor data sheets are I_{SAT} and V_{CE}. I_{SAT} is the base current required to saturate the transistor. V_{CE} is the voltage drop through the transistor and is typically 0.7 V. This value is needed for current calculations.

BJT LED Driver Applications

Figures 6.2 and 6.3 show how you can use an NPN or PNP BJT transistor to control LEDs when more current or voltage is required than the Arduino pin can provide. Arrows indicate the direction of current flow.

Figure 6.2

BJT applications: R1 = 300 ohm, R2 = 100 ohm.

© 2014 Cengage Learning®

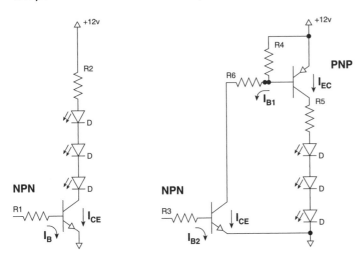

Figure 6.3

BJT transistors with 12-volt power supply: R1 = R3 = R6 = 300 ohm, R2 = R5 = 240 ohm, R4 = 10 K ohm.
© 2014 Cengage Learning®

In both the NPN and PNP cases, the transistor is turned on to illuminate the LEDs. A digital high turns on the NPN transistor, whereas a digital low turns on the PNP transistor. In Figure 6.3, the NPN transistor used with the PNP transistor isolates the Arduino's pin from the 12 V supply.

Each LED needs its own current limit resistor. You might think that the LEDs can be connected in parallel with a single resistor. This doesn't work because the current takes the path of least resistance and flows (mostly) through a single LED. (Some current flows through each path—even high-resistance paths.) Uneven current causes uneven illumination. You can use this transistor technique to drive devices that require more than the 20 mA current that the Arduino can supply. Inductive loads, like motors and relay coils, require a "snubbing" diode in parallel with the load.

FET Transistors

FET transistors typically have four pins: source, drain, gate, and substrate (aka body). However, most come in three pin packages with the source connected to the substrate internally. See Figure 6.4 for the symbols and pin names.

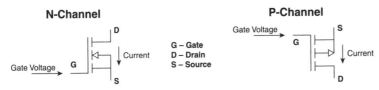

Figure 6.4

FET transistors.
© 2014 Cengage Learning®

Unlike the BJT, the voltage at the gate rather than current controls the FET transistor. For the N-channel device, a positive voltage (relative to the source) applied to the gate permits a large current flow from the drain to the source. For the P-channel device, a negative voltage (relative to the drain) at the gate allows a large current flow from the source to the drain.

Figure 6.4 shows the direction of current flow through N-channel and P-channel FET transistors. No current flows through the gate.

Transistors are nonlinear devices that have several regions of operation. Because we are using transistors as switches, we want to operate them in the saturated region. Standard FETs require relatively large voltages, 10 Volts, to fully turn on (saturate). FETs compatible with 5 V are referred to as *logic level* transistors.

The data sheet parameters of interest for a FET are V_{SAT} and R_{DS}. V_{SAT} is the voltage required to saturate the FET. R_{DS} is the resistance in the current path from drain to source when the FET is saturated.

FET Transistor Driver Applications

Figures 6.5 and 6.6 illustrate how you can use a FET transistor to control LEDs. In these examples, the FET transistors must be logic-level devices so that you can control them with just 5 Volts.

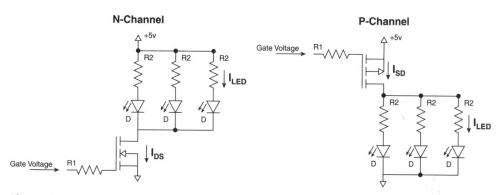

Figure 6.5

FET applications: R1 = 220 ohm, R2 = 200 ohm.

© 2014 Cengage Learning®

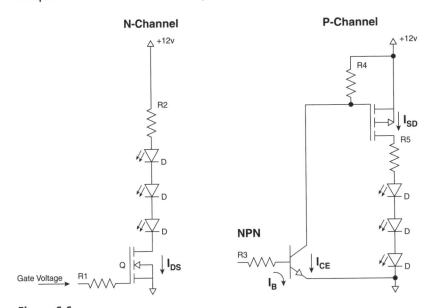

Figure 6.6

FET applications with 12-Volt power supply: R1 = R3 = 220 ohm, R2 = R5 = 510 ohm, R4 = 560 ohm.

© 2014 Cengage Learning®

The gate of the FET looks like a capacitor electrically. Very little current flows through the gate of a FET. Current only flows when the gate voltage changes, and a series resistor must be used to limit the peak current during the switching phase.

Unlike the voltage drop of a BJT, the critical parameter for a FET is the internal resistance (R_{ds} or R_{sd}). The internal resistance varies from FET to FET and must be looked up in the device's data sheet. You can calculate the voltage drop through the transistor by multiplying the current through the transistor by the internal resistance. The voltage drop through a FET is smaller than through a BJT.

Figure 6.5 shows how to use N-channel and P-channel FETs to control LEDs. In both cases, the transistor is turned on to illuminate the LEDs. A digital high turns on the N-channel transistor, whereas a digital low turns on the P-channel transistor.

You can use this technique to drive any device that requires more than the 20 mA of current the Arduino can provide. As with a BJT, a "snubbing" diode is needed for inductive loads. As with the previous figures, arrows indicate the direction of current flow.

Figure 6.6 illustrates the use of FET transistors for switching voltages above Vcc. Similarly to the PNP BJT case, the P-channel FET requires a second transistor to isolate and protect the Arduino pin. This transistor is shown as a BJT, but you could use another FET instead. (The BJT is slightly cheaper.)

Low-Side or High-Side Switch?

You can choose to place a switch (the transistor) between the device you are controlling and the ground. This is called *low-side switching*. NPN and N-channel devices are better for low-side switching.

The other choice is to place the switch between the power source and the device you are controlling. This is *high-side switching*. PNP and P-channel devices are better for high-side switching.

Some components, like common anode LED arrays, require high-side switching. Other devices, like common cathode 7-segment displays, require low-side switching. You can control high-voltage devices, motors, and many other devices with either low-side or high-side switching, whichever is more convenient.

TRANSISTOR SELECTION GUIDELINES

As previously discussed, the data sheet is the ultimate source for device information, but there are thousands of different transistors. Nobody has time to read and compare thousands of data sheets. Let's look at the criteria you use to select a transistor to use as a switch.

Once you have picked the characteristics your transistor needs, an efficient way to find a transistor device is to use a distributor's device selection tool. Be sure to select a device that is in stock and not expensive. Not all devices can be purchased as single devices. Some devices can only be bought by the reel or tube. Avoid devices that are listed as end-of-life or obsolete.

Summary of transistor considerations:

- BJT or MOSFET or "logic level" MOSFET
- NPN/N-channel or PNP/P-channel
- Current
- Voltage
- Package style
- Cost and availability

BJT or FET?

The first choice to make when selecting a transistor is BJT or FET. Advantages and disadvantages of each (when used as a switch) are summarized in Table 6.4.

BJT is a good choice for a general-purpose transistor used as a switch, especially for small currents. These transistors are available and inexpensive. In addition, they are relatively less static sensitive. For larger currents or when a BJT can't meet your needs, consider a FET.

FET transistors have a lower internal resistance and voltage drop. They can handle more current with less heat generation. They are more static sensitive and a bit more expensive. By FET, we mean Metal Oxide Semiconductor FET (MOSFET) and not Junction gate FET (JFET). For higher current applications, consider a power MOSFET.

For LilyPad (or other 3.3 V users), FETs require more voltage to operate (in the saturated region) as a switch than you have available. Select a BJT transistor instead.

Table 6.4 Select Transistor Characteristics

BJT Advantages	BJT Disadvantages
Cheap and common	Runs hotter (higher voltage drop)
Less static sensitive	Higher "on" voltage drop
Easy to use	
Can be saturated at 3.3 V	

FET Advantages	FET Disadvantages
High input impedance	Static sensitive
Cooler	May not be 5 V controllable
Low "on" voltage drop	Can't be saturated with 3.3 V
High current switching	

© 2014 Cengage Learning®

Current and Voltage

The next consideration is the amount of current you need to control and the power supply voltage. You will reach the current limit of a BJT before you reach its breakdown voltage. The main consideration with a BJT is heat dissipation; you may need to select a device that can handle more current that you need to get adequate cooling. See the section "Power Dissipation and Heat Sinks," later in this chapter.

Perhaps you have chosen to use a FET. Typically a FET that can handle your current needs can handle more than your voltage requirements. Select a part that can handle the amount of current you need to control, and add at least 20–25% for margin. Verify that this part can handle more than your supply voltage. (Remember to look for logic-level devices if your control voltage is 5 V.)

Package Style

Discrete transistors are three-pin devices. Select a thru-hole package style for bread-board convenience. SMT (Surface Mount Technology) transistors are small and require special tools. Due to their small package size, heat management is more difficult. Transistors in SMT packages are unsuitable for solderless breadboards.

Check the data sheet for the pinout of your transistor. There is no standard pinout! Don't guess or assume. Even similar devices in the same package may have different pinouts. (You've been warned.)

Power Dissipation

The package of a device can transfer heat to the ambient air. Some packages can dissipate more than others. But you won't know how much power you need to get rid of as heat until you do some calculations.

BJT

The collector-emitter voltage, V_{CE}, is the parameter of interest because the majority of current flows through this path. We can neglect the base current, which is 100 to 1,000 times smaller. (If the base current is not much smaller than the collector current, add the base current to the collector current to calculate power.)

V_{CE} is usually shown in a graph in the data sheet, but our case is simpler. Because we are operating the transistor as a switch in the saturated region, V_{CE} will be V_{SAT}. V_{SAT} is specified in the data sheet as a single value and is typically 0.7 V.

For BJTs, power is the saturated voltage drop across the transistor times the current through it.

$P = IV_{SAT}$

MOSFET

For FETs, the voltage drop is not a fixed value and depends on the device's internal resistance. The voltage across the drain-source junction is determined by the drain to source resistance, or R_{DS}. Select a MOSFET with a low R_{DS} for low power.

For MOSFETs, power is current squared times resistance. $P = I^2 * R_{DS}$

A low input capacitance also indicates that the gate can be switched from the full-on (lowest resistance) to the full-off (highest resistance) state quickly. Slow switching leaves the MOSFET in a mid-resistance state, dissipating more power, and potentially overheating it. For this reason, motor drivers and other high-power applications require special switching considerations. Refer to Chapter 7 for more detail.

Power Dissipation and Heat Sinks

The question, "Do I need a heat sink?" is commonly asked. You won't know the answer until you do a little math. Relax. The math you need is simple arithmetic with a touch of algebra. First, calculate the amount of power your transistor will need to dissipate.

Caution

> Transistor package temperatures can be hot enough to burn. Don't touch them.

Like electrical current, heat flows from sources to sinks—that is, from areas of high temperature to areas of low temperature. Electronic components, like transistors, are heat sources. The amount of electrical power they consume must be dissipated as heat to the surrounding environment, usually the ambient air.

Thermal resistance, like electrical resistance, impedes the flow of thermal energy from source to sink. The thermal resistance is indicated on the data sheet. Two thermal resistance values are supplied: one from the junction to the case and the other from the junction to ambient air.

Thermal flow is calculated like electrical current flow. The difference in temperature between the junction and the ambient air is equivalent to the voltage difference. Thermal resistance from the junction to the package is in series with the thermal resistance from the package to the ambient air.

Unlike electrical circuits, any heat that cannot flow fast enough causes the package temperature and ultimately the junction temperature to rise. You can improve heat flow if you lower the (local) ambient air temperature by adding a fan. You can use a metal heat sink to lower the package to ambient air resistance and improve heat dissipation. When using a heat sink, use a heat sink compound to get the best heat transfer possible.

Let's look at a concrete example. Find a data sheet for a 2N2222A (in a TO-18 package). (Links to data sheets for both the transistor and heat sink are included.) P_d, at 25 C ambient, is 0.5 Watt. Power less than this does not require a heat sink. But if you need to handle more power or have a hot environment, you need a heat sink.

Let's assume your calculations show that you need to dissipate 0.75 Watt. This is on the high side for a 2N2222A, and we could use a different device instead. But for illustration purposes, let's do the math using a heat sink.

Starting with the ambient temperature of 25°C, we add the temperature rise for the heat sink and then for the case to junction. We arrive at an operating junction temperature. If this is within acceptable operating range, our heat sink is acceptable.

$T_j = T_a + P_d * R_{th}$

In words, the temperature (of the junction) equals the ambient temperature plus the power (to be dissipated) times the thermal resistance (junction to case plus case to air).

$T_j = 25\ C + 0.75\ W * 100\ C/W + 0.75\ W * 83.3\ C = 25\ C + 75\ C + 63\ C = 163\ C$

Our calculation shows that the operating junction temperature is 163°C. The data sheet shows that the operating range maximum is 175°C, so our device is within its operating parameters. Note that the case (package) temperature is 100°C; water boils at 100°C. Don't touch it!

A cool junction is a happy, long-lasting junction. The package is hot enough to burn if touched, even if brushed accidently. Consider selecting a device designed to handle more current or a different package style for cooler operation.

You can find the transistor data sheet at one of the following:

www.st.com/internet/com/TECHNICAL_RESOURCES/TECHNICAL_LITERATURE/DATASHEET/CD00003223.pdf

http://media.digikey.com/pdf/Data%20Sheets/ON%20Semiconductor%20PDFs/P2N2222A%20Rev3.pdf

You can find the heat sink data sheet at either of the following:

www.newark.com/aavid-thermalloy/322400b00000g/heat-sink/dp/18M8045

www.aavid.com/products/standard/322400b00000g

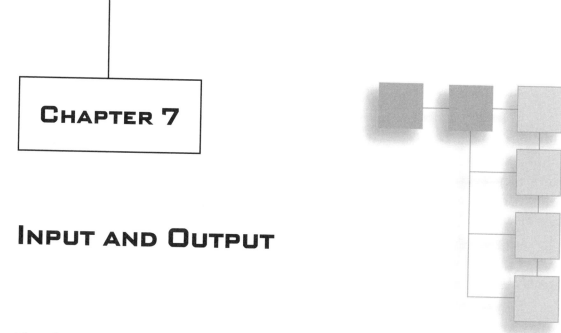

CHAPTER 7

INPUT AND OUTPUT

This chapter answers the following questions:

- What are input and output?
- What's the difference between digital and analog?
- How do I know if my circuit will draw too much power?
- Does my Arduino run on 3.3 Volts or 5 Volts?
- Can it run off of a battery?
- How do I hook up things like LEDs, switches, and buttons?
- How do I connect to a servo or motor?
- What should I do if I run out of pins?
- Can two Arduino boards talk to each other?
- What are some sample circuits I can use for my own projects?

WHY I/O?

Understanding Input/Output (I/O) is the key to making your Arduino fun. Unless your Arduino is flashing lights, running motors, and making noise with sirens or speakers, it's hard to tell that it's doing anything at all. Of course, you want buttons to push, knobs to turn, and sensors to trigger so the Arduino will respond to you.

I/O is where the Arduino shines. Arduino's flexible and programmable I/O makes it suitable for nearly any project with a minimum of additional circuitry.

However, flexibility comes at a cost. The Arduino must be told how you want to use it. But before you can do that, you need to know yourself. Let's take a detailed look at what I/O means and then look at some specific examples of how to hook things up.

INPUT

Input is anything that your Arduino looks at. It's not *really* looking; it's responding to voltage levels. We'll still use the analogy, though. *Input* includes the things you might expect, like switches and sensors. It also includes surprising things like serial data streams through the USB port or via a wireless connection.

The meaning of these inputs is entirely up to you and your program. The Arduino doesn't care what the signals mean. It only knows that your program says that a change in one (input) pin is supposed to make a change in another (output) pin.

Output pins come in one flavor: digital. Input pins come in two flavors: analog and digital. Digital signals have two stable states that can be thought of as on and off, high and low, or active and inactive, whichever makes the most sense to you.

Analog signals take on any voltage level from ground to the supply voltage and don't have distinct states. Because your Arduino makes decisions based on digital values, analog signals must be translated into a form it can understand using the ADC or Analog Comparator.

Digital

Digital input signals are either high or low, usually referred to as *signal state*. Your Arduino can look at static signal levels and make decisions based on their state or level. This type of decision is referred to as *level-sensitive logic*.

When signals change between states, in-between voltage levels are temporarily created. Digital signals are synchronized internally with the clock to prevent them from changing unintentionally during the transition period.

In addition to static signals, your Arduino can look for changes in signal levels. It can detect positive or negative transitions with aptly named edge-sensitive logic.

Rather than looking at a level or a transition, your Arduino can look at a serial data stream. Serial data streams are series of high and low signals that have meaning based on their position in a frame. We discuss serial data streams later in this chapter.

The Highs and Lows of Digital Signals

Digital signals are either high or low. A *high* is a signal whose voltage exceeds the minimum high voltage threshold. A *low* is a signal whose voltage is below the maximum low voltage threshold. Signals that are between these thresholds are not guaranteed to be high or low. They may be seen as either (but not both) with no predictability. The data sheet spells out the threshold levels in the "Electrical Characteristics" section.

Analog

Analog signals take on any voltage level from ground to the supply voltage (Vcc) and don't have distinct states. Analog pins connect the input signal either to the Analog Digital Convertor (ADC) or the Analog Comparator.

Analog signals are always inputs and can be looked at in three ways. The first choice is to convert the analog signal to a digital value using the ADC. The ADC converts your analog level into a number that can then be stored or used to make decisions. Once the level is in digital form, your Arduino can use the information just like any other number.

Assigning meaning to analog inputs is a little trickier than digital signals. Analog signals typically come from a sensor, transducer, microphone, voltage divider, or other inherently analog device. Therefore, the meaning of the signals depends on the nature of the attached device.

The significance of a number derived by the ADC depends on what is attached. A light or temperature sensor provides a voltage level (no surprise), as do many other types of sensors. Once the signal is converted to a number, that number needs to be scaled and converted to a standard unit to be meaningful to a human. (We will discuss scaling in Chapter 9, "Writing the Code.")

In some cases, you may care only about the relative value. For your robot to "find the light," you don't need to convert the reading to a standard unit. You just need to know if a bigger number is brighter or darker.

The other two ways to look at analog signals involve the Analog Comparator. The Comparator can detect an input higher or lower than a reference, or it can compare two inputs.

The Comparator doesn't distinguish between degrees. It can't tell if a signal is a little higher or much higher than the reference. Likewise, it can't tell if two input signals are nearly the same or much different.

Comparators have a variety of uses that may at first be difficult to envision. They can detect a signal crossing an arbitrary voltage level, including a potentiometer-set level. As an example, you could use a knob-controlled potentiometer to set the minimum light level for turning a table lamp on or off.

The Comparator can compare two sensor outputs to detect the higher level. This comparison is done very fast and without the need to convert each sensor's output to a number first. Be aware that the downside to speed is oscillation. Limit the frequency of software actions triggered by the comparisons to avoid oscillations. You can use methods similar to debouncing a switch, covered in Chapter 9.

You can use Comparators to detect logic levels that are not Complementary Metal-Oxide-Semiconductor (CMOS) compatible. Only one threshold level is available, so set it at the midpoint between logic levels. Use separate level-conversion devices if you need more than one signal.

A built-in analog multiplexer, shared by the ADC and Comparator, allows monitoring of multiple inputs without additional circuitry. When the ADC is using the multiplexer, only the input pins (AIN0 and AIN1) are available to the Comparator. When the Comparator is using the multiplexer, the ADC is disabled and can't be used. If you need both the ADC and the Comparator, they have to take turns.

Timing and Counting

Timers and counters are related, but *counters* count electrical events. When those events are based on time, like the clock, it's a *timer*. The number of events in a period of time is a *rate*. Table 7.1 shows which function to use to find your answer.

Table 7.1 Timer and Counter Uses

Question	Answer
How many?	Counter
When?	Timer
How long?	Timer
How often?	Counter and timer

© 2014 Cengage Learning®

Real Time

You and your Arduino live in the real world where, like it or not, some things must happen on a schedule. *Real time* refers to things that are happening at ordinary speed. Nearly everything you do with your Arduino happens in real time. *Real-time programming* is a fancy name for using a high-speed processor to control human-speed processes.

The alternative to real time is simulated time, which can speed up or slow down time. Computer games often use simulated time, a concept you are already familiar with.

Although what you ultimately control will happen in real time, simulated time sometimes provides a faster way to debug your programs. If your program has long waiting periods when nothing is happening, temporarily speeding up time allows you to see actions at a speed you can pay attention to. Other times, slowing time down is more useful.

Use constants for delay times so you can easily manipulate time for both debugging and fine-tuning. Be sure to use a separate constant for delay times, which must not be changed this way with a comment to remind you why. For example, delays associated with a motor and calibrated for a specific turning angle must remain real time.

Timer/Counters

Your Arduino has at least three independent built-in timer/counters, each with slightly different capabilities. Each timer/counter can be clocked by an external source or by the system clock. On the Uno, an external clock source is input on signals T0 (Uno pin 4) and T1 (Uno pin 5).

You can use the timer's prescaler to reduce the system or external clock rate by dividing it by a power of 2. A slower clock accommodates longer periods.

External clocking provides a way to count events. Of course, the only events your Arduino is able to see are electrical. Occurrences that you want to track must somehow be converted to electrical signals. Measuring a rate involves simply counting occurrences per time interval. From a rate, you can calculate speed and distance.

Each timer/counter generates two Pulse Width Modulation (PWM) output waveforms. These waveforms are not completely independent; they share a time base (frequency). Pulse widths, and therefore duty cycle, are independent.

Keeping track of time doesn't require the use of external pins. Your Arduino can provide accurate real-time relative time from the system clock. But it won't remember the time through a reset or power removal.

If you must have absolute time instead of relative time, consider using a battery-backed-up Real-Time Clock (RTC) module. The RTC module has the added advantage of keeping track of day of week, month, and daylight saving time changes. An RTC module does consume I/O pins.

Timer/counter 0 is often used by Arduino time-related functions, including `delay()`, `millis()`, `micros()`, and `delayMicroseconds()`. Other uses have conflicts with these functions. This isn't too much of an inconvenience because two other timer/counters are available. If you plan to use these time functions, select timer/counter 1 or 2 for your other uses.

Linear Speed Calculation

You can determine Revolutions Per Minute (RPM) by counting revolutions and dividing by time. RPM is a measure of angular speed. That's how fast a motor or wheel axle is turning.

Suppose you want to know *linear speed*, or the speed along the ground. Your axle is inside a wheel rolling along the ground. The wheel must roll one of its circumferences in distance to turn one revolution. Linear speed is a simple calculation of RPM multiplied by the circumference of the wheel, assuming no slippage and a 1:1 gearing ratio.

Interrupts

Interrupts are special input signals that tell the program to stop what it's doing now and react immediately. After the special action assigned to the interrupt has been completed, the program resumes operation from the point where it was stopped.

Signals on dedicated interrupt pins or digital pins programmed as pin change interrupts can trigger an interrupt. Dedicated interrupts allow direct jumps (vectors) to individual Interrupt Service Routines (ISRs).

Pin change signals are grouped with one interrupt per group. The exact source of the interrupt is stored in a register and needs to be sorted out before the real action starts. This adds a step to the ISR and is just a little more complex.

Lots of interrupts are available; pick dedicated ones for critical functions. Spread the pin change interrupts across different groups to minimize the decoding necessary. Refer to Chapter 9 for examples of using interrupts.

OUTPUT

All Arduino outputs are digital signals. That means they are either high or low or tri-state (high impedance). They can be relatively static signals that don't change very often. They can be serial data streams, or PWM signals, sometimes mistakenly called *analog signals*.

PWM outputs are a special case of digital signals that are modulated. These signals can be filtered to form analog waveforms. PWM also offers a handy means for motor control. Refer to Chapter 9 for a motor controller example.

SERIAL DATA STREAMS

Serial data streams can be inputs, outputs, or both—perhaps at the same time. A *data stream* is a series of levels, edges, or frequencies that carry some meaning. The tricky bit is recognizing and extracting the meaning.

Serial data streams are information-carrying signals that conform to a set of rules called a *protocol*. Protocols specify everything about the signals. Without the protocol, the signals are meaningless.

You need the serial data streams to be sequences of digital levels. Serial Peripheral Interface (SPI) and Two-Wire Interface (TWI) are protocols that specify transmission at convenient digital signal levels. These protocols are already Arduino friendly.

Coded Messages

Messages communicated over the SPI and TWI interfaces must be kept short—8 bits—to fit within a single frame. Just 8 bits provides $2^8 = 256$ possible codes, with each code representing one message.

Every shield (or other connected device) has its own set of codes or sequence of codes. These codes are not standard, and any similarity is purely coincidental.

The Atmel microcontroller data sheet explains the SPI and TWI protocols in detail. Although not truly a protocol, the USART section explains serial communications in general.

The USART is capable of both synchronous and asynchronous operation. It's used most frequently in asynchronous mode, in which the clock is generated internally and synchronized to the data rather than being carried on a separate wire. The Arduino serial library uses this mode. The serial library is discussed in Chapter 9.

Serial data protocols share many features, and you can look up standard protocols in any convenient source. Some devices may have special requirements, such as a default TWI address or SPI Slave Select polarity. If so, they are detailed in the device's data sheet.

Many communication protocols use analog signals that are not compatible with ordinary logic families. Use a shield for them.

Shields are available for many popular protocols, including Ethernet (802.3), Bluetooth (802.15), wireless Ethernet (802.11), and other wireless protocols. Many Arduino shields use the SPI protocol or TWI protocol to exchange data with the Arduino. Shields are discussed more in Chapter 13, "Expanding Your Horizons with Shields."

All these protocols are transmission protocols. They don't specify what happens to the data that is transmitted. The data may be treated any way you like, or it may be subject to another protocol.

The IEEE 802 Standard

The IEEE 802 standard specifies many communication protocols, transmission media, and data rates. 802.3a is similar to the original Ethernet, whereas 802.11 is a wireless communication protocol of various data rates and transmission frequencies.

The name *Ethernet* has stuck and now is used to indicate any of the Ethernet frame–formatted 802 standards. 802.11 is commonly called wireless Ethernet. Be aware that not all 802 standards are Ethernet.

Serial Protocol Addressing

Transmission protocols are in the delivery business. Many communication protocols, like TWI and wireless Ethernet, require both the transmitter and the receiver to have unique addresses. For Ethernet (and other 802 standards), these are Layer 2 Media Access Control (MAC) addresses, not IP addresses. However, Internet Protocol (IP) addresses must be unique, too.

TWI uses 7-bit addresses, with most slave devices having a predefined address. The device data sheet lists the address that the slave will respond to. Some addresses are reserved and shouldn't be used. (The 328P data sheet contains many of the protocol details.)

If the protocol does not use addresses, it still needs a way to identify the receiver when more than one is present. SPI uses a Slave Select signal to identify the receiver and the device that should reply.

Many shields use the SPI to exchange information with the Arduino. Typically, the Arduino acts as the bus master, while each shield is a slave device. As master, the Arduino provides the clock signal used for both transmit and receive. This clock is provided only during the data exchange. It stops during inactive periods.

Unless you need the Arduino to act as a slave, you must define the Arduino's Slave Select pin as an output whether you use it for the SPI transfer or not. The Arduino acts as a slave device if Slave Select is an input and is pulled low (active) by another device.

Some shields can have any pin selected (via a jumper) to be its Slave Select pin. Other shields use the default Slave Select pin with no convenient way to change it. To use multiple shields at the same time, the Slave Select signal for each shield must be unique. Any digital pin (or analog pin programmed as a digital pin) will do. In addition, the software must be modified to use the correct pin for the Slave Select.

Serial Protocol Master

The Arduino can't act as a USB master; you need a USB host shield for that. USB isn't your only communication option. You can use the SPI, TWI (aka I^{2}C), or Universal Synchronous/Asynchronous Receiver/Transmitter (USART).

SPI and TWI are bus architectures that require one and only one master at a time. So who's the boss? TWI supports a master arbitration process that allows the connected devices to elect one as bus master. Bus arbitration is one of the trickier acts to pull off. Be aware of and plan for recovery from special situations like hung buses, resets, and multiple simultaneous masters.

For TWI, you could let the attached TWI devices arbitrate, but you don't need to. Only one master is ever necessary for data transfers in either direction. You can configure one Arduino as the full-time master and the other devices, including other Arduino boards, as slaves.

SPI does not support master arbitration. You need to pick which Arduino is the SPI master because all Slave Select lines originate at the master. Other devices (including other Arduino boards) can be slaves.

SPI and TWI communication is between master and slave, not between slaves. Communication between slaves is not typical, but it's possible. Any information to be passed between slaves must pass to the master first. Then in a separate communication, the master can relay the information to the destination slave. If the master is not present, the slaves can't communicate.

Connections

Serial buses must be properly connected to work. The way these bus signals connect isn't obvious, so let's take a closer look.

For any of these serial interfaces to work correctly, the connected devices must share a common ground reference. This isn't necessarily a wire. The devices might be connected to the same chassis system, like a car. They might have a physical connection to earth ground for long-distance connections (greater than 1,000 feet). The ground reference might be carried on the shield (wire and foil wrap) of the connecting cable. The devices might share a power supply, which is typical for most hobby applications.

Good signal quality depends on a good-quality ground reference. The best approach is to wire all the ground references together at a single point. Separate earth references, chassis ground, and cable shield ground should be considered low-quality grounds.

The ground point is traditionally a lug attached to the chassis to which ground wires are brought. If you supply your project using AC rather than a DC brick, you must use this approach to ensure your safety. Be certain that you use the correct AC ground.

Only one ground reference to each Arduino (or other device) is needed regardless of the number of serial interfaces in use. Multiple ground connections create their own problem: ground loops.

TWI Signal Connections

For TWI, all the SDA (Serial Data) signals connect to each other. Likewise, all the SCK (Serial Clock) signals connect.

TWI uses open-collector drivers with pullup resistors, with at least one set of pullup resistors needed. Smaller value resistors allow faster switching speeds with sharper, cleaner signal edges, but they consume a little more power. Larger value resistors consume less power but take longer to switch. It's a trade-off that depends on your bus capacitance. 4.7 K ohm is typically specified for TWI.

If you're using a mix of devices powered by different supply voltages, use pullups to the lowest supply voltage. Test your connections before you hook up a 5 V device to a 3.3 V device, especially an expensive one. If you accidently drive 5 V to the 3.3 V Arduino, you will likely damage it.

SPI Signal Connections

The SPI Clock (SCK) signals, the master, and all slaves connect to each other. As long as the devices operate from the same supply voltage, these pins can be directly connected to each other.

All the slave data input signals connect to each other and to the Master Out Slave In (MOSI) signal. All the slave data output signals connect to each other and to the Master In Slave Out (MISO) signal.

Slave Select (SS) signals must be unique and connect from a separate pin on the master to each slave. (Remember: SS is almost always active low.)

An SPI slave might have a signal named Serial Data In rather than MOSI. Likewise, MISO would then be named Serial Data Out.

SPI-capable devices such as shift registers can also be daisy chained, with long chains possible. For shift-out registers, connect MOSI to data in on the first shift register with data out going to data in of the next shift register. For shift-in registers, connect data out to data in, with the last register's data out connected to MISO. Connect SCK and SS for all devices in parallel.

USART Connection

The USARTs are intended for point-to-point communication. It's not a bus, and only two devices can be attached. Communication is peer-to-peer and not master-slave.

The USART's whole purpose is to allow independent systems to exchange information. Even so, some coordination is required. Clock sources, baud rate, number of data bits in a frame, parity, and use of start and stop bits must be in agreement and configured in advance. They can't be negotiated automatically.

The RX (receive) signal on Arduino #1 connects to the TX (transmit) signal on Arduino #2, and the RX signal on Arduino #2 goes to the TX signal on Arduino #1. XCK (clock) signals connect to each other, if used. Pins can be connected directly.

Remember that a ground connection is required for all serial interfaces.

Arduino-to-Arduino Conversation

Making an Arduino talk to another Arduino is not difficult. Use the USART, SPI, or TWI for connection. Connections are like those discussed earlier and are summarized in Table 7.2.

Table 7.2 Signal Summary for Arduino Interconnection

SPI Master	Direction	SPI Slave
MISO	←	MOSI
MOSI	→	MISO
SCK	→	SCK
SS	→	SS
TWI Master	**Direction**	**TWI Slave**
SDA	1, 2	SDA
SCK	→2	SCK
USART 1	**Direction**	**USART 2**
RX	←	TX
TX	→	RX
XCK	3	XCK

Note 1: Signals are bidirectional (only one direction at a time).
Note 2: Each signal requires a 4.7 K ohm (or so) pullup resistor.
Note 3: A signal may come from either device or not be present at all.

© 2014 Cengage Learning®

THE HARDWARE PIECE

Know your supply voltage. Some Arduino models, like the LilyPad and Due, require a 3.3 Volt power supply. Most others require a 5 Volt power supply. The information page for your Arduino indicates the acceptable input voltage range. The necessary voltage is conveniently silkscreened onto the board.

5 Volts applied to an Arduino designed for and powered by 3.3 Volts will damage it. That includes input signals, not just Vcc (power). Signals should not exceed Vcc by more than 0.5 V.

To use your Arduino to monitor or control something, you need to physically connect it. The simplest and easiest way is to directly connect your sensors, switches, ICs, LEDs, and other devices to the pins of the Arduino.

Every input to the Arduino is an output from something else and vise versa. Input or output, you need to know if you can connect your stuff directly to its pins. To decide, consider two things: voltage and current. When you interconnect other devices, you need to do similar checking.

Voltage

For each signal (or each signal type), compare the driver's minimum and maximum high output voltage to the receiver's minimum and maximum high input voltage. If the driver's output is within the receiver's acceptable range, everything's okay. Repeat the comparison for the driver's low output voltage range. If the voltages aren't compatible, you can't directly connect them.

Open-drain (or open-collector) devices can't drive a signal high and require a pullup resistor to provide the output high signal level. Because the pullup resistor and not the driver determines the output's high voltage level, open-drain devices can convert voltage levels.

Arduino outputs (other than TWI) can't be programmed as open-drain, but they can emulate the function with software. To pull the signal low, the pin is configured as an output and driven low. The rest of the time, the pin is configured as a high-impedance input to let the signal float.

Any open-drain signal can use internal or external pullup resistors to pull open-drain input signals high. The internal pullup resistor allows a switch (or open-collector device) to connect directly to an Arduino input pin without additional components. A usual switch application provides a connection to ground when closed. When open, the output floats, and the pullup resistor pulls the signal level to an acceptable high.

Voltage thresholds of the Arduino's digital pins are specified in the Atmel data sheet. Your Arduino is a CMOS device, and the threshold levels are proportional to the supply voltage. The data sheet gives this information in a relative format and is summarized in Table 7.3.

Table 7.3 Arduino I/O Voltage Requirements

Supply Voltage	Min. High Input	Max. Low Input	Min. High Output	Max. Low Output
5 V	3.0 V	1.5 V	4.2 V	0.9 V
3.3 V	1.98 V	0.99 V	2.3 V	0.6 V

Limits are proportional to power supply voltage.
© 2014 Cengage Learning®

For example, the maximum voltage level for a low input is $0.3 * Vcc$. If your Arduino runs on 5 Volts, the maximum level for a low input is 1.5 Volts. To be reliably seen as a low, the input must be less than 1.5 Volts.

Similarly, the minimum high voltage level is 0.6 * Vcc. If your Arduino runs on 5 Volts, the minimum level for a high is 3.0 Volts. Signals between 1.5 Volts and 3.0 Volts are considered either high or low, but which one is not guaranteed!

For a 5-Volt Arduino, the maximum output low voltage is specified as 0.9 Volts. The minimum output low voltage is not specified but will not be lower than 0 Volts. Minimum high voltage is 4.2 Volts. The maximum high voltage level is not specified, but it never exceeds Vcc.

If your Arduino runs on 3.3 Volts, the maximum level for a low input is 0.99 Volts, and the minimum level for a high is 1.98 Volts. The maximum output low is specified as 0.6 Volts. The minimum output high voltage is 2.3 Volts.

Current

Output drivers have current limits. Unlike voltage, current can flow from a driver or be drawn into it. Only maximum current is specified; there's no minimum.

Most devices, like logic gates or other ICs, have high input impedance. That means they require little current to operate. Other devices, like LEDs and transistors, require more current. Use Ohm's Law to determine how much. Go back to Chapter 6, "How to Read Specification Sheets," if you need a refresher about Ohm's Law.

For an Arduino input pin, the input impedance is high, as is characteristic of CMOS devices. The current draw will be small (1 microamp).

If the internal pullup resistor has been selected, there is more current flow. The resistor provides a 20–50 K ohm path to Vcc, providing a maximum of 250–100 microamps when the driver is low. That's still in the small range.

For an output pin, the Arduino can supply (source in the high state) or draw (sink in the low state) at least 20 milliamps of current subject to some conditions (below). The absolute maximum current for an output pin is 40 mA. Current above this damages your Arduino. Keep your current draw to 20 mA or lower.

There are collective limits on the combined current source and draw for specific groups of pins. The group limits depend on your Arduino's microcontroller model. Sorry, but there is no easy cheat. You need to do the math.

Combined current sourced by Arduino pins is subject to limits specified in the Atmel data sheet. For the Atmel ATmega328P, the total current source/draw from all sources can't exceed 200 mA, which is the absolute maximum rating for the chip.

For the Atmel ATmega328P, the total current sourced (high state) by ports C0–C5, D0–D4, ADC7, and RESET should not exceed 150 mA. Also, the total current sourced by ports B0–B5, D5–D7, ADC6, XTAL1, and XTAL2 should not exceed 150 mA.

Combined current draw by Arduino pins is also subject to limits specified in the Atmel data sheet. For the Atmel ATmega328P, the total current draw (low state) for ports C0–C5, ADC7, and ADC6 should not exceed 100 mA. The total current draw for ports B0–B5, D5–D7, XTAL1, and XTAL2 should not exceed 100 mA. The total current draw for ports D0–D4 and RESET should not exceed 100 mA.

Exceeding these limits compromises the output voltage level (best case) or damages your device (worst case). Compromising the voltage level means the high voltage will drop or the low voltage will rise.

These limits are stated in the data sheet for the 328P. They may seem arbitrary, but there's a valid engineering reason underlying them. Other microcontroller models may have different limits.

Analog Inputs

Analog inputs are similar to digital inputs, except that they don't have pullup resistors. The voltage limits are the same. All analog pins can be used as ordinary digital I/O instead and then have all the features of digital pins, including pullup resistors.

Analog inputs are also high impedance, meaning they draw little current. This prevents your source from being loaded and potentially changing what you're trying to measure. Like digital inputs, analog inputs are a voltage. Often used for sensor inputs, analog inputs need to remain within the voltage limits of the Arduino.

Some AC analog signals have positive and negative voltage swings that must be changed to remain within 0 to 5 Volts. If the voltage swing is less than 5 Volts, you can add a DC bias to shift the center point to 2.5 Volts. An AC-coupled voltage divider can be used to add DC bias.

For larger signals, an operational amplifier (Op Amp) can add bias as well as scale the signal. Zener diodes limit voltage and can be used to protect the input from extremes.

Unlike digital inputs, analog inputs may have frequency and sampling issues. Periodic signals must be sampled faster than the Nyquist rate, or aliasing will result. *Aliasing* is the effect of high-frequency signal components looking like and distorting lower-frequency components.

Conversion of an analog signal to a number takes time. The best sampling rate the Arduino can provide, with default clock settings and using `analogRead()`, is about 9 KHz. The practical upshot is that your Arduino is capable of recording reasonable telephone-like voice, but not music.

Keep in mind that you need to store your recorded data somewhere. Your Arduino's memory isn't big enough for more than a fraction of a second's worth of data. Where are you going to keep all this data?

In the audio world, sophisticated compression techniques are used to reduce the file sizes and bit rates. To be fast enough, special-purpose hardware engines (processors) do most of the work.

To summarize, audio recording requires special-purpose hardware and extra memory. There's a shield for that! If you want to make your Arduino a music recorder/player, invest in a shield.

Power

Power is the last piece to consider. For the Arduino, if you remain within the current limits, you won't have a problem. For your other devices, power is calculated by current times voltage ($P = IV$) or an algebraic variation using Ohm's Law ($P = I * I * R$, $P = V * V / R$).

Every device has a power limit. Even axial-lead resistors have a power limit, usually 1/4 or 1/8 watt.

As hinted at already, total power is also a consideration. Your computer's USB port has a power limit (5 V × 500 mA = 2.5 watt). Every power supply has a current limit above which the voltage will be compromised. In addition, some of the available power should be held in reserve.

When operating your Arduino by battery, power becomes a larger consideration. Batteries have an energy capacity. The amount of energy available depends on a number of factors, including cell size, battery age, chemical composition, initial charge, temperature, and drain rate. More current draw depletes the available energy faster.

Pin Assignment Guidelines

Before you can tell your Arduino how to program the pins, you need to assign meanings to the pins you are using. Configure all unused pins as (digital) inputs with the pullup resistor enabled. (This is the recommended configuration stipulated in the Atmel data sheet.) Default IDE configuration for unused pins is input without pullup.

All pins have alternate functions. However, the exact pin functions depend on the microcontroller IC model your Arduino uses. These pins are labeled on the board schematic, but they're much easier to find if you know what you're looking for.

Table 7.4 summarizes the special-purpose pins by signal name for the Uno. The signals are easier to find on the schematic once you know the signal name they are hiding behind. Not all signal names are shown on the schematic.

The schematic is available on the Arduino website. Some Arduino models use a second Atmel microcontroller as a USB interface. Be sure to find the main Atmel microcontroller, which might be drawn smaller than the secondary one. (Hint: The main microcontroller is shown attached to the headers on the right hand side of the page.)

Table 7.4 contains the signal names for the Uno. Other Arduino models have similar names. Multiple copies of the same interface are distinguished from each other by a number added to the end of the signal name.

Table 7.4 Special-Purpose Pin Names

Interface Name	Signal Names	Uno Pin Names
SPI	MISO, MOSI, SCK, SS/	12, 11, 13, 10
USART	RXD (D0), TXD (D1), XCK	0, 1, 4
USART in SPI mode	MISO (RXD), MOSI (TXD), SCK (XCK)	0, 1, 4
TWI	SDA, SCK	A4, A5
External interrupt	INT0, INT1	2, 3
Analog Comparator	AIN0 (positive input), AIN1 (negative input)	6, 7
ADC	ADC0, ADC1, ADC2, ADC3, ADC4, ADC5	A0, A1, A2, A3, A4, A5
Timer/counter 0 External Counter Input	T0	4
Timer/counter 0 B PWM	OC0B	5
Timer/counter 0 A PWM	OC0A	6
Timer/counter 1 External Counter Input	T1	5
Timer/counter 1 Input Capture Input	ICP1	8
Timer/counter 1 A PWM	OC1A	9
Timer/counter 1 B PWM	OC1B	10
Timer/counter 2 A PWM	OC2A	11
Timer/counter 2 B PWM	OC2B	3

The official name for PWM signals is Output Compare Match X Output, but that's a name only an engineer could love.

In asynchronous mode, the USART XCK pin is not needed and may be used for something else.

In SPI as a master device, SS must be set as an output. A different pin controls SS for each slave. SS is usually active low and may be indicated by a /.

© 2014 Cengage Learning®

Assign any needed special-purpose pins first. If there is a conflict between special-purpose pins, it may be difficult to share them.

It is possible to use the USART for program download and use it for something else during program execution. Consider selecting an Arduino Mega if you need multiple USARTs.

If you use the USART pins (D0 and D1) for any purpose other than digital outputs, plan to disconnect them before downloading programs. Conflicts during download are a commonly reported problem. Save yourself from the frustration.

If you are not using the USB interface to communicate with a PC (as a serial monitor port, for example), you can use D0 and D1 (the USART serial interface) without conflict.

After the special-purpose pins, assign analog input pins and PWM pins. From the remaining pins, select your digital I/O, reserving D0 and D1 if possible. If you must use D0 and D1, assign them as outputs. Remember that the analog input pins can also be used as digital I/O pins. Configure leftover pins as (digital) inputs with the pullup resistor enabled.

If you run out of pins, you can expand digital pin output capacity with an additional component. Using a shift register, like the one detailed in Chapter 6, allows many devices (eight per shift register) to be controlled with a group of three or four pins. Shift registers can be chained together (serial out to serial in) in strings of 20 or more. (That's 160 digital outputs at the cost of just three I/O pins!)

You can expand input pin capacity with additional components (multiplexers or shift registers), but it is a little more difficult. You must verify input timing in addition to voltages and currents. Specifically, verify setup and hold times. Rapidly changing signals are difficult to capture this way unless they are latched.

Analog inputs can be expanded with external ADC chips and DAC chips. External ADCs provide greater resolution than offered by the built-in 10-bit ADC. External DACs offer similar advantages. Twelve-bit DACs can provide more voltage control than the alternative of filtering an 8-bit PWM signal. Both ADC and DAC devices are available with SPI or I2C interfaces.

Write down your pin assignments in your handy-dandy notebook. This is your I/O map. You need this map when you program your Arduino. Be sure to note the intended use of the signals in addition to the pin number and signal name.

Verify that you are within the collective current limit for your pin groups. Swap digital I/O around to stay within the limit if you need to.

THE SOFTWARE PIECE

After you have determined that the voltages and currents of the pins you have selected are okay, you need to tell the Arduino. So far, it's just been your secret.

Obviously, you can't talk to your Arduino and explain to it what you want. Programming all the individual registers would be tiresome. Fortunately, there is a faster and less error-prone way. You guessed it—function calls.

The Arduino standard and special-purpose libraries provide functions for nearly all your I/O needs. Typically, one group of function calls programs the pins for input and output as required. Another set is used to set/read the signal levels during operation.

Refer to Chapter 9 for more information on using functions to set up and use I/O. Refer to Chapter 8, "The IDE," for information on physically connecting your computer to the Arduino.

Beyond downloading code, the connection to your computer provides a serial port that you can use to monitor or control your program. The simplest use is providing output messages (from your Arduino) to let you know what your program is doing or to display data it has collected.

EXAMPLES

Most projects consist of independent circuits connected to the Arduino's pins. This section presents a collection of circuits that can be copied to suit your needs.

We also revisit our examples from Chapter 3, "From Idea to Project," this time selecting sample circuits from our collection to provide project control.

Sample Circuits

A number of circuits are handy for projects, and we explore those next. You can mix and match these pieces to suit your needs. You can find the software piece that accompanies them in Chapter 9.

Transistor Drive Circuit

Chapter 6 looked at using transistors and open-drain buffers to drive LEDs. LEDs are noninductive loads. Inductive loads need a snubbing diode.

Transistor Drive Circuit with Snubbing Diode

You can use a transistor drive circuit to control an inductive load, like motors and relay coils. Unlike LEDs, current wants to keep flowing after the signal is switched off. This leftover current needs to go somewhere.

The usual method is to put a diode in parallel with the motor or coil. This diode goes by many names, including flyback, snubbing, freewheeling, catch, and suppressor.

Figure 7.1 shows how to place a diode to suppress these unwanted currents. This circuit could be driven by an Arduino pin or connected to a switch (with pullup).

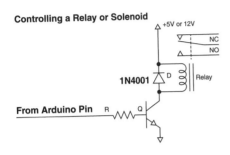

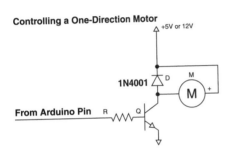

Figure 7.1
Transistor drive circuit with snubbing diode.
© 2014 Cengage Learning®

The NO label on the relay pin means this is the "normally open" pin. When the relay is not energized, this pin is open and is not connected to the common pin. The NC pin is "normally closed" and is connected (to the common pin) when the relay is not energized. When the relay is energized, the NO contact closes, while the NC contact opens.

H-Bridge Motor Controller

The standard bidirectional DC motor controller is called an *H-bridge* or *full bridge*. An H-bridge can be found as a specialized IC or built out of transistors, relays, or switches. The general idea is that the power and ground connections are reversed to reverse the motor. There are several full-bridge shields and breakout boards available for the Uno. (Allowable control signal combinations vary. Refer to the shield or breakout board's data sheet for details.)

The motor controls for the H-bridge driver circuits can attach directly to pins. Two digital pins control direction of motor rotation. One PWM pin controls the motor's speed by changing the pulse width (duty cycle) on the enable line. A typical H-bridge driver circuit is shown in Figure 7.2.

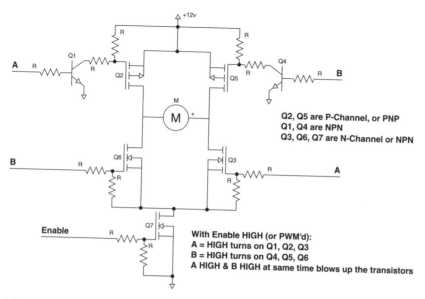

Figure 7.2
H-bridge driver circuit.
© 2014 Cengage Learning®

Real-Time Clock

You can build the RTC as a circuit or purchase it as a module. This module is backed up with a battery and can remember the time (and day, date, and year) through resets and without external power. You can track daylight savings automatically.

Figure 7.3 shows how the DS1307 RTC is connected. This circuit connects to the Arduino using the TWI. As we discussed previously, TWI devices need an address. The RTC chip uses the address 0x68.

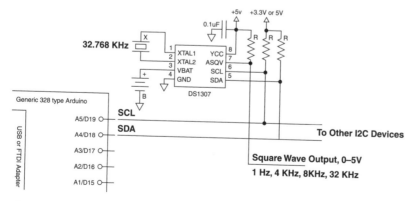

Figure 7.3
Real-Time Clock circuit.
© 2014 Cengage Learning®

Shift Registers

Shift registers provide an easy way to expand output capacity using the SPI or software-emulated SPI signals. SPI signals are MOSI, SCK, and SS, and the emulated signals are dataPin, clkPin, and latchPin. Both sets of signals are shown in Figure 7.4, but only one is connected.

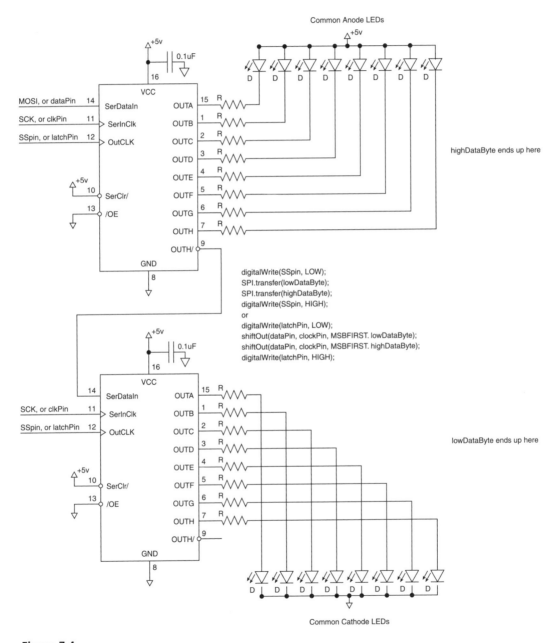

Figure 7.4
Shift registers.
© 2014 Cengage Learning®

Two registers are shown chained together. Much longer chains (20 registers or more) can be formed, providing many more output signals with no additional control pins required.

The top shift register controls the LEDs with low-side switching. The bottom shift register controls the LEDs with high-side switching. It doesn't matter if the top shift register is 2-state or open-drain. The bottom register needs pullup resistors if open-drain devices are used.

The polarity of the control signals is also different. The top row of LEDs turns on with an output low. The bottom row of LEDs turns on with an output high.

It's unusual to mix signal polarities and low-side/high-side switching in a single design as was done for illustration purposes. If you have a reason to mix them, make careful notes to avoid confusion. (Add notes to your schematic, too.)

Multiplexed LED Drivers

Shift registers provide a convenient way to control tons of LEDs. When each output controls a single LED, you inconveniently need many shift registers. But LEDs can time-share control signals with a technique called *multiplexing*.

Each LED is illuminated (or not) for a brief moment in turns. Because the turns are brief and repeated, the human eye sees the LED as on and not flashing. In reality it's flashing, but very rapidly.

Large numbers of LEDs are often arranged in rows and columns to provide a matrix display. Special-purpose LED matrix displays integrate numerous LEDs into a single package, typically up to eight LEDs wide and eight LEDs tall (8 × 8 matrix). They may be single color, dual color, or RGB (Red, Green, Blue), which can be blended to produce many colors.

LED arrays are arranged with the rows sharing the same anode (positive) control, while the columns share the same cathode (negative) control. (If rotated 90 degrees, rows and columns are swapped.) When the row anode is driven high and the column cathode is driven low, an individual LED turns on. Usually LEDs are controlled one column at a time. The columns are cycled through sequentially and repeatedly. Because of the quick repeat and persistence of vision effects, it will appear as if the whole array is continuously illuminated.

Your LED matrix may be wired differently. Read its specification sheet for details and recommended voltages and currents. Driver chips such as MAX7219 have suggested circuits.

Individual LEDs or clusters of LEDs forming arrays, integrated LED matrixes, or some arbitrary arrangement are just a few of the possibilities. You can build physically large arrays by mounting individual LEDs (or clusters of LEDs) in a spaced-out pattern.

Regardless of the physical arrangement of the LEDs as matrixes or individual components, special-purpose ICs make control and multiplexing easy. You can use ICs such as MAX7219 to control 64 LEDs in a single 8 × 8 matrix. One driver is needed for each color, so two-color LEDs need two devices, and RGB matrixes require three.

The MAX7219 is really like eight shift registers in one device with multiplexing control. It provides multiplexed driving control for one 8 × 8 matrix, or eight common-cathode seven-segment displays (with their decimal points).

Other special-purpose control ICs provide other features. TLC5490 or WS2801/WS2803/WS2811 devices provide individual PWM control of each LED, allowing fading effects or brightness control.

Wireless Remote Control

A Radio Frequency (RF) wireless remote control provides a means to control a device at a distance. In the example shown in Figure 7.5, a local pushbutton controls a light at a remote location. Distances of up to about 300 feet are supported.

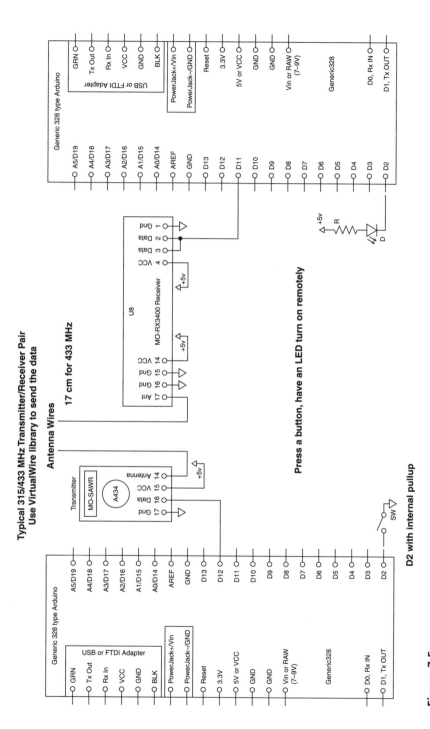

Figure 7.5
Wireless remote control.
© 2014 Cengage Learning®

Infrared (IR) is an alternative to RF but is limited to line-of-sight. Sunlight and some flourescent lights interfere with IR. Because the IR beam is narrow and connection is limited to line-of-sight, about 25 feet is the practical distance limit.

Marquee

You could make the marquee from a dot-matrix display or an array of shift register–driven LEDs mounted on a panel. This circuit uses a dot-matrix display that employs the SPI signals for control.

The marquee driver is a set of three digital pins that attach to special-purpose LED drivers that act like a shift register chain. The SPI pins shift data into the drivers to take advantage of the microcontroller's built-in hardware support.

SPI is not just for serial communication with other microcontrollers or shields. It's a good choice anytime data is serially shifted. Hardware support provides convenience and speed.

The marquee is composed of four 8 × 8 LED arrays side by side. Each LED array is driven by a MAX7219 LED display driver. This driver cycles through the columns quickly so that the LEDs appear to be on at the same time, even though they aren't. Figure 7.6 shows how the display drivers can be attached to the SPI pins to control the LED arrays forming the marquee.

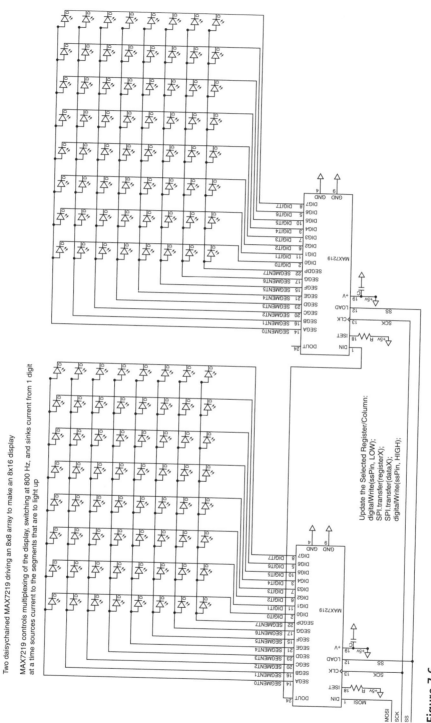

Two daisychained MAX7219 driving an 8x8 array to make an 8x16 display

MAX7219 controls multiplexing of the display, switching at 800 Hz, and sinks current from 1 digit at a time sources current to the segments that are to light up

Update the Selected Register/Column:
digitalWrite(ssPin, LOW);
SPI.trasfer(registerX);
SPI.trasfer(dataX);
digitalWrite(ssPin, HIGH);

Figure 7.6
Marquee driver circuit.
© 2014 Cengage Learning®

Adding USB Ports

Making the Arduino become USB master requires a USB host shield. Software control of a USB host is not trivial. Libraries that come with the shield help, but an understanding of the bus's protocol is required.

Adding slave USB ports, on the other hand, is relatively easy, as Figure 7.7 shows. You can add slave USB ports to the Arduino using FTDI or CP2102 modules. TWI or a software-emulated serial interface connects the Arduino to the module and, ultimately, to the host.

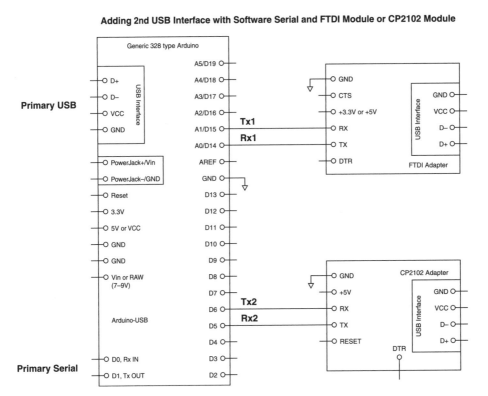

Figure 7.7
USB slave ports.
© 2014 Cengage Learning®

Operational Amplifier with DC Bias

Figure 7.8 shows an Operational Amplifier (Op Amp) circuit. This circuit provides (noninverting) amplification and adds a DC bias.

AC Coupled Non-Inverting Amplifier with 2.5V DC Offset

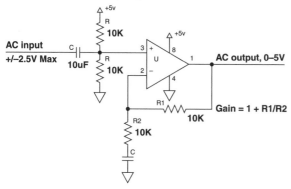

1/2 typical dual op-amp

Figure 7.8
Operational Amplifier with DC bias.
© 2014 Cengage Learning®

Op Amps are usually powered with positive and negative supply voltages, allowing the signal to be centered around 0 volts. DC bias is needed to center the signal around 2.5 Volts when the Op Amp is supplied with just a positive voltage.

Touring the circuit from left to right, the input is AC-coupled using a capacitor. Any DC component the signal has will not pass through the capacitor. A new DC bias is set at 2.5 Volts with a voltage divider (resistors) with the AC component of the input signal added to it.

AC signals in excess of 5 Volts are clipped. That is, peak signal levels are limited to remain within 0 V to 5 V, distorting the signal. Small signals are amplified with the gain set by R1 and R2. The gain is used to scale the output signal to the desired range.

Op Amps are easy-to-use amplifiers that can be used for buffering, active filtering, and scaling (including amplification) of AC signal. Basic Op Amp circuits are not hard to build, but they can be used in too many ways to be covered in detail here.

There are other Op Amp configurations, including inverting amplifiers. Keep in mind that inversion doesn't really change most AC signals in meaningful ways.

Wire OR/AND

Wire logic allows signals to be combined without active logic devices. Some signals, like switch closures, can be combined without additional components. Logic signals need to be either open collector or diode protected. Figure 7.9 shows a variety of wired logic circuits.

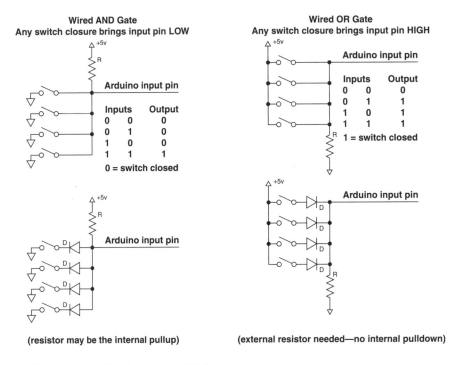

Wired AND Gate
Any switch closure brings input pin LOW

Inputs | Output
0 0 | 0
0 1 | 0
1 0 | 0
1 1 | 1

0 = switch closed

Wired OR Gate
Any switch closure brings input pin HIGH

Inputs | Output
0 0 | 0
0 1 | 1
1 0 | 1
1 1 | 1

1 = switch closed

(resistor may be the internal pullup)

(external resistor needed—no internal pulldown)

Diodes provide electrical isolation between input devices:

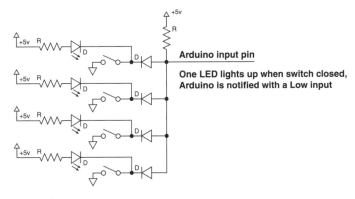

One LED lights up when switch closed,
Arduino is notified with a Low input

Figure 7.9
Wire logic.

There are numerous ways to build logic circuits with only resistors and diodes. That's the way logic circuits were built before there were active electronics (transistors). Unlike digital logic, wired logic can't be cascaded because of power loss.

Sadly, wire logic is a tough topic for a search engine to find. Try *diode logic* and omit the words *wire* and *wired*. Don't get carried away; you shouldn't need more than the occasional OR or AND.

Keypad

The keypad is a useful input device, but it takes a little explanation of how it's used. All C (column) pins are programmed as outputs and driven high. All R (row) pins are programmed as inputs with pullup resistors. Connections to a keypad are shown schematically in Figure 7.10.

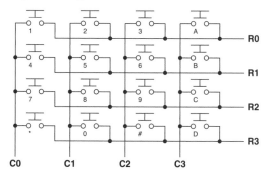

Typical 4x4 Keypad

Keypad buttons are multiplexed/scanned:
Pins are pulled High with internal resistors
One column pin is pulled Low with output pin,
Row pins are read, pressed switch reads as Low
Repeat for remaining columns

Figure 7.10
Keypad.
© 2014 Cengage Learning®

To read the keypad, drive one column at a time low and then read the row pins. Only the column and row combination that produces a low at the row pin is the pressed key. You must continually poll the keypad, or you'll miss key presses. *Debouncing* (short time delay) is required to prevent multiple key presses registered for a single press.

Potentiometer and DC Bias

Figure 7.11 shows how you can use a potentiometer (variable resistor) to set an analog level. You can use ordinary fixed-value resistors in series with a variable resistor to limit the range of the voltage adjustment range.

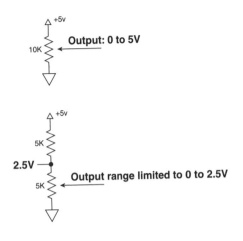

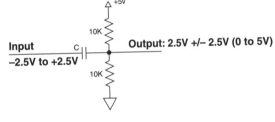

Figure 7.11
Potentiometer and DC bias circuits.
© 2014 Cengage Learning®

The third circuit in this figure shows how to add DC bias to an analog signal. DC bias shifts the center voltage of an oscillating AC signal to a more useful place. You can set the DC bias with a variable resistor circuit similar to the first two shown in the figure.

An AC signal can be biased to be centered around 2.5 V. Without shifting, the negative portion of the original signal would be lost. Negative voltage can't be applied to the Arduino's input pin without damaging it. The negative portion of the signal could be suppressed with a diode, but shifting the center point allows the entire signal to be preserved.

Rotary Encoder

Rotary encoders provide information about how much a knob is turned. Multiple switches inside the encoder open and close as the knob is rotated. The number of switches varies from two to eight.

The switches inside the encoder open and close in a particular pattern. This pattern repeats as the knob is turned. The number of pattern repeats varies by device. Some devices provide a pattern that typically repeats between 12 to 20 times per revolution. Other devices have exactly one pattern per revolution.

Only one switch inside the encoder changes at a time. This type of encoding is called *Gray encoding*. Gray sequences have a big advantage over other types of encoding because only one switch at a time changes. You know what the change will be because you know the sequence.

If you use the proper monitoring technique, you don't need to debounce the rotary encoder's switches. Figure 7.12 shows how you can connect a rotary encoder using the external interrupts.

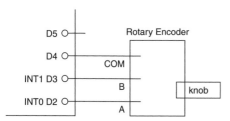

Uses Interrupts in Rotary Encoder Library
to detect clock edges as the knob turns
www.pjrc.com/teensy/td_libsEncoder.html

Figure 7.12
Rotary encoder.
© 2014 Cengage Learning®

Multiplexing

Time-division multiplexing allows a device or set of devices to be shared among a group of other devices or signals by taking turns. A small group of control signals selects one of the shared devices at a time.

The cost of driver ICs, the board space they occupy, or the input/output pins they connect to can be saved this way. Unless you have a reason to add multiplexing, don't add needless complexity.

Figure 7.13 shows how multiplexing permits one set of drivers to power several groups of LEDs by having them take turns. Each group of LEDs forms a seven-segment digit.

Only one digit will be selected at a time using the Digit X Enable signal. These are the signals controlling the transistors on the top and bottom of the diagram.

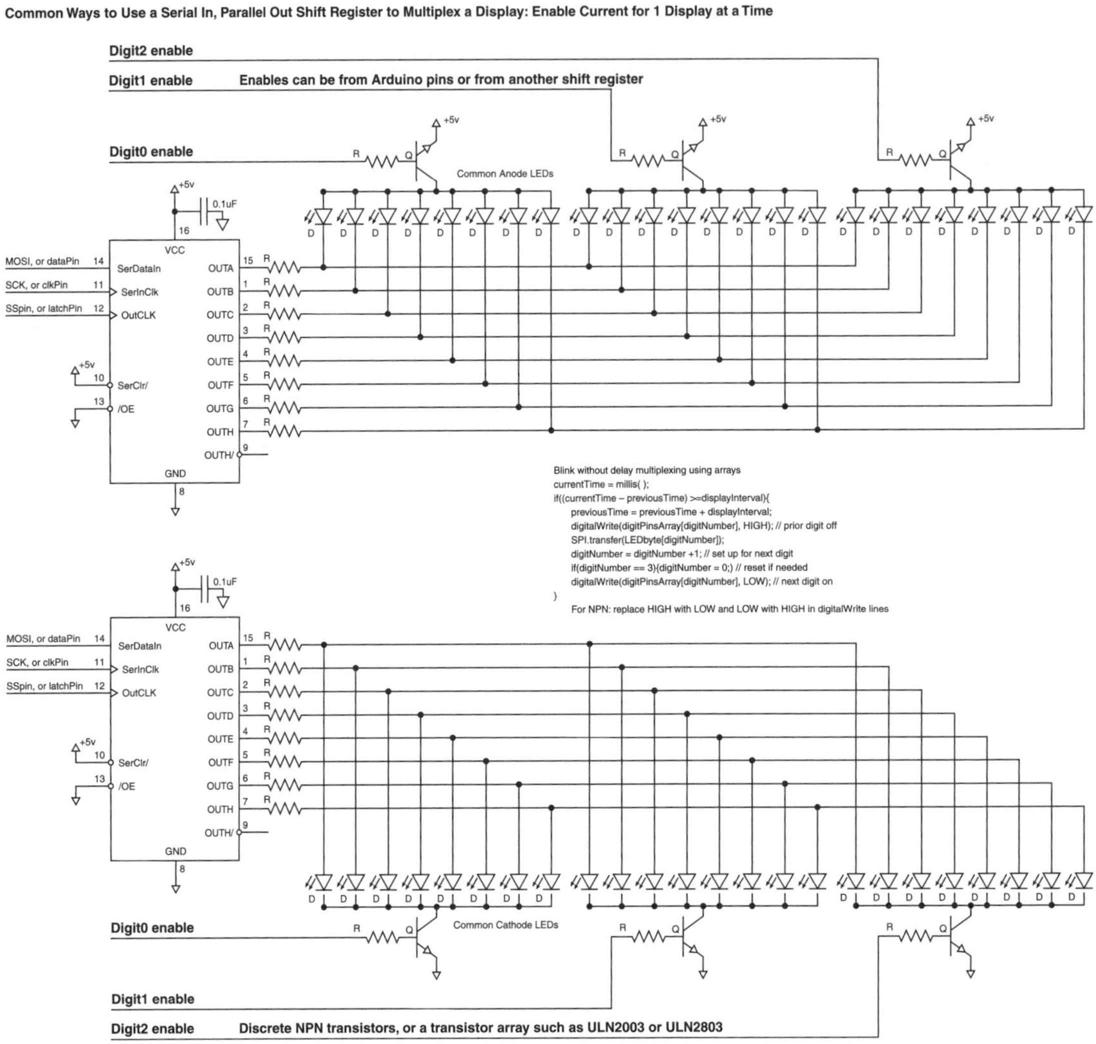

Figure 7.13
Multiplexed drivers.
© 2014 Cengage Learning®

The digits are connected to the driver all the time. The transistor for only one digit will be on at a time. If you cycle through the controls fast enough, it looks like all the digits are on at the same time. If the cycles are too slow, the digits flicker.

A code fragment, included in Figure 7.13, shows how this multiplexed driver circuit might be controlled.

The Traffic Light Example (Part II)

Let's revisit the examples from way back in Chapter 3. This time let's concentrate on mapping the I/O to pins and selecting a drive circuit where needed. We will talk about the programs to run these examples in Chapter 9.

If you recall from Chapter 3, the traffic light has three LEDs and a pushbutton switch. Each LED needs its own output pin, and the switch needs an input pin. Four digital pins should do nicely. Let's pick pins 2 (switch), 4 (green), 5 (yellow), and 6 (red). Refer to Figure 3.6 for a schematic.

LEDs are diodes that produce light when current flows in the forward-biased direction and require a minimum current to illuminate. The forward-biased voltage drop of LEDs varies and is typically 2.2 V for red, 3.2 V for green, and 3.7 V for blue.

If you connect the LED directly to the pin of the Arduino, it draws too much current. To avoid damaging the Arduino, operating output current should not exceed 20 mA on any pin. You need a series resistor to limit the current. Resistors come in standard values, with 220 ohm the closest approximate value.

You can use any value resistor larger than 220 ohms as long as enough current flows to light your LED. Check the LED's data sheet for the minimum, or try a few resistor values to see which you like best. Use Ohm's Law if you prefer an exact value. But remember that resistors are available only in standard values and with 1–5% tolerances.

The only other external component required for this design is a switch. For the switch, use the internal pullup resistor (20 K ohm minimum), which provides the current limit.

A traffic light is really a timer. The time component of this design is completely internal to the Arduino and doesn't use pins.

Battery Power

Power demands of this circuit are modest. Let's look at the power budget to determine if it can be run from a battery and approximately how long the battery will last.

From the Atmel data sheet, the microcontroller draws 9 mA at 8 MHz, with the unnecessary internal circuitry disabled. This isn't exactly the case because your clock runs at 16 MHz. In addition, you are drawing 20 mA from an I/O pin for each LED. Only one LED is on at a time, but one LED is always on.

Occasionally, you need a bit more current (0.3 mA) for the switch. The switch is used so little of the time that it can be accounted for with the margin you're adding. Adding it up and rounding up, you get 30 mA, to which you will add 20% for a margin. The final result is 36 mA.

Battery capacities are specified in amp-hours. Consider four AA batteries. In series, the voltage adds up to 6 volts, which is the minimum required for the Uno. Each battery has a 2000 mAH capacity, with a typical drain of 50 mA. Although the total capacity adds up to 8000 mAH, you get merely 2000 mAH at 6 V because the batteries are connected in series. (The weakest link limits the total battery capacity.)

You lose some power to the voltage regulator (1 volt of the 6 supplied). That's about 80% efficiency. The voltage regulator must dissipate any unused power, and some power is lost to the regulation process.

If you divide battery capacity by the power draw, you can calculate battery life. (2000 mAH times 0.8 efficiency) divided by 36 mA current draw yields a life of 44 hours, or about two days.

In real life, you won't get this level of performance. Battery voltage sags as current is drawn, and the voltage regulator drops out (stops providing the 5 Volt output). Five AA batteries providing 7.5 Volts is a better choice, but even these eventually sag enough to drop out. Dropout occurs before the battery capacity is exhausted.

Now consider some techniques for extending battery life. Because the biggest load comes from the LEDs, reduce their draw first. You can use more efficient LEDs that require less current to illuminate. (To benefit, the size of the current limit resistor needs to be increased to the maximum possible.) Any efficiency gain here translates directly to battery life.

High-efficiency LEDs draw 5 mA rather than the 20 mA that are allocated. That's one-fourth of the power draw, lengthening your battery life to eight days.

You can get some power savings from the microcontroller. For this project, little processing power is needed. Because the microcontroller is CMOS, reducing the clock rate lowers its power consumption proportionally. The easiest way to do that is to reduce the clocking rate globally using the prescaler. The prescaler can divide the system 16 MHz clock to 62.5 KHz. The power consumed is reduced to less than 0.15 mA.

The best power-saving approach is to select high-efficiency LEDs and scale down the system clock. Using only these two approaches, you can extend the battery life to about eight days. Unless you have rechargeable batteries or buy them in volume, consider using a power brick.

Puppet Show Example (Part II)

The puppet show example from Chapter 3 requires a lot more than a switch and a couple of lights. This is a more complicated feat to pull off, and it's harder to do in your head. First, review the parts you need to connect and the type of I/O they need.

Puppet show parts:

Curtain motor (bidirectional)	Two digital pins plus one PWM pin with driver circuit
Music source	Salvaged MP3 player with control circuit and one digital pin
Speaker	Driven by MP3 player (no pins)
Marquee	Group of three digital pins with shift register chain (SPI pins)
Spotlight	Digital pin with driver circuit
Motors for bears (bidirectional)	Two digital pins plus one PWM pin with driver circuit
Momentary switch	One digital pin

Shopping from the sample circuits, you need a marquee, a couple transistor drive circuits, four H-bridge circuits, and a button.

One H-bridge is required for each motor. You can use two dual full-bridge shields from Dipmicro or two Sparkfun TB6612 breakout boards. This shield uses pins 8, 9, 10, 11, and 13, and there is no good way to change them. Unfortunately, you can't stack two shields because you need a way to use different pins!

Breakout boards provide circuits similar to shields, but they are meant to be wired rather than stacked. You can use any pin, but you need to keep the nature of the pins the same. For each motor, a PWM pin controls speed, and the two other digital pins control direction.

For music, use an old MP3 player played through powered PC speakers. There is no sophistication here. Turn the power on at the start of the show, and turn it off at the end with a transistor switch.

For the marquee, use a dot-matrix display that utilizes the SPI signals for control. There's another problem, though. The SPI pins are 10, 11, 12, and 13, which conflict with the motor shield pins. You can use software to emulate the SPI function, which allows you to select any pins, or you can use two H-bridge breakout boards.

This problem does highlight one of the bigger issues with shields. Although shields boast of plug-in convenience, it doesn't always work out. Often, shield pins conflict with each other or with pins with dedicated functions, like the TWI or the SPI.

D0 and D1 have been reserved for use as a serial debug port. That way you can print messages as the program proceeds. As an alternative, you can use LEDs as an indication. Words are easier to understand because a computer is attached anyway.

The spotlight is always on when the music is on, so you can use the same control pin. It has its own drive transistor.

Table 7.5 shows how you can assign your Uno's I/O pins. You need the I/O map when you write the code.

Table 7.5 Puppet Show I/O Map

Pin	Use	Direction	Pin	Use	Direction
0	Reserved (serial monitor RX)	I	10	Marquee Slave Select	SPI O
1	Reserved (serial monitor TX)	O	11	Serial out	SPI O
2	Motor 3 –	O	12	Serial in	SPI I
3	Motor 3 speed	PWM O	13	Shift clock	SPI O
4	Motor 3 +	O	A0	Motor 4 +	O
5	Motor 4 speed	PWM O	A1	Motor 4 –	O
6	Motor 2 speed	PWM O	A2	MP3/spotlight	O
7	Motor 2 +	O	A3	VIP button	I pullup
8	Motor 2 –	O	A4	Motor 1 +	O
9	Motor 1 speed	PWM O	A5	Motor 1 –	O

© 2014 Cengage Learning®

Pinball Machine Example (Part II)

The pinball machine uses the bottom-up approach and is perfect for adding a piece of circuitry at a time. You can use a Mega2650 because it offers more I/O pins.

You can reuse the circuits from the puppet show and add scoring targets. Most pinball targets are just switch closures; software takes care of the fancy bit.

Active bumpers don't need microcontroller intervention; the switch contact triggers a transistor-controlled solenoid directly. The microcontroller still needs to know about it if the bumper is meant to score.

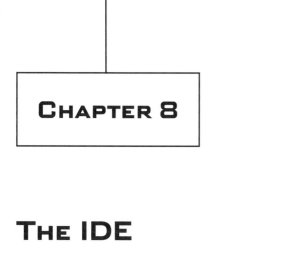

CHAPTER 8

THE IDE

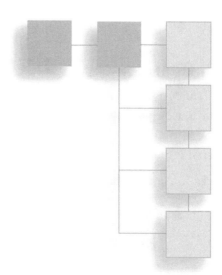

This chapter will answer the following questions:

- What is the IDE?
- Where do I get a copy?
- Where should I put the files?
- What could possibly go wrong?
- What are the key features?
- Where are the C features I'm used to seeing?
- What other programming environments are available?
- Where do I write my code?
- What happens when I click on the Verify button?
- What happens when I click on the Download button?

The Integrated Design Environment (IDE) provides a user-friendly way to program your Arduino. An editor, compiler, programmer, serial port, and various tools are among the built-in features that give the IDE its "integrated" name.

The IDE was originally designed for nonengineers to use. As such, some features of the C and C++ programming language are hidden from the user. For the nontechnical user, this saves a lot of looking at cryptic bits of code you don't need to and probably shouldn't change.

If you happen to be an experienced programmer or engineer, you may find that particular "feature" frustrating. You don't need to worry, because all those pieces are there. They're just hidden; we'll show you where later.

IDE Installation

You can find links to the IDE installation guide, download page, libraries, and troubleshooting guide on the Getting Started tab on the main web page at www.arduino.cc. Separate pages are included for Windows, Mac OS, and Linux, and a good effort is make to keep them up to date. There is little point in duplicating them here.

As a young adult with a computer, you're likely to have already successfully downloaded a million different things from the Internet. The Arduino download and installation is pretty straightforward.

If you do need a little help, the guides on the Arduino page will walk you through all the steps from downloading the IDE files to downloading your first program to verify it's working correctly. If you don't like the official installation guide, you have other choices.

If you bought an Arduino cookbook or project book, it will have a section on the IDE. Books can't keep up with changes that happen after they are published. (Some have associated websites or author sites that try.) Arduino models that appear after the book is printed certainly won't be in it. This brings us back to the web.

Many Arduino distributors and Do It Yourself (DIY) project sites also have IDE installation guides. These sites eventually lead back to www.arduino.cc for the software. Makeprojects.com has a particularly good version for Windows, with screen shots of the Arduino web page and step-by-step directions. Use the site's search bar (found when you click on the magnifying glass) and type "Arduino IDE."

For those who need to see it done, there are YouTube videos. Specifically search for "IDE" and "Arduino" to distinguish IDE videos from project videos.

Start with the directions on the official Arduino site. If you have difficulty, finding another set of directions online isn't hard. Feel free to use as many sources as you wish, but it shouldn't be necessary. The installation phase usually goes smoothly. The first big question is this: where should the files go?

File Location

A frequently asked question is, "Where should the IDE be located?" The short answer is that it usually doesn't matter. The longer answer is that it's traditional to install applications, like the IDE, in the Program Files folder for Windows systems or the Applications folder for Mac OS systems.

For Linux, location does matter, and you should follow the directions for your particular version carefully. The absolute pathnames must be exact.

For Windows or Mac OS systems, just because it's traditional doesn't mean you have to do it. Some people prefer to have the IDE on the desktop. As long as the folder structure remains intact, it doesn't really matter. There are advantages to following traditions. Other people have proven they work, and you shouldn't have issues.

ARDUINO CONNECTION TO COMPUTER

Let's discuss physically connecting your Arduino to your computer. Models of the Arduino that are equipped with a Universal Serial Bus (USB) connector can be connected to your computer through a USB cable.

Models of the Arduino that don't have a USB connector can be connected to your computer with a USB serial interface card. Most models that don't have a USB connector have a group of six pins that plug into a USB serial interface card. Some models must have pins soldered into holes on the PCB first.

These pins are not keyed. The names are stenciled onto the interface card and on the Arduino. If you plug the interface card in incorrectly and power it up, you may damage something. Pins connect per Table 8.1.

Table 8.1   USB Adapter to Arduino Pin Connections

USB Adapter	Arduino
+5V (or 3.3V)	+5V (or 3.3V)
GND	GND
CTS	GND (tells the adapter that it is clear to send data to the Arduino)
RX	TX (Arduino transmits, USB receives)
TX	RX (USB transmits, Arduino receives)
DTR	DTR (Data Terminal Ready—a low level from the USB resets the Arduino)

© 2014 Cengage Learning®

COMMON INSTALLATION PROBLEMS

The installation process of the IDE usually goes smoothly, but just in case, here are discussions on some of the most common problems.

Be sure to check the Arduino troubleshooting page for your specific problem. You can sometimes find the solution to your problem faster using a search engine than by hunting through the Arduino pages. Although an on-page search box exists on some Arduino pages, a search engine turns up better results.

Topics are added to the Arduino pages as they are encountered. If you can't find your problem, you can ask your distributor's support team or ask about it on the forum. See Chapter 12, "Bragging Rights and Pleas for Help," for directions on submitting a question for optimal results.

You can't anticipate every problem you might encounter, but you can anticipate some. This section looks at some of the problems you might encounter as a new user.

I Can't Find the IDE

Windows likes to hide downloads in a download folder. Unless you tell Windows to put the files somewhere more reasonable when you unzip them, the IDE will end up in the download folder, too.

More generally, the IDE will be where you installed it. Maybe you can't remember. The quick way to find it is to search for "Arduino" and look for the executable file. The executable is inside nested folders and has the cute little Arduino symbol next to it. (At least the Windows version has one.)

When you find the IDE, add a link (shortcut) for the executable file to your Start menu or desktop so that you don't need to hunt again. Because you could have installed the IDE anywhere, more specific directions on where to find it aren't possible.

I Can't Find the Sketch I Saved

Your sketches are stored at the default location. The default location is specified in the File>Preferences menu of the IDE. Your program files (sketches) are not stored where the IDE is.

The default location on our machine is the C:\Users\Owner\Documents\Arduino folder. The exact path will be different on your machine. To find your sketch, open the IDE and use the drop-down menu. Note the current setting before you change it to what you want it to be. You can then move any previously saved files to where you want them.

The default location is also where the IDE looks for user-defined library files. These include libraries you need for a shield. Storing libraries in the default location, rather than with the Arduino files, allows you to use them with different versions on the IDE.

I Want to Install Multiple Copies of the IDE

You can have multiple versions of the IDE installed at the same time. They don't share anything with each other and are independent.

You can run multiple instances (windows) of an IDE at the same time. Only one of them can use a particular Com port at a time. Other than competing for Com ports, the IDE versions are independent.

You can have multiple Arduino boards connected to your computer at the same time. The simplest case is one Arduino per PC Com port. You can usually use a USB hub to connect multiple Arduino boards to the same PC port. Each hub connection will be uniquely identified by a Com port number. Unfortunately, some USB hubs don't work for Arduino connections.

To make Arduino boards talk to each other, use Two-Wire Interface (TWI), Serial Peripheral Interface (SPI), or serial interface. Don't use the USB; an Arduino can't be USB master.

My Arduino Is Not Recognized. I Get an Unknown Device Error

Driver issues are the usual cause of unknown device errors. Finding and installing the correct driver version for your Arduino model is the most challenging part of using one. It's almost a guarantee that you will have driver issues at some point.

Operating system and physical hardware differences prevent having one set of directions for installing drivers across all computer platforms. There are separate directions for most operating systems on the Arduino Getting Started page. Even when you follow the directions exactly, the driver installation isn't always successful.

Don't despair! Someone has figured out how to do this crucial step and posted directions.

Finding those directions presents a challenge of its own. Although the Arduino site has a search tool, you may have better luck with a different web search tool, like Google. Google understands Windows 7 as a single term, whereas the Arduino website search function does not.

Try rebooting your computer and resetting your Arduino. Rebooting doesn't always work, but enough forum entries say that a reboot fixed the issue to be worth trying.

Try power-cycling your computer. (Turn it off and then back on.) Power-cycling is not the same as a reboot; it's stronger. Yes, I know that shouldn't make a difference. Drivers manipulate the hardware registers in your computer, and sometimes that isn't a clean process.

You are in pretty good shape if your computer recognizes that the Arduino is attached and the IDE can see it, too. That doesn't guarantee that you will be able to download sketches. Verify that the correct Arduino board type is selected in the IDE. Also verify that the port number is correct.

If you need help beyond these tips, you can find it through forums and tech support from your distributor. Discussions about drivers appear on most Arduino forums, including the official Arduino forum. Someone there has had your problem before. Sadly, the solution may not be there because no one bothered to post it after they found it!

Use a search engine to find the solution more rapidly. Even when the answer is there, it may be hard to pick out from all the other posts. Some of the posted solutions aren't completely accurate. Even so, they may be close enough to be called hints.

Upload or Download

Do you upload code or download it? It's really just a matter of perspective.

If you are computer centric, you will obviously download code to your peripheral Arduino. If you are Arduino centric, you will upload code to your slick new toy. Referred to either way, it's the same process.

Strictly speaking, it's the perspective of the initiating device that counts. Because your computer or programmer initiates and controls the process, it's a download. But use whichever term you prefer.

I Can't Put a Sketch on Arduino

I'm assuming you have made it past the last section. Your computer and the IDE should be able to see your Arduino. Sometimes things can still go frustratingly wrong. Be sure the correct board type and Com port are selected in the IDE.

Your Arduino is equipped with a group of LEDs. These tell you what Arduino is doing during a download. One LED is labeled Rx, which blinks when frames are sent to the Arduino. Another LED is labeled Tx, which flashes when frames are sent back to the computer from the Arduino.

If your Arduino is connected via a USB serial adapter, these indications are reversed. Tx flashes when frames are sent to the Arduino. Rx flashes when frames are sent back to the computer from the Arduino.

During a "normal" download (without an adapter), the Rx LED flashes frequently, and the Tx LED flashes regularly but less frequently. The computer is sending lots of information to the Arduino, which is responding with acknowledgements. If no Tx flashes are occurring, the Arduino isn't recognizing the download.

The problem could be that the Arduino is not responding to the reset signal used to initiate the download. If it continues to run the old sketch instead of responding to the download, that's likely the issue.

You can sometimes get around the problem by pushing the reset button after initiating the download. Timing is critical, so try it a couple of times. If a simple reset push does not work, try holding down the reset button until the IDE gives the `Binary sketch size` message and then releasing it.

Select Verbose Messages in the IDE's File>Preferences menu to get wordier descriptions. If you need to ask for help, these will be necessary.

If Rx doesn't flash, your sketch isn't making it out of your computer or to your Arduino. Check your selected Com port, cabling, and drivers.

If you attempt a download to a device without a bootloader, you get an error message. An official Arduino model from a reliable distributor has a bootloader installed on it when you get it.

If you bought a black market bootleg Arduino, you might have an Arduino without a bootloader. If your Arduino doesn't have a bootloader, you must use an AVR In-System Programmer (ISP) to install one. If you prefer to change the sketch without using a bootloader, you still need to use the AVR ISP programmer.

You may have a defective Arduino. It doesn't happen often, but it does happen. Contact your distributor's technical support for assistance.

I Bought a Chip with No Bootloader

To program a microcontroller chip with no bootloader, you need to install it into an Arduino or use a protoboard to build the minimal Arduino circuit.

You need a programming tool such as the Atmel AVR ISP MKII. (You also need to set the programmer in the IDE's Tools>Programmer menu.) You can use the programmer to install a bootloader or use it to install a program without a boot sector. Either way, the only way to get it working is with a programmer.

Once you acquire your programmer, you need to connect it to the In-Circuit Serial Programming (ICSP) pins on your Arduino. If you don't have ICSP pins or holes to install them into, you can't use the programmer. One option is to use individual wires to connect the programmer to header pins on the Arduino.

The ICSP pins are not keyed, so be absolutely sure that you connect your programmer correctly. The red lead on the MKII goes to the pin 1 end of the ICSP pins. Pin 1 is labeled.

The MKII programmer does not supply power to the Arduino. Power must be supplied separately. You can use a USB connection to the Arduino to supply power, or you can use a power brick. A battery pack with three AA or AAA batteries also works.

Verify that the correct board type is selected, using the IDE's Tools>Board menu. Once everything is connected correctly, use the IDE's Tools>Burn Bootloader command. If you accidently install the wrong bootloader, just follow the same steps to burn the correct one.

If you have a working Arduino, you can use it as an ISP. You can find the best directions at www.gammon.com.au/forum/?id=11635. (Thank you, Nick!)

My Version of Windows Complains

Windows likes to complain about something. Launching the application usually causes Windows to gripe. When installing drivers, Windows warns you it's risky. If you want to use your Arduino, get used to Windows complaints and do it anyway.

One Window complaint not to ignore is "unknown device." This error message means that the Arduino driver is not installed correctly. See the previous section on unknown device errors.

IDE Look and Feel

The IDE has the look and feel of practically every graphical text editor you have ever used. From the start, it feels familiar. Across the top of the window is a series of tabs, and below the tabs are icons for the popular actions. The main space of the window is the code editor area. The narrow strip at the bottom provides compiler messages.

Tabs

The usual things are found under the File, Edit, and Help tabs. For most commands, the keyboard shortcut is shown. (Use the menu if the shortcut doesn't work or work as expected. As the less popular interface, keyboard shortcuts aren't exercised as vigorously.)

Two features worth pointing out on the File tab are examples and preferences. All the example programs from the learning section of www.arduino.cc are there. You don't need to type them. They are presented in alphabetical rather than logical order to make them easier to find.

You can edit examples, but they are read-only files. To edit them, you need to save your version under a different (hopefully descriptive) name. The IDE reminds you to use a new name. The blink example provides a quick way to verify that your Arduino is installed and connected correctly.

The preference feature allows you to change the default sketchbook location. The sketchbook is the directory that your programs are saved in by default. It's also where the IDE expects to find user-defined or shield-specific libraries.

The Edit tab has what you would expect and a few additional commands to format your code. The Help tab presents a copy of information available on the Arduino website.

There are three copy options. Copy for Forum preserves the text colors, bold font, and text formatting used by the IDE. Copy as HTML insets HTML tags instead of preserving the text colors, fonts, and text formatting. Copy captures the text, including whitespaces.

The Sketch tab offers the ability to divide your sketch into more manageable pieces. The Sketch>Add Files drop-down menu item adds a tab to the Edit window of the current sketch. Sketch tabs are a useful way to segment your sketch into comment, declarations, setup, loop, and functions sections. These tabs provide a quick way to move between code sections without endless scrolling.

The IDE's Tools tab has some useful features. You set the board type, Com port, and programmer type using this tab. You launch the serial monitor tool or initiate the bootloader burn using this tab.

Auto Format pretties up your file to be more readable with white spaces inserted. It can also help with debugging because mismatched parentheses ( ), brackets [ ], and curly braces { } stand out more. Conditional statements with a "do nothing" semicolon also stand out. Or rather, they won't stand out, indicating that there isn't a conditional section.

The Tools tab also has a scary-sounding Fix Encoding and Reload command. This command changes ASCII to UTF-8 encoding and is intended for Asian characters that aren't properly represented with ASCII.

Main Window

The largest space in the IDE is the code editing window. This is the window your actual sketch appears in. The window usually has a single tab (named with the filename). Multiple tabs can be created with the Sketch>Add Files drop-down menu. (Each tab is labeled with its filename.)

The IDE has some features that help a beginner. Color identifies some names or words as special. Auto Format neatens up the sketch, and using indentations of various levels indicates code line groups. Automatic highlighting of a mating parenthesis, bracket, and curly brace helps to identify mismatched pairs.

As you type, the IDE changes the color of the text to indicate special words. Keywords and (standard) function calls are shown in orange, whereas macros are shown in blue. Comments, including code sections that have been commented out, are shown in gray.

Indentations on new lines indicate the group the current code line is expected to be in. If you don't like the automatic indentations, you can change them as you go or auto format when you're done.

Find, copy, cut, paste, and replace are available, as they are with any reasonable editor. The IDE's features won't win it editing product of the year, but they are certainly adequate.

Icons

A series of icons below the tabs provides a quick way to perform popular actions. Moving the mouse over the icon will display the verbal interpretation of the icon.

Compiler

The bottom section of the IDE provides comments from the compiler. By tradition, compiler comments are terse and cryptic. If you're lucky, you will see happy white text telling you the size of your file.

If you're unlucky, you will see error messages spewed out in orange. The compiler might highlight the place where it thinks the error is. It is almost certain to be wrong. Refer to Chapter 9, "Writing the Code," for suggestions on debugging your code.

Messages regarding the status of the download also display in this window. You can use a verbosity setting to give more wordy descriptions of what went wrong. (Hold down the Shift key while clicking the upload icon to select the verbose mode or use the File>Preferences drop-down menu to select it.)

Verify and Download Functions

Verify performs a lot of steps, which boil down to converting your sketch into machine code and placing it into a temporary directory. This process may take longer than you expect because many things you don't see are happening. You don't need to concern yourself with all the details, but to make it work properly, you must select the correct board type. The machine code is stored in a temp directory as a `.hex` file.

Download checks to be sure nothing has changed since the last `.hex` file was created. If anything has changed, the verify process is repeated. The `.hex` file is then sent via the selected Com port to the Arduino attached to it. Successful download will be verified if the Verify After Upload preference is selected in the File>Preferences menu.

To see everything the IDE is doing during verify and download, select the verbose options in the File>Preferences menu. (You can make the compile window bigger by dragging the top border upward.)

Conversion of C code (like your sketch) into machine code follows a build process. The build process has many steps, which are described by two different web pages. Consult the FAQ section of www.arduino.cc for links to them. Fair warning—these pages will be difficult to understand unless you are already familiar with software builds in general.

Alternatives to the IDE

If you don't like the IDE for whatever reason, you have choices. Atmel offers a suite of tools that you can use instead. Because the IDE is open source, other versions of the IDE have been developed by programmers unhappy with the IDE experience. There is also a plug-in for Microsoft Visual Studio. The plug-in is free; Microsoft Visual Studio is not.

Atmel Studio

You can download Atmel Studio, parts of which were formerly known as AVR Studio, from www.atmel.com. You can use this tool with AVR microcontrollers (like the Arduino) and other microcontrollers that Atmel makes.

Many tools are incorporated into Atmel Studio. Because this tool is intended for engineers and professional programmers, it has more features than you need.

IDE Clones for Programmers

Because the IDE is open source, other versions of the IDE have been developed by experienced programmers for experienced programmers. Because of its open source nature, this collection will change over time, like the current flavor of Linux does.

Alternatives exist for those unhappy with the original IDE. Here are some of the IDE alternatives in no particular order:

- MariaMole
- Microsoft Visual Studio
- Codebender
- RobotC
- Eclipse
- Sublime Text

NOTES FOR C (AND C++) PROGRAMMERS

This section is not for those new to programming, and you can safely skip it. It discusses where the files and functions that experienced programmers are used to seeing have been hidden.

If you are already a C or C++ programmer, you may find some of the features of the IDE confusing or annoying. The location of `main()`, the use of unconventional conventions, automatic prototyping, and the lack of direct compiler control might cause some irritation at first. (There are IDE alternatives if you can't learn to tolerate it.)

main() Location

Every C programmer expects to see a `main()` function. That's where all the action starts. To be a valid C program, `main()` must exist, so where is it?

`Main.cpp` is located in the arduino\hardware\arduino\cores\arduino directory. You can use Notepad++ to view this file. Don't edit this file, or you could break your IDE. If you do break it, download a fresh copy and leave it alone.

Other files of interest to enthusiastic C programmers are located here as well. Have a good look around. Go nuts. But if you break it, you buy it. (Or as mentioned above, just download a fresh copy.)

Unconventional Conventions

By convention, constants and macros are given names in all capital letters. Some of the functions described by the Arduino reference page are actually macros. By defying the naming convention, it's difficult to tell which ones are macros and which ones are functions.

Most of the time, that distinction doesn't really matter. Unless you are trying to squeeze a big program into a tiny space, the larger compiled size of a macro compared with a function isn't an issue. Likewise, unless you are aiming for blistering processing speed, the slightly slower function call compared with a macro won't be a problem.

An improperly constructed macro can burn you worse than a bad function. For example, a macro with insufficient parentheses can cause truly bizarre things to happen. It can misbehave in completely unexpected and perplexing ways.

Any really big problem with a macro (or function) is reported on the forum. Unless you see an issue reported, it's most likely an error in your code and not a broken macro.

Would it be nice to know if you are using a function or a macro? Sure. Could what you are using change from a function to a macro with a future version of the IDE? Yes. Now for the only question of importance: does it matter? No, not really.

All the files and libraries are available. All the function and macro definitions are there for the interested user to see. You could wade through them to figure it out. If you have the time and interest, have at it.

Automatic Prototypes

Automatic prototypes (function declarations) are generated for most types of functions that don't have them. As an avid C programmer, you might come up with a function that doesn't automatically generate a prototype. Of course, as a passionate C programmer, you always prototype your own functions anyway, so this isn't an issue.

Compiler Control

The build process that the IDE uses is described on two web pages, referenced by the Arduino FAQ page. If you want more control over the build process than is provided by the File>Preferences menu, you might want to use an IDE clone (discussed previously).

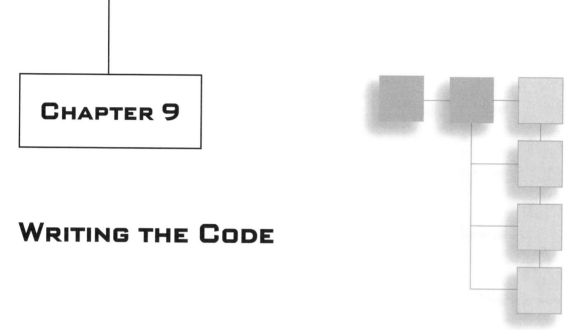

CHAPTER 9

WRITING THE CODE

This chapter answers the following questions:

- How do I get started?
- Why do I need a plan?
- How do you define Input/Output (I/O)?
- What is polling, and why is it used?
- What are interrupts, and why are they used?
- What could possibly go wrong?
- How do I know the code is working?

THE SKETCH

An Arduino program is called a *sketch*. The name is meant to be friendly and inviting, especially for nonengineers, who are the intended users of the Arduino. The sketch contains the directions your microcontroller follows to run your project.

It's tempting to open the Integrated Development Environment (IDE) and dive into a sketch without advance planning. Go ahead! Play with your Arduino. Have some fun trying it out.

For those of you who made it through Chapter 8, "The IDE," without loading a program and need additional incentive, I double-dog dare you! You can't learn to use your Arduino if you're afraid of it.

"Blink," one of the IDE's built-in example sketches, is a good place to start. It requires no external components, and you can't damage your Arduino or yourself with it. Go ahead and try it. Then modify it to flash slower or wait longer between flashes or blink your initials in Morse code.

Next, add a pushbutton (or fake one with a 220 ohm resistor) and try the "Button" sketch. Take a look at any of the sample sketches that catches your attention. You can download a sketch to your Arduino; the worst thing that could happen is that it won't work.

It doesn't make sense to go through all the examples now. They are intended to demonstrate particular techniques, not to be a beginner's tutorial. You could go years (or a lifetime) without needing some of them.

If you do need a particular technique, the closest example or one from the playground (http://playground.arduino.cc/) could be a convenient starting point. Even if you start with an example, you still need a plan for your own project.

Save Early. Save Often.

There are few sounds more unnerving than the fresh quiet of a blackout. The best defense against power glitches and blackouts is a habit of saving frequently. Although power supply isn't an issue for laptops, regular backups let you recover from human-caused or self-inflicted catastrophes.

Accidental deletes, mid-edit distractions, major changes, and bad ideas sometimes cause unrecoverable problems. Returning to the last backup copy is usually better than starting over.

Always keep a copy of your latest working program. Use a copy for edits. Save your work often, right from the beginning of a project. Succinctly phrased, save early, save often. (This is good financial advice too.)

THE PLAN

Before diving straight into writing the sketch to control your project, some planning will make the process go more smoothly. The first part of the plan is to select an approach. That is the general overall method that determines the sketch's basic structure.

First consider the nature of the problem. Can you write step-by-step directions for a friend to follow to run your project? Does more than one thing have to happen simultaneously most of the time? Does a normal routine happen most of the time, with the occasional interruptions? Is the main purpose to move data around? Does your Arduino need to communicate with a device that's not a slave? Do you need sleep modes?

The structure of your program needs to suit the nature of the job you're trying to complete. Some programs are procedural, whereas others are monitoring or interrupt driven. Let's look at some basic types, keeping in mind that no program uses purely one approach.

Step-by-Step

Step-by-step programs are perhaps the easiest to understand. These programs follow a set procedure. You start with step 1, and when you're done with that, you move on to step 2. And so on. When you finish the last step, you return to step 1. You can do any process that you can describe in steps this way.

Procedural programs are writer friendly. They might not be the most efficient technique possible, but they are easier to debug than other types of programs. The advantage and disadvantage of step-by-step programs is that they can do only one thing at a time.

Monitoring

A monitoring structure suits programs that must watch or control multiple things at the same time. Although the order in which conditions are tested is fixed, the order in which actions are performed varies. They will likely be different each time the program is run.

The main feature, a monitoring loop, quickly looks at a series of conditions to see if actions are needed. This technique is also called *polling*. The actions can be performed immediately or flagged for later execution. These programs perform actions on an as-needed basis. Monitoring programs are the best choice when anything can happen at any time.

Smaller monitoring loops are useful for adding time-based features to other program types. They can monitor the time without tying up the microcontroller's processing time in idling loops.

Monitoring programs can be a challenge to debug because the order of execution varies. Use LEDs or a serial monitor port to make the Arduino tell you what it's up to. Be sure to check for things that didn't happen and should have.

Interrupt-Driven

You can add an interrupt (aka exception) to procedural or monitoring programs to handle the unusual condition. Interrupts should be relatively rare occurrences. If your application needs frequent interrupts, consider an interrupt-driven structure.

An interrupt-driven structure is normally idle (or housekeeping) but leaps into action when interrupts are generated. Frequent events needing immediate action are suited to this structure.

Data transfer systems can be interrupt driven to maximize throughput. Interrupts are generated (and serviced) when data buffers empty or fill. This maximizes data transmission because the data doesn't have to wait for the microcontroller to get around to emptying or reloading the buffers.

One hazard of this structure is that interrupts happening faster (on average) than they can be handled (on average) will eventually crash your microcontroller. The advantage is excellent response speed.

Sleep Modes

Sleep modes save power; that's all they do. There is no other reason, except perhaps amusement, to make your microcontroller sleep.

Sleep modes are a form of microcontroller operation and not really a program type. Nearly any program type can use them to save power during idle periods. If your microcontroller isn't idle, it's not really appropriate to have it nap.

Sleep modes turn off the clock to sections of the microcontroller to conserve power. Complementary Metal-Oxide-Semiconductor (CMOS) consumes very little power when it's not clocked. Because they aren't really powered off, the Serial RAM (SRAM) and register file remember their state while sleeping.

Waking up takes some time, where time is measured in clock cycles. For the Arduino, the default is 16 K clock cycles. (For a 16 MHz Uno, wake-up time is 1 m sec.)

Your program needs to be structured around the pieces that remain powered up and wake-up conditions. Considering sleep modes in the planning phase allows you to add them after the rest of the program is working without having to do a complete rewrite. Some rewriting and tweaking are needed, but careful planning will let you keep more of your original code.

When the Arduino sleeps, only the microcontroller itself actually sleeps. The power savings might not be what you hoped for. Any microcontroller outputs driven high when the sleep state is entered will remain high. Any floating input pins may oscillate; use the internal pullup resistor to avoid this problem. The 5 V and 3.3 regulators power LED, and the USB/serial driver chip remains on. All of these things consume power even while your microcontroller sleeps.

ANATOMY OF A SKETCH

Before diving into example sketches, let's look at what one looks like in more general terms. Sketches follow a general arrangement. The first line or lines may have instructions to the compiler. They are known as *preprocessor commands* because they are executed before compilation starts. (Once upon a time, a separate piece of software did the preprocessing work. Now it's built in to the compiler.)

These preprocessor instructions are easy to identify because they start with the pound symbol (#). Libraries to include, conditional compilation, and macros are among the compiler actions specified. (Be careful with preprocessor syntax; it's different from ordinary C syntax.)

The top sketch section, outside of both setup() and loop(), defines constants, variables, arrays, and pin names. These items will have global scope; they can be accessed anywhere within the sketch.

Variables are assigned a data type and given an initial value. Although not strictly required, initializing variables is good practice and makes each execution of your sketch predictably the same. (That's a good thing, especially at debug time.) Uninitialized variables typically have a value of 0, but don't rely on it.

Global functions can be prototyped here. Prototypes are to functions what declarations are to variables. Prototypes declare the function's return type and the type of its arguments.

Prototypes are not required by the C programming language; however, they do allow the compiler to perform additional type checks. As one of the preprocessing operations, the IDE will create a prototype for most types of functions that don't have one. (It can't handle all cases.) To be sure you like what you get, write your own function prototypes.

The code snippets that follow show a function prototype and a definition for a trivial example. Be careful with prototype syntax; it differs slightly from function declaration syntax.

Here's the trivial function prototype:

```
int add_six(int x); // Prototype for function that takes and returns an integer
```

Next up is the trivial function definition:

```
int add_six (int x) { // Function to add six to an integer
    x = x + 6; // Add six
    return (x); // Return answer
}
```

Functions (with global scope) can be defined anywhere in your sketch outside of setup() and loop(). They are traditionally prototyped at the top of a program and defined at the bottom or in a library. Remember that setup() and loop() are functions.

Just in case you're wondering, setup() and loop() have already been prototyped for you as void setup(void) and void loop(void). (They return no value and take no arguments.)

Functions and Global Variables

A function's arguments and returned values are not global variables even if the function has global scope; they are passed values. These values are assigned to temporary variables while the function executes. The function has the type and value that is returned, just like a variable has a type and value.

Unlike a variable, a function does not keep its value past the calling instruction line. If the function's value is not captured with a more permanent variable, it is lost. That might be fine. A function call used as an argument in a conditional statement may not need meaning beyond that one test.

setup()

The `setup()` function is the first section after preprocessor commands, global declarations, and function prototypes. This function is intended to set up pin configurations, timers, and serial interfaces (Serial, SPI, Wire [I2C]). It sets output pin levels and initializes anything that needs it.

`setup()` is called once and only once. You are free to put anything you want into this function. It can include running self-checking routines, initializing circuitry or machinery, or anything you want to do once before the program starts in earnest. There are no limitations on what you can put into `setup()`. Remember that variables or functions defined inside of `setup()` have local scope and are unavailable to `loop()`.

Hardware registers programmed in `setup()` retain their values. For example, pins programmed as digital output pins stay as digital output pins unless they're reprogrammed. (You can change I/O pin configuration during operation, but it's not recommended. Set them once in `setup()` and then leave them alone. If you must change them, refer to the datasheet for limitations and issues.)

If you don't have anything you want to put into `setup()`, you still have to define one. The IDE looks for it and complains if you omit `setup()` entirely. You just need to define the function; it doesn't need to actually do anything.

On the other hand, you could put your entire program into `setup()`. In this case, you still need to define a `loop()`, even if it does nothing.

For any program you might need help debugging, follow the more traditional approach. Use `setup()` for setting up your Arduino and `loop()` for the main program.

Where Is main()?

For the C and C++ programmers who are wondering where `main()` went, it's still there. It's the `arduino\hardware\arduino\cores\arduino\main.cpp` file. You can examine it with a text editor (or use a software editor such as Notepad++).

loop()

The second section, loop(), is also a function. loop() is called over and over again as it finishes. As the name emphasizes, loop() runs repeatedly.

Arduino programs rarely terminate. This never-ending approach is common for microcontrollers, especially ones controlling real-world processes. Microcontrollers are single-purpose (one task at a time) machines that are completely dedicated to the job at hand.

loop() does not need to terminate. The never-ending feature can be obtained with a looping construct inside of loop() rather than repeated calls of loop(). In this sense, the name is confusing. loop() can be called continually (repeatedly) or be designed to run continuously (without stop).

You may be wondering why it matters. Most of the time, it doesn't matter. But there are potential problems for the unwary. The difference is in the treatment of local variables and functions.

Variables and functions defined inside of loop() are local to loop(). Local variables don't exist from one function call to another. Each time loop() is called, these variables are re-created. If loop() does not terminate, local variables created within loop() keep their values. (That may or may not be what you want.)

Global variables have a more permanent existence. You can use a global variable to count the number of times loop() is called. A variable local to loop() can't.

Regardless of the program type, all code is written with sequential commands. These instructions are step by step, even when they give the illusion of things happening concurrently. We will talk about this some more with some concrete examples.

Library-Defined Functions

Many useful functions are defined in libraries. Some libraries are specific to C (and C++). There are libraries to perform mathematical functions, handle I/O streams, type-cast, allocate memory, manipulate complex numbers, and many other things.

Some libraries are specific to the Arduino. These libraries contain functions to set up Arduino I/O, set pins high and low, control Pulse Width Modulation (PWM), and other things.

Other libraries are specific to a shield. Shield libraries are available from the shield maker. Shield libraries need to be located in your sketchbook library folder, allowing any version of the IDE to find them. (A preprocessor command to include them is also required in your sketch.)

User-Defined Functions

You are not limited to only `setup()`, `loop()`, and library functions. You can define your own functions. Functions allow a section of code to be used repeatedly. Functions may take arguments, variables, or numbers, to be used during function execution. Arguments are not required.

Functions may return a value. Multiple values can't be returned by a C/C++ function; it's a situation C/C++ doesn't handle well. Use structures, pointers, or global variables if more than one value is calculated by a function. (Global variables are the simplest choice and arguably the best choice for those not comfortable with C programming.)

Place user-defined functions in your sketch, the most straightforward option, or in a user-created library. Creating your own library of functions takes more than copying the functions into a sketch. You need to properly structure the library file using classes, and you must supply a required keyword file.

There is a tutorial on the Arduino website (www.arduino.cc/) for those interested in creating their own libraries. From the main page, click on the blue Learning tab and then on the Hacking link. You should see "Writing a Library" under the Software heading.

Macros

Macros, like the commands to include libraries, are not C (or C++) code; they are preprocessor commands. They tell the compiler to perform actions before the actual compilation starts. (*Compilation* is the translation of C code to binary machine language.) Macros are identified by the pound symbol (#) preceding the name (without a space).

There are several types of macros, and the Arduino libraries are stuffed full of them. You can use function-like macros as you would a function call, including the use of arguments. The preprocessor replaces them with a section of C or C++ code.

For example, the following code line shows how the macro `min(a,b)` is defined. Note that there are no equal signs or semicolons. Syntax for macros is different because the macro is written for the preprocessor.

```
#define min(a,b) ((a)<(b)?(a):(b))
```

Each instance of `min(a,b)` is replaced by `((a)<(b)?(a):(b))`, where `a` and `b` are the arguments. It looks as though the writer was overly fond of parentheses, but these parentheses are needed to prevent odd precedence problems.

This example uses C's conditional construct. The expression preceding the question mark symbol is the condition. The expression to the left of the colon is used when the condition is true. Otherwise, the expression to the right of the colon is used. Although cryptic, the conditional construct is popular with programmers because it's so compact.

What follows are pre-processor example results. Here's the original code:

```
least_value = min(x,y);
```

Here's what it looks like after the preprocessor:

```
least_value = ((x)<(y)?(x):(y));
```

These replacements are literal, just as if you did a replace operation with a word processor. There is no intelligence here. Function-like macros can be difficult to write, but they are just as easy as functions to use.

You can use object-like macros like a constant to hold a number, string, or address. Many Arduino-specific macros are this type, including bit and register names. Your compiler (preprocessor) replaces each object-like macro with its numerical value. Object-like macros are easy to write and use.

Other macros, hidden deep inside the preprocessor, handle special situations related to adapting a program for the hardware it's meant to run on. The IDE provides these adjustment macros for your sketches. They fine-tune the code to accommodate Arduino model and compiler version differences, among other things.

Functions and Macros

Functions and function-like macros are similar and different. They allow sections of code to be reused, but they do so in different ways.

Functions reuse sections of code stored in program memory. Program execution takes two jumps for every function call. The first jump is to the function, and the second is back when it's done. Pipelined processors, like the one your Arduino has, take a small performance hit when executing jumps.

The preprocessor section of your compiler replaces every macro with its definition in a literal way. Therefore, function-like macros duplicate lines of code. This duplication makes your program a little bigger, depending on the macro's size and how often you use it. Macros execute a tad faster because they don't need a jump.

Table 9.1 summarizes some of the differences between functions and macros. 99.99% of the time, you won't care whether you are using a function or a macro. You don't need to know the intricate details because the IDE handles the particulars for you.

Table 9.1 Comparison of Functions and Macros

Functions	Macros
Written in standard C/C++	Written with mix of C/C++ and preprocessor commands
Easy to use	Easy to use
Easy to write	Difficult to write
Reuses code stored in memory	Duplicates lines of code
Requires jumps (small performance hit)	Requires (a little) more memory
Function names are always followed by parentheses	Macro names are traditionally all capital letters. Many Arduino macros don't follow this convention
Examples: `setup()`, `loop()`, `pinMode()`	Examples: `HIGH`, `min(a,b)`, `true`
Straightforward	Rare hidden pitfalls and strange problems
Error messages when compiled	Error messages when compiled

For that rare instance in which you might care whether something's a macro or a function, it's helpful to be able to identify them. Functions always have parentheses, like `setup()` and `loop()`. Some function-like macros also have parameters and use parentheses, like `min(a,b)`. Macros by convention should be named with all capital letters, like `HIGH`, `LOW`, and `OUTPUT`; however, some macros don't conform to this convention, like `true` and `min(a,b)`.

When a naming convention isn't used, it can be difficult to determine if you are using a function or a macro. The only way to tell for sure is to find the definition, which could be in any included library or file. To make things worse, the definition could change from a function to a macro or the reverse with a new release of software or a library update. The good news is that you will seldom, if ever, care.

SKETCH EXAMPLES

Nothing is better at illustrating the details of a technique than a concrete example. Once again, you will be revisiting the examples from earlier chapters. This time, you will concentrate on the code that makes them work.

Personal styles of code are a matter of taste. There are some conventions that will help you share your projects with others or get help when you need it:

- Use comments that describe the intended function of your code, starting with a general description at the beginning of the program.

- Structure your sketch like the examples. Put the sketch elements in order, with preprocessor commands first, followed by global declarations, function proto-types, `setup()`, `loop()`, and function definitions.

- Construct your sketch in a way that makes sense to you. Functions, other than `setup()` and `loop()`, are optional. You can make as many additional functions as you like or use none at all.

- Name variables and functions descriptively, or add a decoding key in comments.

- Initialize all variables where they are defined.

- Don't abuse global variables to pass arguments to functions. Global variables may be necessary to return multiple values from a function.

- Follow the whitespace formatting convention or use the Auto Format tool of the IDE. (You can find it in the Tools drop-down menu or by pressing Ctrl+T.)

THE TRAFFIC LIGHT EXAMPLE (PART III)

You can use procedural, monitoring, or interrupt-driven methods to program most projects. Let's revisit the examples we first looked at in Chapter 3, "From Idea to Project," and last saw in Chapter 7, "Input and Output." The traffic light example illustrates how you can use any one of these approaches to solve the same simple problem.

All these techniques are equally valid, but each has its own advantages and limitations. More complex control problems may favor one approach over others.

The time scale in the example code has been compressed to speed up debug time. Once you're satisfied that it's working, you can put in the real times.

Procedural

Running the traffic light is a sequential process with one hiccup: the Walk button. Because you are waiting around anyway, you can monitor the Walk button in the green state. It's the only state where the button should have an effect.

Although you are monitoring the time, this example is procedural. You work on only one step at a time. Until that step is complete, you can't go on to the next one.

There is a library function, delay(), that delays for a period of time what could be fixed or contained in a variable. You could have used this function instead of monitoring the current time. What you gain in convenience, you lose in flexibility. Nothing (except interrupts) happens while delay() executes.

As demonstrated by the Walk button, you can do other things while you wait. The delay() function does not allow other actions to be performed at the same time. The Walk button requires an interrupt for timely processing.

Because you are monitoring time, you don't need an interrupt for the Walk button. You simply need to check the button. You don't need to debounce the button because the nature of the program has built-in delays.

The following code shows the complete example sketch. Let's look at the code for this example. You don't need to include any libraries that aren't already included by default. You don't have any preprocessor commands.

```
// Traffic light example code, procedural approach
// pre-setup; assign names to pins and declare variables
byte red_led = 6;
byte yellow_led = 5;
byte green_led = 4;
byte switch_pin = 2;
// Time-related variables are data type unsigned long
unsigned long red_start_time = 0;
// UL after the time variable ensures you get an unsigned long
unsigned long red_duration = 5000UL; // 5000 milliseconds, 5 seconds
unsigned long yellow_start_time = 0;
unsigned long yellow_duration = 5000UL; // 5 seconds
unsigned long green_start_time = 0;
unsigned long green_duration = 5000UL; // 5 seconds
unsigned long current_time = 0;

// Set up code; runs once
// Define pins as input and output
void setup(){
  pinMode (red_led, OUTPUT);
  pinMode (yellow_led, OUTPUT);
  pinMode (green_led, OUTPUT);
  pinMode (switch_pin, INPUT);
  // Write the input pin HIGH to connect the internal pullup resistor
  digitalWrite (switch_pin, HIGH);
  // Capture the time to start with
  current_time = millis();
} // end set-up
```

```
// Loop code; runs over and over
void loop(){
  // Turn on yellow; turn off red and green
  digitalWrite (yellow_led, HIGH);
  digitalWrite (green_led, LOW);
  digitalWrite (red_led, LOW);
  // Save time yellow started
  yellow_start_time = current_time;
  while ((current_time - yellow_start_time) <= yellow_duration){
    current_time = millis(); // Update current time
  } // Loop until duration exceeded

  // Turn on red; turn off yellow and green
  digitalWrite (yellow_led, LOW);
  digitalWrite (green_led, LOW);
  digitalWrite (red_led, HIGH);
  // Save time red started
  red_start_time = current_time;
  while ((current_time - red_start_time) <= red_duration){
    current_time = millis(); // update current time
  } // Loop until duration exceeded

  // Turn on green; turn off red and yellow
  digitalWrite (yellow_led, LOW);
  digitalWrite (green_led, HIGH);
  digitalWrite (red_led, LOW);
  // Save time red started
  green_start_time = current_time;
  while ((current_time - green_start_time) <= green_duration){
    current_time = millis(); // Update current time
    // If button pushed, skip to yellow
    if (digitalRead (switch_pin) == LOW){
      break;
    }
  } // Loop until duration exceeded
} // End loop
```

The first section defines global variables to hold pin numbers. Using variables instead of pin numbers allows you to change pins, if you need to, in just one place. Variables to hold the time and the duration of each cycle phase are also defined and initialized.

The setup() function is next. This function sets the input and output pins, turns on a pullup resistor for the input, and captures the start time. This function executes only once.

The loop() function has three steps. Step 1, the yellow phase, turns on the yellow LED. The green and red LEDs are turned off. Although the red light should already be off, turning it off here keeps two lights from being on accidentally.

Then you monitor the time while you wait for the phase time to elapse. Monitoring the time is not the same as being idle. The millis() function is repeatedly called and the result tested.

Step 2, the red phase, turns on the red LED. The green and yellow LEDs are turned off. Again, time is monitored until the phase time elapses.

Step 3, the green phase, turns the green LED on. The yellow and red LEDs are turned off. Then the button and the time are monitored until the phase time elapses or the button is pushed. If the button is pushed, skip to the end of step 3.

loop() ends here, and control returns to the main program. loop() is immediately called again, leading you back to step 1.

This code example shows just one way to write a procedural program. It's a useful starting point for programs that need to monitor the time to decide when to move to the next step.

You could have monitored anything instead of time. You could monitor a sensor input, a serial interface, the internal temperature sensor, a digital input, or some combination of events.

The function millis() uses timer 0. Select another timer, if you need one, to avoid conflicts.

Monitoring

Like most monitoring programs, the monitoring example performs some setup and then enters a monitoring loop. The monitoring loop tests a series of conditions to see if further action is required. The loop then repeats.

The following code shows another way to control the traffic light. This example uses a monitoring approach. Let's take a look at the example in detail.

```
// Traffic light example code using a monitoring approach
// Presetup, assign names to pins and declare variables
byte red_led = 6; // Use pin 6 for red
byte red_state = 0;
byte yellow_led = 5; // Use pin 5 for yellow
byte yellow_state = 0;
byte green_led = 4; // Use pin 4 for green
byte green_state = 0;
```

```
byte switch_pin = 2; // Use pin 2 for switch
unsigned long red_start_time = 0;
unsigned long red_duration = 5000UL; // 5000 milliseconds, 5 seconds
unsigned long yellow_start_time = 0;
unsigned long yellow_duration = 5000UL; // 5 seconds
unsigned long green_start_time = 0;
unsigned long green_duration = 5000UL; // 5 seconds
unsigned long current_time = 0;

// Set up code; runs once
void setup(){
  pinMode (red_led, OUTPUT);
  pinMode (yellow_led, OUTPUT);
  digitalWrite (yellow_led, HIGH); // Turn on yellow
  yellow_state = 1; // Remember yellow is on
  yellow_start_time = millis(); // Note the time
  pinMode (green_led, OUTPUT);
  pinMode (switch_pin, INPUT);
  // Writing an input pin HIGH connects the internal pullup resistor
  digitalWrite (switch_pin, HIGH);
} // End setup

// Loop code; runs over and over
void loop(){
  current_time = millis(); // Capture the time
  if (yellow_state == 1){ // Is yellow light on?
    // See if it's time to turn it off
    if ((current_time - yellow_start_time) >= yellow_duration){
      digitalWrite (yellow_led, LOW); // Turn it off
      yellow_state = 0; // Store its state
      digitalWrite (red_led, HIGH); // Turn on the red light
      red_state = 1; // Store its state
      red_start_time = current_time; // Store the time of the change
    } // End yellow duration check
  } // End yellow light check
  if (red_state == 1){ // Is red light on?
   // See if it's time to turn it off
   if ((current_time - red_start_time) >= red_duration){
     digitalWrite (red_led, LOW); // Turn it off
     red_state = 0; // Store its state
     digitalWrite (green_led, HIGH); // Turn on the green light
     green_state = 1; // Store its state
     green_start_time = current_time; // Store the time of the change
   } // End red duration check
 } // End red light check
```

```
if (green_state == 1){ // Is green light on?
  // See if it's time to turn it off or if the switch was pressed
  if ( ((current_time - green_start_time) >= green_duration) || (digitalRead
(switch_pin) == LOW) ) {
     digitalWrite (green_led, LOW);// Turn it off
     green_state = 0; // Store its state
     digitalWrite (yellow_led, HIGH); // Turn on the yellow light
     yellow_state = 1; // Store its state
     yellow_start_time = current_time; // Store the time of the change
  } // End green duration or switch press check
} // End green light check
} // End loop
```

The first part of the program is just like the procedural version. Some additional variables, which serve as flags, are defined and initialized. These flags keep track of which light is on and modify the action slightly on each pass through the loop. Only one flag is meant to be set at a time.

The setup() function sets the input and output pins, turns on a pullup resistor for the input, and captures the start time. The yellow LED is lit, and the yellow flag is set. This function executes just once.

loop() captures the current time. It tests each flag in the sequence: yellow, red, and then green. For the flag that is set, the current time is tested to see if it's time to change the lights. When it's time, the lights are changed, the start time is captured, and the flags are updated for the next phase of the cycle.

During the green phase, in addition to the other tests, the button is tested to see if it has been pushed. When a push is detected, the next phase is cycled to as if time had expired. As with the previous example, the button is monitored only when the green light is on. Because you are monitoring the button, no interrupts are needed.

The time scale has been compressed for debug convenience. Once you're satisfied that the program is working as intended, you can adjust the time using the variables.

Interrupt-Driven

Time-base interrupts form the basis for this program, because the traffic light is essentially a timer. Timer 1 will be set up to interrupt periodically, once per second. You will count the number of interrupts to keep track of time and drive your traffic light cycle.

A counter, aptly named *seconds*, is incremented once per second by the Interrupt Service Routine (ISR). This variable counts the time through the cycle. You can make each phase of the cycle last as long as you want by counting the seconds. The counter is reset back to zero to restart the cycle.

Now that you have the general idea, let's look at the example program in detail. This program is not like the others because interrupts require some special handling.

The following code shows the program listing. At the top of the program are preprocessor commands. You need to include the libraries that support interrupts.

```
// Traffic light example using timer-based interrupts to change the lights
// Timer 1 is used to generate periodic interrupts based on counter match A

// Need avr-libc library for interrupts
#include <avr/io.h>
#include <avr/interrupt.h>

// Use macros rather than variables to name pins to allow use in ISR
#define REDLED 6
#define YELLOWLED 5
#define GREENLED 4
#define SWITCHPIN 2

// Variables used in ISR must be declared as volatile
volatile byte seconds = 0;
volatile byte green = 0;

// Set up pins as outputs and inputs
void setup()
{
  pinMode (REDLED, OUTPUT);
  pinMode (YELLOWLED, OUTPUT);
  pinMode (GREENLED, OUTPUT);
  pinMode (SWITCHPIN, INPUT);
  // Writing an input pin HIGH connects the internal pullup resistor
  digitalWrite (SWITCHPIN, HIGH);

  // Globally disable interrupts
  cli();

  // Set up timer 1 counter control registers A and B
  // Normal port mode, Waveform generation mode 4
  // CTC -Clear on Timer Compare match
  // Divide by 1024 prescaler
  TCCR1A = 0;
  TCCR1B = 0x0D;

  // Set compare match A register to match in 1 sec
  OCR1A = 15264;

  // Enable timer 1 output A compare match interrupt
  TIMSK1 = 0x02;

  // Enable global interrupts
  sei();
```

```
  // Set up the serial monitor port so that debug messages can be sent
  Serial.begin(9600);
}

void loop()
{
  // Monitor the walk button in the green state
  if ((green == 1) && (digitalRead(SWITCHPIN) == LOW))
  {
    seconds = 0;
    // Let me know someone pushed the button
    Serial.println("Walk button pushed.");
  }
  // Print seconds so I can monitor the cycle
  Serial.println(seconds);
}

// This is the Interrupt Service Routine for timer 1 A compare
ISR(TIMER1_COMPA_vect)
{
  // Keep track of elapsed time
  seconds++;

  // Yellow light on at 0-5 seconds
  if (seconds == 1)
  {
    green = 0; // Don't monitor walk button
    digitalWrite(GREENLED, LOW);
    digitalWrite(YELLOWLED, HIGH);
  }
  // Red light on 6-10 seconds
  if (seconds == 6)
  {
    green = 0; // Don't monitor walk button
    digitalWrite(YELLOWLED, LOW);
    digitalWrite(REDLED, HIGH);
  }
  // Green light on 11-15 seconds
  if (seconds == 11)
  {
    green = 1; // Monitor walk button
    digitalWrite(REDLED, LOW);
    digitalWrite(GREENLED, HIGH);
  }

  // Restart cycle
  if (seconds > 16) seconds = 0;
} // End ISR
```

Unlike the previous sketches, you use macros to hold the pin numbers instead of variables. You can't use variables inside of ISRs without declaring them as volatile. *Volatile* tells the compiler to store the variable in RAM rather than a register, making it available to the ISR.

Because the pin numbers aren't going to change during program execution, there is no reason to make them variables. Using macros allows the preprocessor to substitute the numeric pin number while still providing the convenience of using the pin number in only one location.

You can't use some functions inside of an ISR. Without digging into the details of a function, it's hard to tell if it will work. `Serial.println` didn't work inside the example ISR.

As useful as library functions are, they can sometimes produce mysterious and unexpected problems. These problems aren't really mystifying if you understand the code hidden behind the function. But let's assume for now you don't want to or can't examine the function is detail. So what can you do?

If your function call doesn't compile or doesn't behave as expected during an ISR, you can try a couple of techniques. Use macros where possible instead of variables. In the example code, `pinMode()` doesn't compile with variables as arguments inside of the ISR. Macros work just fine, and no logical change to the program is needed.

If using macros doesn't work, rethink the logic of your program to place the function call outside of the ISR. If you must have information only available inside the ISR, you can use a volatile variable as a flag to pass the information back to your main program.

Look for a similar way to do the job. Perhaps you would like to print a debug message during an ISR and `serial.println()` doesn't work. You could use a variable to pass an error code back to your main program and print the message corresponding to the error there. Or you could use an LED attached to a pin as an alternative indicator. Be creative; there is always another way.

In this example, you next declare two volatile variables. One is used as the counter to keep track of time. The other is used as a flag to indicate the green cycle, during which you need to monitor the Walk button.

Next comes the `setup()` function. `setup()` initializes the I/O like the previous examples, except that macros rather than variables hold the pin numbers. Then the interrupts are configured.

Before configuring interrupts, you disable them globally. Near the end of `setup()` and after everything is properly configured, you re-enable them.

For this example, timer 1 generates interrupts every second. You need to use the prescaler to divide down the system clock, or interrupts happen too fast. The prescaler can divide the clock by 1024.

16 MHz divided by 1024 gives a frequency of 15625 Hz. For 1 second, the timer needs to count from 0 to 15624. When the count reaches 15624, you want to generate an interrupt and reset the counter to 0.

TCCR1A and TCCR1B are the timer 1 control registers that control the prescaler, mode of operation, and reset condition. The prescaler is controlled by the clock select bits in TCCR1B. You can set these bits using a number of techniques.

You could set the bits with an OR operation of the register contents with the prescaler setting and then place the result back into the control register.

```
TCCR1B |= 0x05;
```

You could set the bits one at a time using predefined macros to shift a 1 into the proper position. The result is set with an OR operation as above. CS11 stays as 0 and doesn't require an instruction.

```
TCCR1B |= (1 << CS10);
TCCR1B |= (1 << CS12);
```

You could figure out the entire contents of register A and B using the register bit definitions in the data sheet. Then you can set them with a single code line for each register. For example, these two lines set normal port mode, waveform generation mode 4, clear on timer compare A match and divide by 1024 prescaler. Refer to the data sheet for details on what these settings mean. If you were setting a bit at a time, you would need more lines of code in addition to the ones above for these other settings.

```
TCCR1A = 0;
TCCR1B = 0x0D;
```

Our preference is to configure the registers once, and our code reflects that. You can use any method or combination of methods that you are comfortable with. These registers are read/write. If you don't know what your register contains, you can read it and print the result to the console port. This is especially useful for debugging.

The count match is set in the OCR1A register. Earlier you calculated the count to reset on as 15624 for 1 second.

Next, you enable timer 1 to generate interrupts when the count matches the value set in OCR1A. Now that everything is set up, you re-enable interrupts. The last line sets up the serial monitor so that debug messages can be sent to the serial monitor port.

loop() doesn't have much to do. During the green phase of the cycle, loop() monitors the Walk button. You can't print the value of seconds in the ISR, but you can print it in loop(). Because the value is changing, you know the ISR is running. A single value of seconds prints multiple times because loop() runs more than once per second.

After loop(), the last part of the sketch is the ISR. The ISR keeps track of time using the variable seconds. This variable is used to turn the lights on and off when it reaches certain counts. The cycle has been shortened for debug purposes.

PUPPET SHOW EXAMPLE (PART III)

The sequential nature of a puppet show suggests a step-by-step approach for the sketch. Providing a full-length code example for the puppet show isn't very helpful. It's too complex with the pieces interspersed to be readable. More usefully, let's discuss the marquee, motor controller, and analog input pieces separately. Because we haven't discussed it before, we'll talk about how to read and scale an analog signal.

The Marquee

The marquee is built from LED matrixes driven with MAX7219 drivers, with one driver device per LED matrix. The 7219 drivers contain fourteen 8-bit registers. Six registers provide configuration and control. The eight others correspond to one column of the display each, with one bit mapping to one LED.

Some display drivers, like the MAX6953, include a built-in font set. Built-in fonts provide a quick way to get started and eliminate the need to define your own font set.

Although convenient and a quick way to get started, built-in fonts don't support all features. Scrolling by a whole character at a time is possible, but not the smoother scrolling of a single column at a time. Reverse video may or may not be provided. Vertical scrolling isn't possible with the built-in font. To add smoother scrolling or other features, you need to define your own font set.

You aren't committed to a single font set. You can use the built-in font set and later add your own. The differences are only in software and don't require tedious rewiring. Using the built-in font mixed with your own font is possible but difficult. You would need to reconfigure display driver control registers on the fly to switch between them.

Font Set

The first step to driving the marquee is to build a font for it. The font defines which LEDs are on and off for each character you want to display. Each character is a series of columns, stored as numbers, with the LEDs set on or off.

Your font could use a fixed number of columns for each character, or it could represent wider characters, like W, with more columns. The number 1, the uppercase *I*, and the lowercase letter L could share one narrow character or be separate characters. A narrow space between letters could be built in to your font or added as a separate character. Unless your character width is fixed, you need to store the width with the rest of the character data.

Your font may include only the characters you actually use, or it may contain all alphanumeric characters. The numbers 0–9, uppercase letters, a space character, and limited punctuation make a reasonable font set.

In short, your font set is a collection of data for each character you want to display. It includes column definitions and, unless fixed, the number of columns.

You can use any software constructs you want to store your font. You can use one array for each letter or one huge array with groups of data for fixed-width characters in alphabetical order. You can use structures that conveniently store different types of data together.

A font set is a large amount of data, so use a method you understand and are comfortable with. You need to find data for an individual character to construct your display strings. Think about how you will identify one particular character from that mass of data.

Figure 9.1 shows one way to define a font. Each character in this example is made up of five columns and does not include a space between characters. A 1 indicates an illuminated LED. A hexadecimal number represents each column with the Most Significant Bit (MSB) corresponding to the topmost LED. Five hex numbers make up each character in the font.

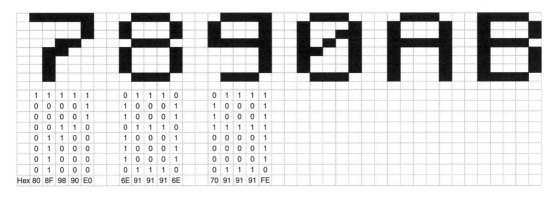

First 2 characters are then stored as:

```
byte fontArray[] = {
0x80, 0x8F, 0x98, 0x90, 0xE0, // 7
0x6E, 0x91, 0x91, 0x91, 0x6E, // 8
0x70, 0x91, 0x91, 0x91, 0xFE, // 9
:
:
} // end fontArray
```

Figure 9.1
Font definition—giant array.
© 2014 Cengage Learning®

In this example, the entire font is stored in one giant array. Display messages could take the form of an index into the font array. They could instead be ASCII characters that your program converts into an index.

The next code shows another other way to store your font definitions using an array for each character. An array name can't start with a digit. Special characters, like numbers and punctuation, need special names. Your display message might be stored as ASCII characters. Your program would then translate each ASCII character to an array.

```
byte digit_7[] = {0x80, 0x8F, 0x98, 0x90, 0xE0} // 7
byte digit_8[] = {0x6E, 0x91, 0x91, 0x91, 0x6E} // 8
byte digit_9[] = {0x70, 0x91, 0x91, 0x91, 0xFE} // 9
```

Note that the font data is the same as the previous example. The LED illumination pattern remains the same regardless of the method that stores the information.

The following code shows how a font can be stored as structures. Structures are useful because they allow mixed types of information to be stored together. A particular character can be stored as an individual structure or as part of an array of structures. The example shows how to store a character as part of an array of structures.

```
/* Define a structure with an ASCII character, column width, and column definitions as
an array. Call the structure myfont just in case font is a reserved word. */

struct myfont { char c; byte w; byte columns[5]; };
// Define the font set as static since it won't be changing
static struct myfont number[10] =
{
{'0', 5, { 0x7E, 0x89, 0x91, 0xA1, 0x7E }}, // 0
{'1', 5, { 0x01, 0x61, 0xFF, 0x01, 0x01 }}, // 1
{'2', 5, { 0x63, 0x85, 0x89, 0x91, 0xF1 }}, // 2
{'3', 5, { 0x43, 0x89, 0x89, 0x9D, 0x76 }}, // 3
{'4', 5, { 0xF8, 0x08, 0x08, 0xff, 0x08 }}, // 4
{'5', 5, { 0xE1, 0x91, 0x91, 0x91, 0x8E }}, // 5
{'6', 5, { 0x7E, 0x98, 0x98, 0x98, 0x4E }}, // 6
{'7', 5, { 0x80, 0x8F, 0x98, 0x90, 0xE0 }}, // 7
{'8', 5, { 0x6E, 0x91, 0x91, 0x91, 0x6E }}, // 8
{'9', 5, { 0x70, 0x91, 0x91, 0x91, 0xFE }} // 9
};
```

The first element of the structure is the ASCII character the structure represents. The second is the width of the character in columns. The remaining elements are the column definitions.

Like the previous examples, your program needs to identify and extract the correct character data. Unlike with the previous examples, you can use the ASCII character stored with the character data to identify the correct entry.

With any character set, be sure to include a default character for when you are missing a character definition. A square, a dash, or a question mark would be good default options. Any character that's not part of the normal set would work. Blanks would be a poor choice because they are too common.

Although the syntax looks complicated, it's not as bad as it seems. The following line of code shows how to refer to the second column of data for the 7 character. You might use a line like this to copy your font into the display string. The number of columns is part of the font structure, so you can use a loop with `number[7].width` as the upper limit to copy all the columns. This structure can accommodate characters of various widths.

```
display_string[current_column] = number[7].columns[2];
```

As an alternative to creating your own font or using a built-in one, you can use a library font. Read the documentation for the library carefully. For your letters to display correctly, you need to understand the format the font is stored in.

If you make a mistake and your letters appear upside down or backward, you can correct the problem in software. That advice applies equally to a library font or your own font. Compensating in software for wiring errors is often easier than rewiring. If you plan to make multiple copies of your design, and even if you don't, be sure to document any errors you find and how you corrected them.

Display Messages

Now that the mechanics of how to form letters are stored in the font, it's time to decide what your marquee is going to say. Your program can display one message from a set of fixed messages, or it can display a message entered through the serial port.

The display message can be stored in any convenient format. It might be a string of ASCII-represented characters or a series of index numbers or code numbers. The message format must be compatible with the font set format. The display message character must identify the corresponding font character.

Give the identification process some thought. This is one of the more complex tasks in controlling the marquee. Keep your C book handy. You may find it helpful to study pointers, arrays, and structures because these constructs make the control job easier.

Caution

Use an array of char rather than strings to avoid string implementation issues.

Beware: C considers a string to be an array of char, but the Arduino has some oddities there. String may work, but char always works. Use an array of char to hold strings and avoid the issues.

Display String

Once you have decided on the message, the next step is to translate that message into the display string containing the bit pattern. Each character of your message needs to be converted to a bit pattern using your font set. The bit patterns are packed together to form a display string.

The display string is constructed like an old-fashioned line of type is built. For each letter of your message, your program picks out the bit pattern specified by the font. Those columns of data are packed onto the end of the display string, while keeping track of how many total columns are used.

The exact software techniques used will be highly dependent on how the font definition and message strings are structured. The result will be more or less the same: one set of data with one byte corresponding to each column of data to be displayed.

If you want to display a symbol or picture rather than a text message, you might choose to put the LED pattern directly into the display string. In fact, you can do exactly that for all your messages and dispense with both the font and the display message. Clearly, you give up flexibility for simplicity. You still need to know how many total columns wide your display string is.

The last step is controlling the physical display. If your display string is wider than your display or if you want to add effects like scrolling, you need to pick which part of the display string to show. The display window picks off the part of your display string that is written to the display's control registers.

Display Window

The display window corresponds directly to the physical display. The display window has the same number of columns as the display, with one bit per LED. This is the data that is sent to the control registers of the displays. You can't change the size of the window because it corresponds one to one with the physical display.

The display window selects the part of the display string you want to appear on your physical display. You are free to choose any portion of the display string you want to show.

For horizontal scrolling effects, the display window slides over the display string and picks off the data to show. The window doesn't actually move; the data copied to the window starts and ends at successive positions in the display string.

The analogy is good once you understand it. You see only what appears in the window and not what's to either side of it. The rest of the display string is still there and unchanged. You just don't see it until the window "moves."

Figure 9.2 shows how the font, display string, and display window work together. The row at the top of the figure shows the display string column numbers. The display message appears with the font corresponding to each character. This data is packed together to form the display string. The brackets at the bottom of the figure show what appears in the display window.

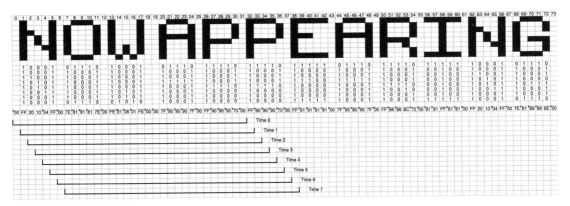

Figure 9.2
Completed message display.
© 2014 Cengage Learning®

You can achieve horizontal scrolling effects by selecting successive sections of the display string. You can accomplish other effects by manipulating the display string columns as they are copied to the display window. Reverse video can be achieved by 1s complementing the columns' data. Vertical scrolling effects can be achieved by bitwise shifting the columns' data. (This is one case where you probably don't want sign bit extension.)

If you want to scroll the first word onto the display, pad the left side of the display string with blank characters. If you want to scroll the last word of the display, pad the right side of the display string with blank characters.

You can achieve nearly any effect you can think of by manipulating the display window. The display string doesn't change unless you want to update the display message. Then the display string is rebuilt using the same process.

Motor Controller

The most common DC motor controller is the full bridge, as discussed in Chapter 7. Built as a special-purpose Integrated Circuit (IC), the full bridge allows the motor to run forward, reverse, or brake. Some H-bridge ICs allow two separate power sources to be used: one for the control and another for the motor. An enable signal allows speed to be controlled without sacrificing torque.

To control a motor with software, two digital pins and one PWM pin are used. The digital pins are used together to set the direction or brake. The PWM pin controls the enable line. The higher the duty cycle of the PWM signal, the faster the motor turns.

You can use the cryptically named analogWrite() function to control the PWM signal. This function takes two arguments: the pin number and a number representing duty cycle. Duty cycle is the amount of time the signal is high relative to the entire cycle time. The signal frequency remains the same, at about 490 Hz.

analogWrite() is not the only way to set up PWM signals. You can write timer/counter registers directly to achieve control not accommodated by this function.

Changing the settings for the timer/counter associated with the PWM signal changes the duty cycle. The duty cycle is really a count match signal. The signal goes high when the counter reaches the stored value and remains high until the counter is reset or rolls over.

Changing the count at which the counter resets changes the duty cycle by changing the cycle time. Using the prescaler doesn't change the duty cycle, but it can cause the cycle time to be too long, resulting in noticeable flicker or surging.

You can use a counter for other purposes and still use it to control PWM signals, but they are not independent. You need to set the count match to get the duty cycle you want.

The following example shows how to use the serial monitor port to control two motors with a dual H-bridge.

```
//Serial Control 2 dc motors
char buffer[5]; // ru000 to ru255, rd000 to rd255, lu000 to lu255, ld000 to ld255
//buffer>parameter
// PICK PINS so that analogWrite is available for the enablePin
const int motor1Pin = 3; // H-bridge leg 1 (pin 2, 1A)
const int motor2Pin = 4; // H-bridge leg 2 (pin 7, 2A)
const int enablePin = 9; // H-bridge enable pin
const int motor3Pin = 10; // H-bridge leg 1 (pin 2, 1A)
const int motor4Pin = 11; // H-bridge leg 2 (pin 7, 2A)
const int enablePin2 = 8; // H-bridge enable pin
byte incomingByte;
byte speed;

void setup()
{
Serial.begin(9600);
```

```
// Motors
pinMode(motor1Pin, OUTPUT);
pinMode(motor2Pin, OUTPUT);
pinMode(enablePin, OUTPUT);
pinMode(motor3Pin, OUTPUT);
pinMode(motor4Pin, OUTPUT);
pinMode(enablePin2, OUTPUT);
// Disable them
analogWrite(enablePin, 0);
analogWrite(enablePin2, 0);
}

void loop() //
{
if (Serial.available() > 4) {   // Got 5 bytes in?
incomingByte = Serial.read();
if  ((incomingByte == 'r') || (incomingByte == 'l'){ // Got a good start character
buffer[0] = incomingByte;
buffer[1] = Serial.read();
buffer[2] = Serial.read();
buffer[3] = Serial.read();
buffer[4] = Serial.read();
}   // Done capturing a good message
// Set right motor direction
if (buffer[0] == 'r'){
  if (buffer[1] == 'u') {
      digitalWrite (motor1Pin, HIGH);
      digitalWrite (motor2Pin, LOW);
   }
  else{
      digitalWrite (motor1Pin, LOW);
      digitalWrite (motor2Pin, HIGH);
   }
} // End right direction
// Set left motor direction
if (buffer[0] == 'l'){
  if (buffer[1] == 'u') {
      digitalWrite (motor3Pin, HIGH);
      digitalWrite (motor4Pin, LOW);
   }
  else{
      digitalWrite (motor3Pin, LOW);
      digitalWrite (motor4Pin, HIGH);
   }
```

```
} // End left direction
// Now the speed
// Convert digits to numbers, multiply by 100/10/1, and add together
speed  =((buffer[2]-48)*100)  +  ((buffer[3]-48)*10)  +  (buffer[4]-48);  //  check
asciitable.com for conversion
// What are we doing?
Serial.print("moving motor ");
Serial.print (buffer[0]);
Serial.print (buffer[1]);
Serial.print(speed);
// Which motor is to move?
if (buffer[0] == 'r'){
analogWrite(enablePin, speed);
}
else{
analogWrite(enablePin2, speed);
}
// Maybe a 'b' case to move  both together?
} // End loop
```

Scaling Analog Level/Volume Knob

The volume knob for a serial message-controlled MP3 player provides a good example for reading and scaling an analog level. The volume knob controls a variable resistor-set voltage level. This is the simple voltage divider as discussed in Chapter 7.

The analog signal level is converted to a number. The result needs to be scaled so that the maximum and minimum voltage levels correspond to the maximum and minimum volume control levels.

The analog voltage varies from 0 volts to 5 volts, which your ADC sees as the numbers 0 to 1023. That needs to correspond to a digital range of 0 to 99 that the MP3 player uses for volume. To scale the knob volume to a usable MP3 player setting, divide the ADC result by 1023 and multiply by 99. (Or multiply by 99 and then divide by 1023, to avoid unnecessary loss of precision. Mathematically, it's the same.)

There is a map() function that can do the scaling for you. But if you understand basic algebra, you can probably do it faster yourself. Use a floating-point number to store the calculation results, and type cast back to a byte when you're done.

For our MP3 player, the current volume level will read back as a number from 0 to 99. But you can't set the level directly. The only controls are to increase volume by one or decrease volume by one.

To adjust the volume set on the MP3 player, you must read and scale the knob voltage level. You also need to read the volume on the MP3 player. Then you need to adjust the MP3 player volume one level at a time until it matches the level set by the knob.

You need to periodically read the volume knob and readjust the MP3 volume. You need to strike a balance between fooling around with the volume too much and being responsive enough to satisfy the person adjusting the volume knob.

The following is example code for setting the MP3 volume. Consider this a code fragment and not a complete example. Code to flush the serial interface, control song choice, and start/stop the player is required but not shown in the example.

```
// MP3 analog volume example code
// Read an analog knob and use level to adjust MP3 volume with serial messages

#include <SoftwareSerial.h> // Include library with serial emulation function

// Presetup. Assign names to pins.
byte mp3_RX = A2;
byte mp3_TX = 9;
byte volume_knob = A3;

// Declare variables (and initialize)
byte current_volume = 0;
byte scaled_volume = 0;
int knob_volume = 0;

//Set up variables to hold MP3 commands
byte volume_up = 0xE9;
byte volume_down = 0xE8;
byte volume_query = 0xA4;

// Declare variables for mathematic calculations
float x = 0; //scratch variables
float y = 0;

// Function prototype of volume adjustment function
void adjust_volume( byte target, byte start);

// Call library function to emulate serial interface in software
SoftwareSerial mySerial(mp3_RX, mp3_TX); // RX, TX

// Set up code; runs once
void setup(){
  pinMode (volume_knob, INPUT);
  mySerial.begin(9600); // Set up serial port for MP3 player
  Serial.begin(9600); // Set up serial debug port
} // End setup
```

```
// Loop code; runs over and over
void loop(){
  // Need to repeat this section periodically in case volume is adjusted.
  // but not too often

  // Read current volume knob setting
  knob_volume = analogRead(volume_knob);
  x = (knob_volume*99)/1023; // Scale to be between 0 and 99
  scaled_volume = byte (x); // Type cast to byte

  // Read current volume level at MP3 player.
  mySerial.write (volume_query);
  // wait for data to come back
  while (mySerial.available() < 1){
  }
  current_volume = mySerial.read();

  // Call function to adjust volume
  adjust_volume (scaled_volume, current_volume);

  delay(1000); // This is a placeholder; don't use in real life

  // Debug printing

  Serial.print("scaled_volume ");
  Serial.println(scaled_volume);
  Serial.print("current_volume ");
  Serial.println(current_volume);
} // End loop

void adjust_volume( byte target, byte start){
  if (target){ // Reads zero when not playing; don't adjust
    // Repeat to adjust difference
    for ( y=abs(target-start); (y == 0) ; y--) { // Adjust volume
      // Adjust MP3 level, one level at a time
      if (target < start){
        mySerial.write(volume_down);
      }
      if (target > start) {
        mySerial.write(volume_up);
      }
    } // End for
  } // End if
} // End function
```

This example shows how you can use the serial port to make debugging easier. Using a software-emulated serial port provides a second serial port for MP3 player control. The slower emulated speed is not an issue here.

PINBALL MACHINE EXAMPLE (PART III)

The nature of the pinball machine lends itself to the monitoring programming approach. Like the traffic light monitoring example, the pinball sketch is a big monitoring loop. Instead of monitoring time, the pinball machine will continually monitor the input pins.

The amount of time to complete the monitor loop will depend on what the microcontroller is doing. It will vary from one pass to next because the inputs will vary.

Because you can't rely on the monitoring loop's time to complete, you need to add time elements another way. Periodic timer interrupts, like those used in the traffic light interrupt-driven example, provide the time base for any time-related elements.

Pin change or external interrupts provide for critical time-sensitive control. Just as interrupts from the timer trigger execution of an ISR, other interrupt sources trigger their own ISRs. As always, keep your ISRs short.

TIME

Your Arduino's sense of time is based entirely on the system clock. Most system clocks are 16 MHz, but some are 8 MHz. The traffic light example used previously is based on the Uno with its 16 MHz clock. (If your system uses 8 MHz, just multiply the time scale by two. Everything happens half as fast or takes twice as long, depending on how you look at it.)

The smallest time unit available with a 16 MHz clock is 1/16 MHz, or 62.5 nanoseconds. That's way too fast to be used for most things. The system clock has a prescaler that slows the clock systemwide. This prescaler is typically used to save power. If you are using the systemwide prescaler, set that up first because the system clock forms the time base for everything else.

Your Arduino is equipped with three (or more) timers, each with its own independent prescaler. In addition to timing and counting, each timer generates the time base for two PWM signals. You can also use each timer to generate periodic interrupts or measure the duration or frequency of a signal.

PWM and timer-based interrupts are not independent. Although it's not impossible to use one timer for both purposes, it would be difficult. You can't tinker with the timer without changing the PWM time base and vice versa.

When Counters Roll Over

Two functions, `millis()` and `micros()`, provide a convenient way to keep track of time. Both of these functions use timer/counter 0. This 8-bit timer regularly rolls over and updates a 32-bit counter containing elapsed time in milliseconds.

Thirty-two bits are a lot of bits, but these counts eventually roll over, too. `millis()` takes 49+ days to roll over. `micros()` takes only 71 minutes.

Does the math still provide the correct value when the counter rolls over? Happily, time calculations using proper techniques are correct even if the counter rolls over.

Time testing is best done with subtraction. Save the starting value with a descriptively named variable like `start_time`. Subtract the `start_time` from the `current_time` to get the `elapsed_time`.

For those who want to see the bits, consider this example where the start time is before the rollover and the current time is just after it. When `millis()` rolls over to 0, 0xFFFF FFFF becomes 0x0000 0000.

`start_time` = 0xFFFF FFF0

`current_time` = 0x0000 0010

`current_time` − `start_time` = 0x0000 0010 − 0xFFFF FFF0 = 0x0000 0020

This result makes sense because 0xFFFF FFF0 is 0x10 counts before the rollover, whereas 0x10 is 0x10 counts after the rollover. Thus, 0x20 is the expected difference.

If you find this a little odd, you're right. But it's just part of doing math with a limited number of bits. Look up binary subtraction if you need additional explanation.

INTERRUPTS

An interrupt is an on-demand transfer of program control to a special piece of software called an ISR. An ISR is similar to a function except that it has no type and returns no value. Global and individual interrupt control registers determine whether the interrupt has an effect or not. The Arduino provides an overabundance of interrupt sources, each with its own ISR. This can be confusing if you try to consider them all at once. Let's break down the problem by considering each type of interrupt separately. But first let's consider the things they have in common.

Registers provide global control of interrupts. Before changing individual interrupt control, you should globally disable interrupts. After everything is set up and individual interrupts are enabled, re-enable interrupts globally.

An interrupt can occur while another interrupt is being serviced. This is referred to as *nested interrupts*. Nested interrupts are disabled by default. When nested interrupts are enabled but not wanted during a particular ISR, disable interrupts globally as the first line of your ISR. Re-enable them as the last line.

The traffic light example does not disable interrupts because only the timer interrupt is enabled. There will be lots of time (one whole second) to process the interrupt before the next one arrives. Each interrupt source has its own control registers and ISR. Details of how to set the control registers for a particular interrupt are included in the data sheet.

Tutorials for interrupts appear on the playground. If you choose to copy a playground example, copy it exactly first. After you have it working, save a copy and then modify it for your own needs. Some playground examples work, and some don't.

Here are some important concepts when using interrupts:

- You must use "volatile" variables, stored in RAM, inside an ISR.

- Use macros (#define) rather than variables for pin numbers, names, and anything that doesn't change.

- Keep the ISR short.

- Don't interrupt more often than you need to or faster than can be serviced.

- Disable interrupts globally. Set up a specific interrupt and enable it. Enable global interrupts.

- More than one way to set up registers exists. Use the way you understand.

- For time-based interrupts, use the timer's prescaler and count to establish the time base.

- Send debug messages to the console port so that you know it's working.

- Get the handler name right. It's the only way to associate an ISR with its trigger. You will only be warned by the compiler once, not once each time the code is compiled.

- For sections of code where interrupts must not occur, disable them globally. Don't forget to re-enable them when you're done.

Time-Based Interrupts

Let's look at timer-based interrupts first. These interrupts are useful for making periodic events happen without tying up the microcontroller's processing time with wait loops and stall tactics. The interrupt-driven traffic light example illustrates the use of timer-based interrupts.

No function calls currently exist to help you set them up and use them. Don't panic. Start with the traffic light example or a tutorial example and expand from there. (Keep in mind that the traffic light example was written for the Uno. If you use another Arduino model, you need to modify it slightly.)

The cryptic register and bit names come straight from the Atmel datasheet. You can look them up there because no other list exists. (At least we couldn't find one.)

You can use any of the Arduino's timers to generate time-based interrupts. Each of them is a little different, so read up on the one you're using. As mentioned in an earlier chapter, some functions like delay() use a timer and will interfere with other uses.

Pin Change Interrupts

You can use nearly every pin as a pin change interrupt, unless it is used for something else. Pin change interrupts are bundled together as shown in Table 9.2, with only one ISR for each group. If more than one pin per group is used for an interrupt, the ISR is slightly more complicated. The ISR must determine which of the bundled pins caused the interrupt before it can get on with the business of servicing the interrupt.

Table 9.2 Pin Change Interrupt Mapping

Interrupt	Group	Control Register
PCI2	PCINT23 to PCINT16	PCMSK2
PCI1	PCINT15 to PCINT8	PCMSK1
PCI0	PCINT7 to PCINT0	PCMSK0

© 2014 Cengage Learning®

Pin change interrupts are triggered by one (or more) of the associated signals changing. Although only one interrupt is provided for the entire bundle, the port can be read to determine the exact pin and whether the signal changed from high to low or from low to high. The interrupt sets flags in a register, but the exact source is not stored.

Signals are synchronized with the clock internally, so edges are lost. Both positive and negative transitions are detected with no differentiation between them. Short transitions, less than one clock cycle long, may be missed entirely.

When interrupts are enabled for more than one pin, the order of interrupts may be ambiguous. If a second signal arrives after the first one but before the interrupt is serviced, there's no way to tell which one arrived first. Write your ISR so that multiple simultaneous sources can be accommodated.

Pin change interrupts are enabled by setting the appropriate bit in the Pin Change Interrupt Control Register (PCICR). The pin or pins you want to trigger the pin change interrupt are controlled by the PCMSKx (Pin Change MaSK 0, 1, or 2) register. The following code illustrates how to use a pin change interrupt.

```
// Program that takes a pushbutton input on pin 8 and uses a PCINT0
// pin change interrupt to toggle the built-in LED on and off
```

```
// Serial monitor port used for debug messages
#include <avr/interrupt.h>

volatile boolean change = false; // Flag to indicate LED change
boolean litup = false; // Flag to indicate LED on when 1

void setup(void)
{
  pinMode(13, OUTPUT);
  pinMode(8, INPUT);
  digitalWrite(8, HIGH); // Enable pullup resistor
  Serial.begin(9600); // Enable console port for messages
  cli(); // Globally disable interrupts while configuring them
  PCICR = (0x01); // Enable PCIE0 group
  PCMSK0 = (0x01); // Enable PCINT0
  sei(); // Enable global interrupts
  digitalWrite(13, LOW); // Start off
}

void loop(void)
{
  // Serial.println("It's alive.");
  if (change) { // If there's a change, toggle light and print it
    Serial.println("We have a change.");
    if (litup) { // If it's on,
      digitalWrite(13, LOW); // turn it off
      litup = false; // Remember it's off
      Serial.println("It's off.");
    }
    else { // It's off, so
      digitalWrite(13, HIGH); // turn it on
     litup = true; // Remember it's on
     Serial.println("It's on.");
    } // end else
    change = false; // Wait for another change
  } // End if
} // End loop()

// Interrupt Service Routine attached to INT1 vector
ISR(PCINT0_vect)
{
  change = true; // New change.
}
```

In addition to setting up the interrupt control registers and enabling interrupts globally, you must configure the pin itself as an input. The built-in pullup resistor is convenient for active low interrupts generated by buttons or switches.

Unlike timer-based interrupts, there are functions to help you with the configuration of pin change interrupts. Two libraries of functions (`PinChangeInt.h` and `PinChangeIntConfig.h`), used together, provide the necessary control. An example on the playground illustrates their use. Search for `PinChangeInt` and not the older `PCInt`.

External Interrupts

Two external interrupts pins are provided. Signals connected to these pins can cause an interrupt on rising edge, falling edge, low level, or toggle. The EICRA register controls which of these conditions generates an interrupt. EICRA stands for External Interrupt Control Register A. I'm not making it up; it's in the data sheet.

The EIMSK (External Interrupt MaSK) register enables and disables the external interrupts individually. Interrupts must be globally enabled for this register to matter.

The EIFR (External Interrupt Flag Register) contains two flags for each interrupt, which are automatically cleared when the ISR is executed. Read the data sheet for detailed information on the interrupt flags. Because each interrupt has its own ISR, you are unlikely to need to examine these flags.

Each of the external interrupts has a dedicated ISR. The IDE identifies the ISR by name, so you must use the exact names.

```
ISR (INT0_vect) {
// Place your code here
;}
ISR (INT1_vect) {
// Place your code here
;}
```

The following code shows how you can use a pushbutton to turn on and off the built-in LED using an external interrupt. Although the example is somewhat trivial, it's a good starting point.

```
// Program that takes a pushbutton input on pin 3 and uses an external
// interrupt to toggle the built-in LED on and off
// Serial monitor port used for debug messages
#include <avr/interrupt.h>

volatile boolean change = false; // Flag to indicate LED change
boolean litup = false; // Flag to indicate LED on when 1

void setup(void)
{
  pinMode(13, OUTPUT); // Built-in LED pin
  pinMode(3, INPUT); // INT1 pin
```

```
    digitalWrite(3, HIGH); // Enable pullup resistor
    Serial.begin(9600); // Enable console port for messages
    cli(); // Globally disable interrupts while configuring them
    EICRA = (0x08); // Trigger INT1 on falling edge
    EIMSK = (0x02); // Enable external interrupt INT1
    sei(); // Enable global interrupts
    digitalWrite(13, LOW); // Start off
}
void loop(void)
{
  // Serial.println("It's alive.");
  if (change) { // If there's a change, toggle light and print it
    Serial.println("We have a change.");
    if (litup) { // If it's on,
      digitalWrite(13, LOW); // turn it off
      litup = false; // Remember it's off
      Serial.println("It's off.");
    }
    else { // It's off, so
      digitalWrite(13, HIGH); // Turn it on
      litup = true; // Remember it's on
      Serial.println("It's on.");
    } // end else
    change = false; // Wait for another change
  } // end if
} // end loop()
// Interrupt Service Routine attached to INT1 vector
ISR(INT1_vect)
{
  change = true; // New change.
}
```

Because switches bounce, a delay might be needed in the ISR to let the signal settle down and not generate too many interrupts. Some delay is cause by the serial.println() calls, so this example works without additional delays. Clean signals, like those from logic gates, should not need delays.

You may have noticed that the pin change and external interrupt examples are remarkably similar. The techniques are the same and not difficult.

As with pin change interrupts, there are functions that may help with external interrupts. Be aware that these functions redirect the ISR from the default handler to another named routine.

Debouncing Switches

Switches have contacts inside that are bent pieces of metal. You may know bent pieces of metal by another name: springs. It's no surprise then that switch contacts bounce.

Each switch closure results in a series of switch closures that settle down as the springs lose energy. The easiest way to compensate for this behavior is to wait 50 msec or so. Programs with built-in delay, like the examples, don't need more.

PROPER NAMES

Signal and variable names should be meaningful to you. One common approach is to string a description together, capitalizing every word except the initial one. (The initial letter is not capitalized because some compilers don't like that.)

An example of a descriptive signal name is `curtainMotorSpeed`. From the previous examples and the words in the name, you can guess the meaning of this variable. The downside to this approach is that the names can become long and cumbersome. Similar names can be hard to distinguish, like `bear2MotorSpeed` and `bear3MotorSpeed`.

A related approach is to use the underscore character as a word separator, like `curtain_motor_speed`. Some prefer this approach as being easier for a human to read. Although it's easier to read, it's harder to type unless you can find the underscore character without having to hunt for it.

An alternate approach is to give the signals a more compact but less descriptive name. When you use terse signal names, place a table in comments just before the variable declaration section to explain them.

STARTING POINT

Start with the Blink example built in to the IDE. This verifies that everything between your computer and your Arduino is working correctly. After you are sure your Arduino and computer are behaving properly, select an example that most closely resembles the approach you have selected.

You can use one of the IDE's built-in examples, an example you found on the web, or an example from a book. If you are typing in an example, copy it exactly first. Makes sure it compiles and runs, if possible. Adapting a working example is much easier than starting with an empty window and writing a sketch from scratch.

Now that you have a starting point, modify it to meet your needs. You can cut and paste between IDE windows. You can combine sections of working programs, but be careful of duplicate variable and function names.

Don't forget to save early and often. Save a named backup before any major change. Save another named backup when the change is working.

Is It Working?

There are two aspects to a properly working program. First, consider an effective strategy or logical method that gets the job done. Algorithm is the hard way to spell "effective logical method." Remember the puzzle with the rowboat, chicken, dog, and bag of seeds? (No? Use your search engine to find "chicken crossing puzzle.") The solution to the puzzle is an algorithm.

The engineering tool for a software algorithm is a flow chart. (We talked about flow charts in Chapter 2, "Tools of the Trade.") Flow charts present in diagram format what your code will do and the branches it will make at decision points. You don't need a formal flow chart, but you do need a written account of what you expect your Arduino to do.

Flow charts help to get the logical method right. Pretend to be your Arduino and follow the flow through every path. (Remember, this is a tool for your own use; there is no right or wrong way to draw one.) If you have to assume something, can't reach a path, or have steps out of order, you have a logic problem.

Interrupt Service Routines

ISRs are usually shown as a separate path to the side in a flow chart. They can occur at any point in your program and require special consideration.

Play the "what if" game with your sketch code. What if the interrupt happened here? Or here? Or in the middle of this?

If there is any point during your program where an interrupt must not occur, add a step to disable it just before that point. Don't forget to re-enable the interrupt when it's okay again.

Once the logic behind the program is mapped out, the second aspect comes into play. For a program to work, the written code must match your algorithm.

Most of the flow chart maps directly to code. A decision point requires a conditional statement. Variables remember numbers and conditions or serve as loop counters. Reading or writing pins also map directly.

While you are writing the code, add statements that can help you debug it later. Have the Arduino tell you what it's doing. For step-by-step programs, have the Arduino tell you which step it's on. For monitoring programs, have it tell you when something happens. For interrupt-driven programs, have Arduino tell you when critical moments occur.

Use the serial monitor port (if you haven't used it for something else) to send out print statements. Print out sensor reading, variables, loop counters, or anything else you want to know. (Print statements may not work as part of an ISR.)

COMPILER ERRORS

Sometimes your code doesn't compile. That's natural. So, what do you do when you get a cryptic error message?

Turn on verbose error message in the Preferences dialog box before you compile. The messages will still be cryptic, but at least you'll have more to work with.

When you compile (verify) your code, pay attention to those orange warning messages. Some of these messages only appear once because the compiler doesn't recompile unless it has to. The first time you verify, make the message window large enough to read, and check anything printed in orange. If the trouble seems to come from a library, it probably won't be a problem. It deserves more thought if it's something you wrote.

Just because it's a warning and not an error doesn't mean it's not a problem. If your ISR handler name is wrong, it only generates a warning (about spelling!) and not an error. Your compiled sketch won't have the ISR associated with your interrupt, and it won't work.

Chapter 11, "Debugging," contains more help on finding errors.

TWO ARDUINO BOARDS CHATTING

The final example in this chapter considers two Arduino boards chatting with each other using the serial port Universal Synchronous/Asynchronous Receiver/Transmitters (USARTs). Because you are using the USARTs, the serial monitor port isn't fully available. However, you can use it to eavesdrop on what a board is sending out. Don't enter anything from the keyboard; that would either have no effect or interfere with the communication signals.

Two instances of the IDE are needed, one for each board. You may need two computers, one for each IDE session. Some computers/operating systems support multiple sessions better than others.

The same sketch is loaded into two Arduino boards. Tx from each board is connected to Rx on the other board. Also connect a ground wire between them. (Connect the signals after downloading the code.)

Open the serial monitor for each board, which resets the boards. You can also manually reset one (or both) of the Arduinos if the conversation doesn't start on its own.

When finished resetting, each board sends out a byte, but only the last board to finish resetting and send out a byte counts. (When the first one finished, the other was still resetting and didn't listen.)

When the sketch receives a byte, it adds 1 to it and sends it out. The range was limited to 48–127 because these are ASCII values for normal printable (viewable onscreen) characters. See www.asciitable.com for ASCII codes.

Note that the `Serial.print()` and `Serial.write()` functions send information through the serial port (TX pin) to the other Arduino.

Use the serial monitor tool of the IDE to snoop on what's being sent. One serial monitor for each board lets you see the entire conversation. Because the sketch sends out the next character, every other number or letter shows on the serial monitor. If you only have one serial monitor, you see only half of the conversation.

This method can be expanded. For example, your Arduino can watch for an incoming message, perform some action based on the message combined with local conditions, and return a results message.

```
/* simple test to receive a message and
    send it back out using hardware UART
    Connect Rx on one to Tx on the other and vice versa */
byte outputLed = 13;
byte incomingByte;
byte numberToSend = 48; // 48 is ASCII 0

void setup(){
  pinMode (outputLed, OUTPUT);
  Serial.begin(9600);
  Serial.write(numberToSend); // Send something out
}
void loop(){
  if (Serial.available()>0){ // Was anything received?
    incomingByte = Serial.read(); // Yes, read the first byte
    delay (1000);
    if (incomingByte == 127 | incomingByte == 128){
      incomingByte = 47;
    }
    Serial.write(incomingByte+1); // Send out the byte that came in, +1
  }
}
```

This same method can be expanded. For example, your Arduino could watch for an incoming message, perform some action based on the message combined with local conditions, and return a results message.

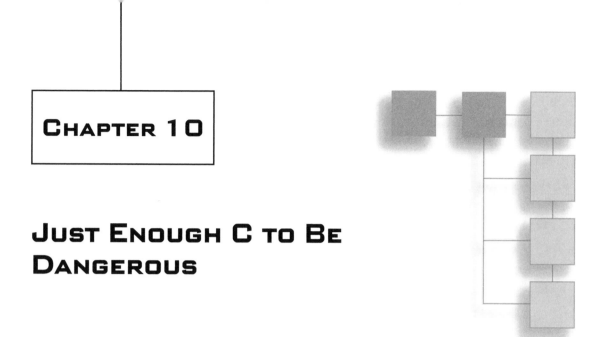

CHAPTER 10

JUST ENOUGH C TO BE DANGEROUS

This chapter answers the following questions:

- Is there an easier way to learn programming?
- Do I have to learn C?
- Just how much C do I need to know?

This chapter provides, as the title suggests, just enough C to get started programming your Arduino in C. Perhaps you don't own or want to own a C programming book. That's okay. This chapter gives you just enough C to write reasonable programs.

This chapter doesn't cover every detail of C and only brushes up against C++. When you're ready, look for a basic C book or a C++ book that follows the language-first approach.

REMEMBERING THINGS

You know your Arduino has memory, and you would like to save something into it. But how do you get your data into the Arduino's memory? That's what variables do.

Variables give a little piece of memory a name so you can use it without having to use awkward address numbers. Later, the compiler converts these names to address numbers. The addresses don't matter to you; you just use the names.

Using Variables

Variables have a type that tells the compiler just how much memory you need and how you want to store your information. You only need four types: byte, int, float, and char. There are other types, but remember that this chapter only has the minimum.

Byte tells the compiler that you only need a little memory: 8 bits to be exact. An int, short for integer, has twice that at 16 bits. Both byte and int variables contain whole numbers; they don't have fractions or decimal points. One bit of int is used as a sign bit, allowing both positive and negative numbers.

Float, short for floating point, is the variable type for fractional numbers and accurate mathematical calculations. Just in case you're wondering, float has 32 bits. But the bits aren't used in the same way. Numbers are stored in floating-point format with a number and an exponent.

You can look up floating-point numbers if you're interested. The compiler handles the details for you, so you don't need to worry about the format.

The last type is char, short for character, which stores an ASCII-encoded character. It also has 8 bits.

Table 10.1 summarizes byte, int, float, and char and a few others. You can use the other types, except for double and string, which aren't recommended. Or you can stick to the four types mentioned, since these are enough for nearly all uses.

Table 10.1 Data Types

Type	Size	Range/Uses
Boolean	1	`true` or `false` only; usually used as flags
Byte	1	Positive integer up to 255
Int	2	Positive or negative integers up to 32,767
Unsigned int	2	Positive integer up to 65,535
Float	4	Decimal number stored as a number and an exponent
Double	4	Same as float in the Arduino; use float instead
Long	4	Positive or negative integer up to 2,147,483,647
Unsigned long	4	Positive integer up to 4,294,967,295
Char	1	ASCII-formatted character
String	variable	An array of char, terminated by a null character
Char [n]	n + 1	An array of char, preferred to string by forum users

Size listed is in bytes; multiply by eight for a bit count.

Picking a Type

How do you pick a type? If you are handling ASCII characters, char is the type for you. Use an array[] of char for words and phrases. Note the square brackets, which we will discuss more in a bit.

If you are counting loops less than 255, byte will do. Byte is the smallest amount of memory allocated to a variable. Byte's size exactly matches the width of registers inside the Atmel chip. The size match allows convenient register reads and tests.

Larger numbers or negative numbers need int. Bigger positive numbers can be stored as unsigned int. "Unsigned" tells the compiler to use the sign bit as another binary digit. Very large positive numbers can be stored as unsigned long.

You are probably thinking that you'll never need 32 bits. But you will. The time functions millis() and micros() need unsigned long variables to store their values. Unsigned long allows for long time measurements: 49+ days for millis(), and 71+ hours for micros().

Type Matching and Casting

For an assignment or calculations, variable types must match. Ordinarily, it doesn't make sense to mix variable types in one C command. Trying to assign a byte variable with a number contained in an int variable will make the compiler complain about type mismatch. In this case, you don't have enough bits.

For the exceptional cases, there are type casting functions that convert between the data types. You may need to type cast an int to a float, using float(), for calculations. See the later discussion on functions.

Making Variables and Assigning Values

Declaration statements at the start of your program create variables and set aside little pieces of memory for you. These pieces of memory contain random nonsense. They can be—rather, *must be*—assigned a value at the same time. (You wanted it simple, so don't argue.)

Caution

One equal sign (=) is always an assignment. Two equal signs (==) are always a test condition. Don't mix them up.

Inside of setup() and loop(), the value of a variable can be assigned (given a value) or tested. setup() and loop() are functions discussed later. Assigning a value uses one equal sign. Testing uses two equal signs. Mixing them up causes hard-to-find logic errors. Following are declaration statements that initialize variables.

```
byte x = 100;
float y = 2.5;
unsigned long max_count = 17597UL;
array int readings[10] = {0, 1, 2, 3, 4, 5, 6, 7, 8, 9}; // supply one value for each
element
array char pet[] = "dog";
```

UL in the code guarantees that you get an unsigned long. It's an Arduino quirk.

The last two entries are arrays. An array is just a group of variables, stored in memory together. When you *declare* an array, you use the number of elements you want inside the square brackets. That's the array's size.

Later, when you *use* array elements, the index numbers inside the square brackets start at zero. The last element's number is one less than the size you declared.

Caution

> Start counting array elements with zero, not one. The last element's index number is one less than the declared size.

The last entry in the table is an array of char named pet. The compiler fills in the size for you, but don't let it! If you want to store something bigger later, you can't. Pick a size large enough to accommodate the longest contents you can imagine and then add one.

An array of char is special; it's one element larger than other array types. The size is the number of letters, plus one for a null character. A null character is '' (single quotes without a space character between them). Null is not 0. Use single quotes for a single character, including the null character.

Use double quotes to assign a value to an array of char. All the array's elements are assigned at once, using the supplied characters and automatically adding a null character. Leftover elements don't contain valid data.

To summarize, use single quotes for single characters. Use double quotes to assign a value to an array of char. (It's complicated; just do it.)

The variable pet in the code sample is four elements long because a null character is added to the end. 'd' is stored in pet[0]. An ASCII null character is added in pet[3].

Ordinary arrays, like readings[], are *not* one element larger. In the code sample, readings[9] contains the integer value 9.

readings[10] is a piece of memory beyond that set aside for readings[]. It can contain some other variable or whatever random garbage is left over in memory. Assigning a value to `readings[10]` could be a disaster if that piece of memory contains something important.

Don't count on the compiler to find array indexes that are out of bounds. Array names are pointers that can contain any valid address, even if it's not the one you meant. To the compiler, it's not an error. Don't worry about pointers; just be careful with your array indexes.

Reading and Writing Registers

A register is a byte-wide piece of memory with a dedicated purpose. Your Arduino has registers that control the use of the I/O pins and their values. You can use their names, just like variable names, to read and write them.

To read and write registers by name, you need to know their names. We're sorry to say, you have to look for the register names in the Atmel data sheet. The IDE provides the translation of the name to an address.

These register names look like random letters, but they are really acronyms. They're not the fun kind that actually spells something, but just the first letters of the register's long name. C is case sensitive; use all capital letters for the register's name.

If you don't want to read and write registers, that's okay. You can set up most of the microcontroller's registers using function calls. We'll talk about functions a little later.

TESTING 1, 2, 3

Much of what your sketch does will be testing values using a condition. Table 10.2 lists the available conditions. The values tested can be contained in a variable or the result of a function call or calculation.

Table 10.2   Test Conditions

Meaning	Symbol	Meaning	Symbol
Equal	==	Not equal	!=
Greater than	>	Less than	<
Greater than or equal	>=	Less than or equal	<=

© 2014 Cengage Learning®

The result of the test will be true or false. Philosophical discussions aside, false is 0. true is *any* non-zero value. Negative or positive doesn't matter. –521 is just as true as 1.

Caution

Don't use a single equal sign as a test condition because it does an assignment instead. Assignment (single equal sign) is always true.

The true/false result of a test condition provides a way for your Arduino to make choices. if statements and loops (for loops and while loops) are the only two you need to know about. (When you're ready, your C book has more.)

MAKING CHOICES

The power of a microcontroller comes from its ability to make choices. Your Arduino can use information from input pins and variables to choose one set of instructions or another.

The test conditions discussed earlier form the basis for making choices. You must frame your options around conditions your Arduino can test for. if and loop statements use these conditions to make decisions.

If I Say So

The first choice-making statement is the if statement. The code lines that follow show the general form. You can use this general form for all your if statements.

```
if (x == y) { // do this if true
}
else { // otherwise do this
}
```

The space between the curly braces { } can contain as many lines of code as you need or none at all. The curly braces are required, even if they are empty. Note the absence of semicolons. Adding a semicolon to an if statement tells your Arduino to test a condition and then *do nothing*.

Caution

Don't add a semicolon to an if statement with curly braces.

The words after the double backslash form a comment. Comments are ignored by the compiler and don't use Arduino memory. Use them to say in English what your code is meant to do.

For the test condition, this example uses (x == y). We could have used anything with a value including a variable (x), a numerical calculation (x + y), or a function call (Serial.available()).

When the test condition is true (nonzero), the code inside the top set of curly braces executes, and the bottom set is skipped. When the test condition is zero (false), the code inside the lower set of curly braces is executed, and the top set is skipped.

Going in Circles

Sometimes we need to wait for data to arrive or time to pass. Often we need to repeat instructions more than once. Loops are what we need. You could get by with one loop command, but two are easier because they don't require you to rearrange your human brain logic.

The two loops you need to know are for and while. You can do just about anything with just these two choice makers.

while

while statements repeat until the test condition is false. Let's look at this in more detail. First, the condition is tested. If it's true, the statements inside the curly braces run once, and then the condition is tested again. This repeats until the test condition is false *when tested*. while loops don't jump out or end in the middle.

If the test condition is false the first time, the statements inside the curly braces never run. Empty curly braces are fine, too.

Caution

while loops execute forever if the test condition is never false.

Beware! If the condition is never false, your Arduino will be stuck in the while loop forever. An example of the while statement is shown here.

```
while (condition){ // Statements here execute until the condition is false.
}
```

If you want to reverse the situation and execute your code until the test condition is true, you can use the not (!) operator. For example, a while loop with a ! (condition) repeats until the test condition is true. Use parentheses around your condition to avoid precedence problems. Not is a (Boolean) operator that changes true to false and false to true.

for

`for` statements have more built-in features. Take a look at the `for` statement. (We'll wait.) You will notice there are three fields inside the parentheses after the keyword `for` and separated by semicolons.

```
for (j = 1; j > 10 ; j++){ // j is a counter (aka index) and can be used inside the for
loop.
}
```

This loop runs 10 times. `j` takes on the values 1 to 11, but the loop exits without running the eleventh time. `j` retains the value of 11 until it's reassigned a different value.

The first field is an initial condition. Each time the `for` loop is encountered, the variable `j` is set to 1. Then `j` is tested to see if it's greater than 10. If it is, execution continues after the closing curly brace. If it's not, the code inside the `for`'s curly braces executes once.

`j` is then incremented. The plus plus sign (++) after the variable is the same as j = j + 1. They mean the same thing, so don't let anyone pick on you for using the one you like. (The compiler mashes them down to the same thing anyway.)

After `j` is incremented, the condition is tested again, and the process repeats until the test condition is `true`.

These three fields form a set with the initialization, test condition, and increment. Be sure to use semicolons to separate them, not commas. (C isn't English.)

Use a test condition that is a range rather than an exact value. Use greater than or equal to (>=) instead of equal (==). That way, a small logic error is less likely to create a loop that never exits (an infinite loop).

The loop counter is an ordinary variable. There isn't anything special about it. You can use it inside the `for` loop for array indexes or calculations. You can also assign it a value inside the loop, but I don't recommend doing so. It's too easy to make logic errors that way.

If you absolutely must end the `for` loop early, assigning an out-of-range value to the `loop` counter will do so at the next test. Be sure you used a range for your test condition.

You could use other things as the initialization, test condition, and increment; C won't stop you. To make life simpler, stick with the simple variable counter. Use separate statements for other things.

THE NATURE OF C

The C programming language is based on the model of functions. Everything written in C is part of a function. (Main() is also a function that has been taken care of for you.)

Well-written functions are standalone sections of code that need only the parameters (numbers or variables) passed to them to do their work. Functions are not required to use parameters, and some don't like setup() and loop() (and main()).

Most functions return a value, but they are not required to do so. Because functions are expected to return a value, they have a data type just like a variable. If the function does not return a value, it has data type void. Both setup() and loop() have data type void.

Returned values and parameters are unrelated. void functions can use parameters. Functions without parameters can return values.

Assign the returned value of a function to a variable. A call of the function without the assignment executes the function without saving the result. void functions do not return a value, so they do not need their returned value stored. To use a void function, simply use its name and supply any required parameters.

Help for the Tyro

Tyro, newbie, rookie—whatever you call yourself, functions are here to help. Functions are sections of code written by someone who (usually) knows what they are doing. The hard work has already been done for you.

You can do nearly everything from setting up I/O pins to reading registers with a simple function call. You supply details, like which pin you want to read from, as parameters. A parameter is a fancy name for a number or a variable.

Supply parameters in parentheses after the function's name when you call it. Some functions are actually macros. They look and work the same way, so you don't care.

Function calls make up the last must-know C. Here is where we use a little tiny bit of C++. Don't worry; it won't hurt.

The C++ wrinkle is in the name. We won't bore or perplex you with the technical details. Just type the names as you see them. C++ functions have a dot (period) in the middle of the name, whereas C functions don't. Here are some examples of functions.

C

```
pinMode (13, OUTPUT);
digitalWrite (3, HIGH);
attachInterrupt (0, blink, CHANGE);
```

C++

```
serial.begin (9600);
wire.endTransmission();
EEPROM.read(0x10);
```

Because someone else wrote these functions, you need directions and an example to use them. Look on the www.arduino.cc Reference tab for function descriptions and usage. The same information is available using the Help>Reference drop-down menu in the IDE.

Don't guess at what functions do or how to use them. Get in the habit of looking at the reference page and examples to learn about them. Look up what you need to know.

Search the forum for any questions you might have. If you are having trouble, someone else has probably had the same problem, too. Try to find the answer on your own before you ask. Just because you're a rookie doesn't mean you have to look like one.

More functions are added with each release, and sometimes the existing ones change. Read the release notes to keep up with changes and additions.

setup() and loop()

You (yes, you there staring at this book) need to write two functions: setup() and loop(). The parentheses remind you that they are functions. They are void functions; they don't return values. They look like this.

```
setup(){ // Your setup code goes here.
}
loop() { // The code you want to repeat goes here.
}
```

Don't worry that these are functions. Think of them as snug, warm places to nestle your code. As the name suggests, setup() is where you place the code you want to do once and only once. Use it to set up your I/O, serial ports, output signal level, timers, shields, and so on.

loop() runs repeatedly, so the things you put into loop() execute over and over. Don't worry that your sketch never ends. It's okay. Your Arduino *loves* to run.

The meaty part of your sketch goes into loop(). This is where the work gets done. Anything that isn't set up belongs in loop(). And anything that is set up belongs in setup().

There are pieces, like variable declarations, that you need to place outside of setup() and loop(). Where you place your code does matter. See the description in the "Order Matters" section that follows.

PREPROCESSOR COMMANDS

Sadly, the first piece of a sketch you come to is the odd one. These are preprocessor commands with their own language and syntax. They aren't written in C.

You can easily identify preprocessor commands by the starting pound sign (#). Fortunately, you only need #define and #include.

#define

The #define statement lets you use a name instead of a number for limits and pin numbers. Names are easier to remember. (This statement has other uses. You don't need them yet.)

```
#define LED_pin 13
```

#include <library name>

The #include statement tells the compiler where to find libraries of functions you used in your code. The IDE includes some standard C libraries automatically.

You need to include special-purpose or shield-specific functions located in other libraries before you can use them. Usually, you only need one or two #include statements to add a special library. You can use the IDE's Sketch>Import drop-down menu to include some common libraries.

In addition to being included in your sketch, shield-specific libraries need to be copied to the correct directory for use. Refer to the directions on www.arduino.cc or the manufacturer's or distributor's web page.

This example allows you to use the EEPROM-specific read and write functions.

```
#include <EEPROM.h>
```

ORDER MATTERS

You need to place elements of your sketch in the correct area and in the proper order. It would be easier to point, but we'll make do with an example. The following code shows a sketch labeled with the recommended locations.

```
// Simple program to show for and while loops

byte x = 0;  // variable for loop count and delay time
byte incomingByte = 0;  // variable to hold input number
byte ledPin = 13;  // use pin connected to L LED on Uno
char outputChar = '0'; // char to print instead of ASCII code

void setup(){
  pinMode(ledPin, OUTPUT); // set up LED pin for output
  digitalWrite (ledPin, LOW); // start with LED off
  Serial.begin(9600); // set up serial monitor port
} // end setup

void loop(){
  // while repeats for as long as serial data is available
  while (Serial.available()){ // check for serial data
    incomingByte = Serial.read(); // read the data
    outputChar = char(incomingByte); // type cast to char for printing
    Serial.println(outputChar); // echo it back out
  } // end while

  // make LED do something interesting while waiting for serial data
  // initialize x = 1; test x < 11; increment x
  // for loop repeats 10 times
  for (x=1; x<11; x++){
    digitalWrite (ledPin, HIGH); // turn on the LED
    delay(x * 50); // wait a bit
    digitalWrite (ledPin, LOW); // turn off the LED
    delay(x * 50); // wait a bit
  } // end for
} // end loop
```

In addition to demonstrating order, this example shows how to use loops for repeating sections of code. The while loop repeats as long as valid data is available in the buffer. Each entered character is echoed back to the serial monitor. When the buffer is empty, execution continues after the while statement.

The for loop follows the while loop. The for loop flashes the built-in L LED on the Uno in an interesting pattern.

The `delay()` function introduces a wait so the light is visible. Don't use the `delay()` function for long delays because the microcontroller can't do anything else while it's waiting. The examples in Chapter 9, "Writing the Code," show how to use `millis()` instead.

The `for` loop must also finish before going on. Because it's the last thing in `loop()`, execution continues back to the start of `loop()`. If the `for` loop has just started when you enter characters via the serial monitor, there will be a noticeable delay before they are echoed back.

Here's the proper order:

1. Preprocessor commands (if needed)

2. Global variable declarations and initialization

3. Function prototypes (`setup()` and `loop()` have already been prototyped for you)

4. `setup()` (required)

5. Local variable declaration and initialization

6. Your setup code

7. `loop()` (required)

8. Local variable declaration and initialization

9. Your repeating code

10. Functions you created (if any)

11. Interrupt Service Routines (ISRs) (if interrupts are used)

Take a look at the examples in Chapter 9 again and see if you can identify the elements just listed. Pay special attention to placement of code sections within the sketch.

OTHER PLACES FOR HELP

Get a C book for beginners to help you with the language syntax and usage. It doesn't need to be a new book. The parts of C you are using haven't changed since the last millennium. You don't need to learn everything; just a little C goes a long way.

Use the online Arduino-specific language reference available at www.arduino.cc under the Reference tab. And take advantage of the examples presented under the Learning tab. Each example contains a description, circuit diagram, wiring chart, and code example. The IDE provides the code for these examples under the File tab, so you don't even need to type them.

Start by modifying an example that you understand. Don't forget to save your program under a descriptive name. Save early, and save often. Keep a backup of your best program so far so that you can go back if you need to.

Search the forum for specific problems. When you are truly stuck, see Chapter 12, "Bragging Rights and Pleas for Help." Use the recommended format for submitting questions for best results.

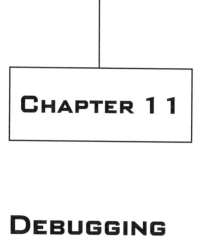

CHAPTER 11

DEBUGGING

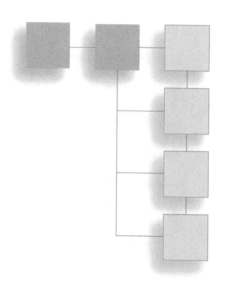

This chapter answers the following questions:

- How do I get my project working without damaging it?
- What's a smoke test?
- Is my project working?
- Why doesn't my project work?
- How do I fix my project?
- What can I do if I can't find the problem?

So far, things have been going well. Your sketch has been written, compiled, downloaded, and running since Chapter 9, "Writing the Code." The hardware powered up without smoke or flames. But you're reading this chapter because something didn't work or work as expected. (Or maybe you want to avoid smoke and flames.)

Finding and remedying problems doesn't take psychic abilities or lottery-winning luck. Debugging takes a systematic approach to testing each part of your project. That means testing your software, hardware, connections, and interaction of the pieces. Testing includes checking the parts that appear to work to be certain that they do indeed work.

Debugging starts with a plan. Connecting everything, crossing your fingers, and hoping for the best while flipping the power switch isn't really a plan. You can prevent some difficult-to-find damage with some simple checks prior to the first power application.

A Systematic Approach

A *systematic approach* means testing or changing only one thing at a time in a planned, orderly fashion. Follow a debug plan. Write down your test results.

Write down what you changed and why. If your change didn't work, what happened? Did you change it back or leave it? Write everything down.

Following a plan and writing down your results also helps if you need to ask for assistance.

The Debug Plan

Perhaps this is your first exposure to a serious debug, so let's look at a generalized plan. Figure 11.1 shows a list of debug steps that is very broad. Simple projects, like your very first one, won't take extensive testing at every step. You can modify this plan to be specific to your project.

You don't need a formal written plan that includes every little detail. But include all the important pieces that you don't want to overlook.

Before you get started, gather your documentation. You need your notebook, schematic or wiring diagram, sketch (program), data sheets or other part information, and anything else that you used for your design.

Software Test

- Check input and output definitions and pin assignments.

- Enable your debug messages.

- Wiggle all the outputs, using LEDs as stand-ins.

- Wiggle all the inputs, using switches or variable resistors as stand-ins.

- Test as many paths through the software as possible using stand-ins.

- Disable debug messages and check that no timing problems occur. Or leave them alone and simply ignore them.

Before Power-Up Hardware Checks

- Match your pin assignments with your schematic.

- Make sure your components are installed correctly.

- Test power connections.

- Check for short-circuits on power signals.

- Measure (unconnected) power supply output.

Hardware Test

- Cautiously apply power to the hardware.

- Measure power supply voltage.

- Test that each control signal (from the Arduino) has the desired effect.

- Check that each input (to the Arduino) has the desired effect.

Integration

- Make sure the hardware and software play nicely together.

Thorough Test

- Test every path through your program.

- Test every hardware signal through its entire range.

Figure 11.1

The debug plan.

© 2014 Cengage Learning®

SOFTWARE TEST

Now that we have a generalized plan, let's look at each piece in turn, starting with the software piece. You did read Chapter 9 first, didn't you?

To test your sketch, you have to write one. It has to compile and download without errors. Chapter 9 will help you write your sketch if you haven't already.

You may have elected to write and debug a section of code at a time. Starting with a small piece of software is an excellent strategy. Your baby sketch (sketch-let? Sketch-tino?) might test just a button, just a buzzer, just the console port, or just a motor control.

A small sketch is quicker to write, and problems are easier to find. The downside is that a working sketch has to be modified and potentially broken to add the remaining pieces. (Save early, save often.)

Another approach is to write the entire complete, complex sketch and test a piece at a time. Leave it unconnected, or temporarily comment out the sections you haven't tested yet. Clearly, some judgment is required. You can't leave control signals floating; they have to be set either high or low.

The advantage of writing the entire sketch at once is that you don't have to mess with a sketch that's working. The disadvantage is that it's much tougher to write and debug.

Compilation Issues

At this point, you probably have a sketch you believe will do the job. But because this is the chapter on debugging, let's assume you have some problems. Missing (or extra) commas, semicolons, parentheses, square brackets, and curly braces often cause compilation problems.

The compiler does its best to highlight the line where the error occurs. But its success rate isn't great. For those new to C, check the syntax of the highlighted line with a book or Internet search. The Integrated Development Environment (IDE) auto format tool can catch mismatched parentheses, square brackets, and braces. Clicking on one piece of the pair highlights the other piece.

Complaints of undeclared variables and undefined functions might truly be missing, or they might be spelling errors. C is case sensitive, so the variable x isn't the same as the variable X.

Placement of declarations inside a function means the declared item is available only while inside that function. Both setup() and loop() are functions, so place your declarations outside of them. Your declared items will have global scope, but extra scope rarely causes problems.

Don't use keywords or already defined words as variable or function names. Some of these are tricky. If the IDE turns your variable or function name a pretty color, you can't use it. When in doubt, you can always add my to the front of the name, like mySerial().

If you have stubborn compiler issues, back up to your last saved sketch version that did compile. Add sections, like complete `if` statements, one at a time until you find the problem. Don't worry that an in-between sketch won't do the job. Hunt your compiler error first.

Temporarily commenting out sections of code provides an alternative. But you have to do this strategically or you'll introduce more errors. Adding sections at a time, like a complete `while` loop, is an easier technique for the novice.

You may have made some creative errors, so step-by-step debug guidelines aren't possible. If you are genuinely stumped, see Chapter 12, "Bragging Rights and Pleas for Help."

pinMode() and digitalWrite()

Input/Output (I/O) is king, so check that each pin you intend to use has two function calls. Make sure there is a `pinMode()` call to make it input or output *and* a `digitalWrite()` call to make the signal level high or low. If input, `digitalWrite()` controls the pullup resistor.

`pinMode()` and `digitalWrite()` are functions that do some things behind the scenes. Order matters. Use `pinMode()` first and then `digitalWrite()`. If you have a signal that doesn't seem to be working, check to be sure you have called both functions and used `pinMode()` first.

Console Port, aka Serial Monitor Port

A *console port*, also called a *serial monitor port*, is a serial port connected to your computer used for debug and control. Using the serial port connected to the Universal Serial Bus (USB) connector provides the most convenient way to get a console port. Connect to it using the Tools>Serial Monitor drop-down menu in the IDE.

Some Arduino models, like the Uno, have only one built-in serial port. Using the serial port as a console port is convenient, but it doesn't allow the serial port to be used for anything else. Fortunately, the SoftwareSerial library provides functions allowing any two pins to be used as a serial port.

Keep the built-in serial port as the console port because it's the one connected to the USB connector. Use an emulated serial port when you run out of built-in ports.

Breadcrumb Trail

Once your sketch compiles, add some extra lines for debugging. Use console port (serial port to your computer) print statements, LEDs, buzzers, or some other means so you know what your Arduino is up to. Think of it as leaving a trail of breadcrumbs that show where your Arduino has been.

These indicators will make the debug task a lot easier and provide confidence that it's right when it does work. Pick key points in your program, like the less common path through a conditional statement.

As you find errors and fix them, you can move your indicators to new points in your program. Don't add too many at one time, though, because it will be hard to pick out the critical one.

Don't overdo print statements. Too many print statements add delay and may change timing relationships. They also scroll by too quickly to read.

It's okay to add conditional statements to limit the print statements to the first occurrence or once every tenth or hundredth time. That's assuming you can add the code without introducing a new bug.

Hardware Test

When the software piece is ready or as ready as you can make it, the debug process continues with adding the relevant hardware piece. Your sketch may not be 100% complete. As long as it compiles and downloads, it's complete enough to do some testing.

But First

It's tempting to plug everything together and hope for the best. But one small error can set you all the way back to the start, with or without the puff of smoke. Dull as it sounds, a few simple tests can prevent expensive, time-consuming, hair-pulling, tooth-grinding frustration.

Put your Arduino aside for the moment and spend some time with your other pieces.

Wiring

The amount of attention your wiring deserves depends on a number of factors. If you are putting together a Printed Circuit Board (PCB) kit you purchased, you can be confident that the wiring is correct. (You still need to verify that your Integrated Circuits (ICs), transistors, diodes, and polarized capacitors are oriented correctly.) If you built your circuit on a wire wrap board late at night by the glow of your TV, it deserves more attention before power-up.

You can visually check wiring of wire-wrap circuits. Using a multimeter provides a more reliable and often faster way to look for problems.

Circuits built on solderless breadboards deserve some attention, too. It's easy to miss the target hole and be off by one row. The miswire causes a short or leaves an open or both. You can check wiring on solderless breadboards either with a multimeter or your own eyes. If this is your first time using a solderless breadboard, test with a multimeter.

If you chose not to check all your wiring, check the power and ground connections as a minimum. If you used sockets, make the initial measurements before populating your board.

Populated board or not, verify the power and ground connections for each device. All the ground connections should measure 0 ohms between them. Power to ground should measure high impedance for populated circuits or open for unpopulated circuits. (Use the positive side of your multimeter on the positive power connection and the negative side on the ground connection.)

Test that your different power supply voltages are not shorted together. The resistance between each different supply voltage and ground should be large. Power connections should measure 0 ohms within a section.

Once your circuit is populated, measure the resistance between power and ground, paying attention to polarity. For a populated circuit, the resistance should measure 10–100 K ohms or more. Measurements of less than hundreds of ohms usually indicate a problem.

If you did wire your circuit by electronic glow, verify at a minimum the power and ground for each IC. If you find errors, check all of your wiring prior to power-up. Use a highlighter to mark off the wires on your schematic as you check them with the multimeter.

Impedance or Resistance

Sometimes used interchangeably, impedance and resistance are subtly different. With DC signals, they are equivalent. *Impedance* is the frequency-dependent version of *resistance* for changing signals.

The impedance of components changes with frequency. Capacitors are high impedance at low frequency and low impedance at high frequency. Inductors are low impedance at low frequency and high impedance at high frequency. Resistors don't change much with frequency.

Pin One

Verify that all your components are installed with pin 1 in the correct orientation. Dual In-line Package (DIP) components in particular are easy to install backward (rotated 180 degrees), often resulting in part destruction if they're not caught before power-up. Devices with leads on four sides offer more exciting wrong choices.

If you can't identify pin 1, check the data sheet. Pin 1 is always marked somehow, but exact methods vary.

PCBs usually have pin 1 identified in some way. Sometimes the pad is a different shape. Sometimes the silkscreen has an outline with a notch or a label for pin 1. If you bought a kit, an assembly drawing shows the orientations.

Photographs of assembled kits found online can also help. Compare your board with the photographs.

Power Supply

Now it's time to turn your attention to the power supply. Verify the power supply's voltage and polarity while unconnected to your circuit. Make sure that your power supply is large enough to supply the current your circuit needs. Check the power supply rating label against your calculated power draw.

Most power supplies are thermally protected. They shut down and stop providing power if too much current is drawn for too long. If your project powers up, runs for a bit, and shuts down suddenly, you may be hitting the power supply's thermal limit.

Make sure all grounds are connected. The Arduino's ground must connect to your circuit's ground and the power supply ground. All power supply grounds connect if you have more than one power supply. Make sure the supply side of multiple power supplies aren't shorted together.

If your power is miswired, even a brief (in human terms) application of power is sufficiently long to permanently damage your electronics. Often, power supply–inflicted damage occurs inside devices at the microscopic level without any outward signs. (Static electricity causes this type of invisible damage, too.) Your damaged parts may fail unexpectedly some time later.

Double-Check

Double-check your Arduino input and output pin assignments. The Arduino is tough but not indestructible. Be sure you used current-limiting resistors with all LEDs. Check for snubbing diodes for motors, relays, and coils. Use drive circuits for motors and relays.

Make sure your sketch programming matches your schematic and your wiring. If you have a habit of documenting or fixing things later, it's later now. If you wait any longer it could be too late.

Moving Parts

Temporarily remove moving parts like propellers, flame throwers, and anything that might pose a hazard if uncontrolled. It's a good idea to disconnect anything that might be damaged by a software bug, even if it's not dangerous.

Use a stand-in indicator, like an LED, to debug these sections of code more safely. Don't attach anything hazardous until you have completed dotting your I's and crossing your T's.

The Smoke Test

The big moment has arrived. It's time to power up your circuit for the first time!

If your circuitry is connected to any Arduino pins, power the Arduino first. Applying voltage to a pin of an unpowered Arduino may ruin it.

Double-check your polarity. Connect the power supply, but be ready to disconnect it. Be alert for the smell of burning electronics, sharp pops, smoke, or other indications of problems. Immediately disconnect the power at the first hint of trouble. If it's a false alarm, there's no harm done.

Caution

Remove power at the first indication of trouble.

If there is a problem, you have probably damaged some of your circuitry. Damage happens in less than a second. You only get one puff of smoke. The second time you apply power, already damaged devices don't often show an indication of trouble.

If you suspect a component is installed backward or has otherwise failed, don't touch it. It could be hot enough to burn you.

Caution

Failed components are hot. Don't touch them.

Measure the power supply voltage while connected. The voltage should measure what you expect.

Low power supply voltage measurements indicate too much current draw; disconnect the power immediately. Recalculate your expected current draw. If your power supply should be large enough for your expected current draw, you might have a wiring error, a failed component, or a component that's incorrectly installed.

High measurements could indicate that you have the wrong supply; disconnect it immediately. Your electronics become damaged by even a brief exposure to a voltage that is too high.

Debugging a circuit that has been abused this way is hard for an experienced engineer. Mark all your active components (ICs) as bad so you don't accidently reuse them. Then replace them.

I know what you're thinking. Yes, some of your ICs might still be okay. But they could also be damaged in ways that are hard to detect and fail later without warning.

If the voltage you abused the circuits with is below the do-not-exceed limit (listed on the data sheet), the components should be okay. Single transistors may fall into this category, as do most passive components. Passive components like resistors, capacitors, and inductors are probably okay. Otherwise, assume that all active components are bad.

If the voltage is what you expect, and you don't smell burning electronics, the next adventure is making sure the project works as intended.

COMBINING HARDWARE AND SOFTWARE

Focus now shifts to connecting the Arduino to the rest of your circuitry. You may have already connected some of your signals. Now it's time to hook up the rest. While you are attaching your wires, check your connections against the schematic. You don't have to debug a wiring error you didn't make.

Hold off on propellers and other hazards until you finish with the dotting your I's and crossing your T's part of the debug. Use stand-ins to prove your control logic and circuits.

The physical connection is only one piece of the puzzle. Your sketch needs to make your project perform the way you anticipated.

Logic Errors

Logic errors pose one of the hardest errors to find. Trace through each path in your code to see that the execution is what you planned. Use your debug messages or indicators to confirm proper execution.

If you don't get what you expect, check for common errors. Make sure you constructed your test conditions correctly. Look for assignment (=) where you should have used the test condition (==).

You may have exited your loop one count too soon or too late. You may get stuck in a loop that never meets the exit condition.

You may have started numbering your array elements with 1 instead of 0. Remember to declare your arrays with the number of elements in the square brackets. Assign them starting with 0 and ending with the size minus one.

Check your if statements for a semicolon. Putting a semicolon in the wrong place tells your Arduino to test a condition and, if true, do nothing. If your condition is true and your Arduino is doing nothing, a rogue semicolon may be the culprit.

Uninitialized variables may give you unexpected results if you fail to assign them before testing them. Always initialize variables when you create them to avoid this problem.

Initial Position

To debug anything, you must have a consistent starting point. That's why we initialize variables. You need to place physical components into an initial position, too.

Robot arms need to start in a home position. Curtains need to start either open or closed. Snack delivery systems need to start at their dock.

Starting at a random point makes debug unnecessarily hard. A random starting point may be an eventual goal, but first start in a consistent place. Then add the piece to bring your machine from a random position to a known position.

See How It Runs

Because your sketch works and your circuitry checked out, putting them together should go smoothly. Smoothly does not mean perfectly, though. Something usually needs a tweak or two.

Frustratingly, sometimes things don't work at all. Take a couple of deep breaths, because you are not alone. Everyone occasionally has this sort of minor catastrophe. Just debug one problem at a time.

The first thing to check is your wiring between your Arduino and the other circuitry. (Again! Ugh.) Does your sketch match your schematic? Make sure you have the correct header hole. When viewed at an angle, the pin numbers may not line up with the holes due to the height of the header. Count the holes from the header end, and remember to start counting with zero.

Make sure your ground connections are solid. All grounds (power supply, Arduino, circuitry) must be connected. If the ground connection isn't good, your signals don't work when they're connected. When disconnected they appear fine. While you're at it, verify the power supply levels and connections.

Once you are positive that your wires are correct and find your sketch still doesn't work, check your sketch to be sure the function calls setting up your I/O are correct. Do your function calls to set up the I/O include both a `pinMode()` and a `digitalWrite()` function call?

Timing issues might also cause the appearance of not working at all. In particular, reading from a serial interface may take a `wait` loop. Make sure your sketch tests to be sure the data is ready before attempting to read it. Then again, leftover garbage may be in the serial buffer, and you may need to flush it before reading your real data.

Your Arduino is doing something; use debug print statements to find out what. Print variables, loop counters, input readings, and any other critical information.

Search the forum for posts about the same sort of issues you are seeing. Compare your sketch with a similar sketch from the forum. Look for comments that indicate something was added to make it work.

Conflicting signals on the serial interface and the USB port might also cause issues. Be sure you use only one or the other of these. (It's possible to use the USB interface to snoop on the TX side of a serial connection.)

Write down what you've done. Take breaks when you get perturbed. Sleep on it. But stick with it. When you get as far as you can go and still can't find the problem, refer to Chapter 12.

DOTTING THE I'S AND CROSSING THE T'S

At this point, everything appears to work, and your project is nearly done. If your project is just for show, and occasional malfunctions aren't a problem, you're done now. Otherwise, it's time to dot the I's and cross the T's.

You may have portions of your code that rarely or never execute under normal conditions. It's time to test them.

Error handlers, special sections of code to cope with problems, need attention. Test them to be sure they properly detect and deal with the crisis.

Thoroughly test control for anything that poses a hazard. If you purchased a kit, follow its directions carefully. If you built your own device, consider all the possible ways it might go wrong and test for them. Research other people's disasters to keep from creating your own.

Caution

Test and operate potentially hazardous items only in clear areas.

Test and operate potentially hazardous items only in an area clear of people, pets, livestock, wildlife, property, and anything soft or breakable. Own and use protective clothing and equipment for all phases of operation, especially testing.

Caution

Own and wear protective equipment for testing and operation.

Sensors and other hardware need to be tested through their entire range. Test your project at the temperature at which it's intended to operate. Test it a little warmer and a little cooler, too.

When you are completely satisfied that everything has been thoroughly tested, you're done. Enjoy your project.

CHAPTER 12

BRAGGING RIGHTS AND PLEAS FOR HELP

This chapter answers the following questions:

- Where can I show off my project to an appreciative audience?
- Where can I find help when I'm stuck?
- Who is the best person to ask for help?

Although bragging seems as far as you can get from pleas for help, the two actually have a lot in common. Both involve sharing all or part of your design and use the same documentation. Even the intended audience is the same.

When bragging, the amount of information you provide is up to you. You can share your entire design or just pieces of it. If you intend to sell your design, you might limit the amount of information you give away. But when you sell it, you need to supply more extensive information. (You also need to answer questions and provide support for your customers.)

When asking for help, you need to provide as much information as possible. The quality of the answers you get depends heavily on the background information you provide and the quality of questions you ask. Who you ask for help also matters.

GETTING ORGANIZED

Before you share your design, you need to organize your information into a recognizable set of documents.

The first important piece is a general description of what your project does. It doesn't need to be anything formal—just a couple paragraphs or a half-page long (or less) description. Describe any input signals or sensors and any output signals, indicators, or actions. This is sometimes called the *black box description* because the inside workings aren't described.

The next piece is to describe the inside workings of the black box. Start with general terms and work your way down to the details. Talk about how it does what it's supposed to do. This piece is sometimes called a *theory of operation*.

Use pictures or drawings to fill in some details. Some things are easier to draw than to put into words. The pictures can be photographs, hand-drawn sketches, or any other picture-based information.

Photographs of your circuits can be the key to finding your problem. Hey, it looks like your chips are in backward! Don't laugh; it's happened.

Include schematic diagrams or the equivalent that show your components and wiring. Provide part numbers for devices, resistor and capacitor values, and pin numbers. Don't forget to include the Arduino model and any shields you are using.

Include your sketch (program) and ensure that it has enough comments that someone who has only read your description can follow it. You don't get credit for confusion. Advice from the baffled is worse than no answer at all.

If you feel your problem involves only your sketch, you're probably right. (I know that doesn't make you feel any better.) But you still need to include other information. It helps to put into context what you intend for your sketch to do. Your approach could be the real problem.

Provide a problem description that goes beyond the phrase, "It doesn't work." What does it do correctly? What does it do when it's not working? When do the problems happen? Do they start right away or only after days of operation? Include any information that might help to identify the problem.

Some problems can be quickly identified by an experienced user from the nature and timing of the symptoms. Use units where appropriate, as in, "The voltage is .4 Volts too low," or "The problem starts after about 45 minutes of operation." Pretend you're a newspaper writer trying to get who, what, where, when, how much, or how many for a story.

Here's a question-posing checklist:

■ What seems to be the problem, or what would you like to know? (Be brief.)

■ What is your project meant to do in general terms?

■ How does your project work in specific terms?

- What does your project look like? (Include pictures or drawings.)
- How is your project wired?
- What does your sketch do in terms of logical steps?
- Can we see your sketch?
- Does your sketch compile? If not, what are the specific error messages?
- When does your problem occur, and what does it do when it's not working?
- What have you tried, and what happened?
- What can you tell us about the details of your problem?

SEEKING YOUR OWN ANSWER

Now that you've organized your information and settled on a question, spend some time looking for your own answer. That might involve searching forums for posts on a particular device, technique, or compiler error code. It might instead involve using good debug techniques and persistence. If you do post your question to the forum, include the things you tried that seemed to have an effect, good or bad.

Some questions aren't really suitable for the Arduino forum. Questions about C or C++ are better answered by a book or an Internet reference.

Some C or C++ questions do belong on the forum. Sometimes the Arduino has C-related quirks that will be discussed on the forum. Questions about Arduino library functions also belong on the forum.

The device manufacturer provides the best answers for questions about specific devices used with the Arduino. Data sheets provide a great deal of detailed information on devices. Don't forget to look there.

Shield makers usually provide information on using their products and provide support for what they make. Check the support page for an answer. Contact customer support for help before posting a shield-related question.

Some shields are little more than holders for Integrated Circuit (IC) devices that do all the work. In this case, looking up the information for the IC may provide the best help. Search for the part number located on the main IC on a shield.

FORUMS

Organized and having exhausted your own resources, it's time to ask for help. But where do you go to meet others with an interest in Arduino projects? You've already guessed the answer: a forum.

Forums are public places in the ancient tradition. They provide a space for people to meet and share ideas. Just like meeting on a street corner, you will meet all sorts of people in a forum.

Moderators keep the discussion on topic and civilized. Some forums have full-time professional moderators, others have volunteer moderators, and still others have no moderators at all.

The Arduino forum (http://forum.arduino.cc/) provides a good place for beginners to start. Volunteer moderators do their best to keep the posts polite, with generally good results.

Nearly every distributer listed on the official distributor's page (http://arduino.cc/en /Main/Buy), including global distributers, provides a forum. These forums often have professional moderators with low tolerance levels for misbehavior. Their job depends on keeping the discussions under control.

Maker and hacker magazines and websites sometimes provide forums. Because these entities don't have a relationship with Arduino, they aren't listed on the official Arduino web page. Your favorite search engine should be able to find them.

PICKING A FORUM

Selecting the correct forum for your question or brag can be just as important as proper documentation. There are lots of forums to choose among, with more popping up every day. Be picky.

Choose a forum that is moderated and requires membership to post on. Examine posted answers for a few questions to see if the answers given are understandable to you. Avoid forums where the tone is critical, unhelpful, or nasty.

Look for structured content. Searching a forum organized by topic is a lot faster than one arranged only by date.

Most forums have how-to-use or how-to-post directions. Check these out before you attempt to post. Remember that these are public places, so don't include your private information.

You don't have to include all the items in the previous checklist. But remember that the quality of the answer you get will depend on the quality of the information you provide. Failure to mention something important is your own fault, not the fault of the person who answers your post.

Don't post the same question on every forum. Wait a day or two for an answer to your question before you assume no one will answer it. The people answering the questions are volunteers with jobs and families. It may take a while for them to get around to you. You can't expect instant service.

An interest-specific forum may provide better results than a general Arduino forum. If your project is a robot, take a look at robotic forums. If your project is a train controller, check out model railroading forums. If your project is a quadcopter, take a look at drone and quadcopter forums. Maker or hacker forums are another option.

Look for recent posts to be sure the forum you selected is still active and hasn't been abandoned. Avoid forums that contain advertisements as posts.

Here's a forum selection checklist:

- Moderator presence
- Membership required for posting
- Polite and helpful tone
- Organized content
- Understandable answers
- Recent posts
- Poster ratings or other indication of quality
- No advertisement posts

FRAMING A GOOD QUESTION

Posing a good question is the key to a quality answer. A question that is too general will lead to an answer that is too general. A question that is too specific might need six other questions to get to the real problem.

Sometimes the best you can do is a general question. That may be the case when you have a stubborn compiler error. If you have compiler issues, be sure to include the entire sketch. Set the IDE preferences to show verbose compiler messages. Cut and paste any error messages into your post.

If your question is about logic, you must include a description of what your logic is meant to do. C allows you to do things that might be what you meant, but also might be logical errors. Taken out of context, it's impossible to tell.

For example, an assignment might be a legitimate test condition for an error handler that takes over when the assignment fails. Clearly, this would be an exceptional condition and unlikely to be one you meant. Examined by itself, an assignment as a test condition seems like a mistake. But it's not necessarily true.

In general, volunteers answer questions posted to a forum. These are real people, and the most interesting question gets attention first. Summarize your question up front. A volunteer doing this for fun isn't going to wade through tons of information to get to your question at the end. You must still include all that information, but state your question at the start.

Phrase your request for help respectfully. Ask for an answer appropriate for your level of experience. If you are a newbie, it's okay to say so. Everybody was new once. If you've done other projects or have a year or two of experience, you can say that instead.

There are some things you should *not* include in your post. Do not post personally identifiable information such as name, age, or address. Do not agree to meet anyone in person. Do not place yourself in dangerous situations. Do not assume your post is anonymous; it's not, so behave yourself.

CHOOSING THE BEST ANSWER

You may receive conflicting answers or advice to your question. Who do you believe? There is more than one way to solve many problems; it's possible that more than one is correct. Pick one and try it. The worst thing that can happen is that it doesn't work. You're not losing much since your system already doesn't work.

Some forums allow users to rate the usefulness of posts or rate posters. The forum may identify usefulness with "karma" or a frequent poster as a "guru" or employ some other unique indicator. Pick a well-rated post. Otherwise, select a post by someone with good karma or guru status.

CONTESTS AND SUCH

Contests clearly present an opportunity to brag for a prize. Be aware that you may be giving your design away when you enter a contest, so ensure the prize is worth it. Read and understand all the rules before you enter.

The playground on www.arduino.cc contains a special bragging section. Click on Playground (in the gray box at the very top of the page) and then scroll down to find the Exhibition section link on the left side of the page. (You could instead use a search engine because this page is a little hard to find.)

If you browse for a while, you will find the more interesting brags are the ones that contain the most information. Posts that are really vague and contain no useful information are boring. Write the interesting post.

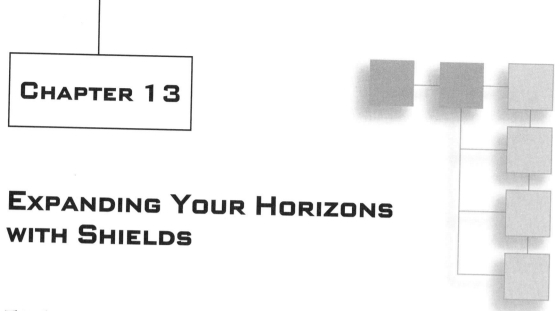

CHAPTER 13

EXPANDING YOUR HORIZONS WITH SHIELDS

This chapter answers the following questions:

- Is there a shield for that?
- Can I use a shield with any Arduino?
- Is a shield my only option?

Shields provide a little bit of hardware with stackable, plug-in convenience. They are a great way to add capability to your Arduino without having to design and build your own circuitry. If you aren't interested in the hardware bits, you can usually get what you need with one or more shields.

Designed for the Uno, shields may or may not be compatible with other Arduino models like the Mega. They obviously can't plug into Arduino models without headers.

Breakout boards supply similar hardware pieces in a wire-up format. They provide more flexibility because the headers don't dictate pin assignment. Most breakout boards require a little bit of soldering.

When necessary, shield makers or distributers supply special-purpose libraries of functions for use with their shields. Other shields use more general-purpose libraries for control. Each shield comes with directions for use, examples, and customer support. For the nonengineer, these are advantages too big to easily pass up.

Shields exist for nearly any feature you might want to add to your Arduino. Some shields are made by Arduino, but many more are made by other companies. New shields come out all the time. (And the less popular ones are discontinued.) Let's explore some shields divided into broad categories.

Communication

Communication protocols allow you to send your information wirelessly, over wires, or even via satellites. To these protocols, your important information is *data* or *payload*. Don't worry about what your information is called; the protocol's responsibility is to deliver it intact to the far end of the link.

The protocols deal with messy details like making sure your entire message arrived and keeping your data in the proper order. Shields provide the hardware pieces for these protocols and take care of many of the protocol details. You only need to provide the data to send and process the received data.

Data doesn't necessarily mean numbers. Data just means the information you want to send. The information you choose to send and receive is up to you, but it is most likely in the form of messages. For the messages to work, both ends of the communication link must agree on what they mean.

A serial communication port, usually the Serial Peripheral Interface (SPI), allows data transfer between the shield and the Arduino. The SPI provides hardware data buffers that might be essential to the proper operation of the shield.

You can buy shields that support Ethernet, Wi-Fi Ethernet, Bluetooth, X-bee, other wireless protocols, cellular phone, power line, or even satellite protocols. They aren't meant to be used together. Pick only one communication protocol at a time.

As with other shields, use the special-purpose libraries, and follow the supplied directions.

Motor Controllers

Ordinary, DC motors require more drive current than the Arduino's pins can provide. This takes a bit of hardware to accommodate. Don't worry; there's a shield for that.

Motor controller shields provide plug-in convenience and drive current. Because their functions are relatively simple, there usually isn't a library that goes with them. Sets of three pins usually control the motor. Two control direction, and one Pulse Width Modulation (PWM) signal controls the speed.

Chapter 9, "Writing the Code," provides an example of a motor controller sketch that you can use with a motor shield.

Although shields are stackable, one of their limitations comes to light here. Stacking motor shields doesn't let you control more motors. Because the control pins of the shield (typically) can't be changed, independent control of stacked motor controllers isn't conveniently possible.

If you need to control a lot of motors, find a shield that lets you select which pins are used for control. For these shields, on-board jumpers provide a means to select which control pins are used. (For shields without jumpers, changing control pins would require cutting and soldering.)

Stepper motors aren't like DC motors. They require a different type of control—a more complex type of control. There are specialized shields for their control, too. Some shields can be stacked to control more motors. Carefully read and follow the directions that come with the shield.

Servo motors require yet another type of specialized control. A PWM-like pulse stream controls their position. You guessed it—there's a shield for that, too.

Robot Driving Bases

Robot driving bases simplify the task of making your Arduino mobile. These bases integrate motors, motor drivers, batteries, gearing, and steering into one compact package. All the mechanical bits and pieces are already there. Some driving bases let you simply plug your Arduino on top of the driving base, and away you go. (That qualifies them as shields.)

There is, of course, a bit more to it than that. But driving bases really do simplify the process. You aren't limited to bases custom made for the Arduino. An Arduino can control other robot driving bases. These need separate wiring and maybe some soldering, too. (They aren't really shields, but they're not bad, either.)

Read the product descriptions to determine which pieces are not included. You may need to add sensors, GPS, radio control, or other things.

Memory

When you need more memory than your Uno provides, there's a shield for that. Selecting an Arduino model with more built-in memory is often a better choice. But there are times when a shield is a good option.

Shields with various types and sizes of memory are available. Because these memories aren't connected to the microcontroller's data bus, the data must be accessed via a serial interface. Usually the SPI provides connection to this memory.

The memories are accessed via a serial interface, so access to them takes longer than the built-in memories. Functions supplied in special-purpose libraries accommodate the longer access times. They also handle addressing issues.

SD card shields are especially convenient for data logging. The shield can load the SD card, and you can move the card to your computer for processing. The File Allocation Table (FAT) file system libraries and functions are required for manipulating files on the SD card.

Refer to the directions that come with your shield. They should include an example sketch that shows how to use the memory.

Music

MP3, MIDI, and music shields provide a way to add music to your Arduino. The Arduino doesn't have native music capability. It lacks some of the vital hardware pieces.

Audio is one case in which a shield is essential. Music without a shield is difficult. The Arduino's 16 MHz, 8-bit processor with no internal DAC and 2 K of SRAM just doesn't provide enough processing power to handle stereo music.

MP3 music shields allow your Arduino to record/play back MP3 files with respectable sound quality. A microphone or an amplifier with speakers is also required.

MIDI shields generate MIDI code sequences that allow your Arduino to be a musical instrument. For actual sound, a separate MIDI-controlled sound generator is required. You might also need an amplifier with speakers.

Display

A display provides an exciting way to interact with your Arduino. Display shields offer a quick and easy way to add this feature.

Right now, display shields provide 7-segment, LED array, LCD, and touch screen displays. Display shields are changing rapidly, with resolution, color, and size improving all the time.

Each shield needs its own special-purpose functions for control. Touch screens are also input devices and more challenging to use to full potential.

Take advantage of the documentation supplied with your shield. The examples and directions let you use your shield's capabilities to best advantage.

OTHER

Other is a broad category that includes everything else. It includes, but isn't limited to, Input/Output (I/O) extender, Field Effect Transistor (FET) drivers, relay board, prototype board, keypad, joystick, battery, Universal Serial Bus (USB) host, and GPS modules. In short, when you need a bit of hardware, there's a shield for that.

There are more types of shields available than can be listed here. www.shieldlist.org provides a list of shields that have been created. The list isn't exhaustive; the page author tries, but he just can't keep up.

Being on the shield list doesn't guarantee that the shield is still offered for purchase and stocked by suppliers or suitable for your function. Absence from this list doesn't mean the shield doesn't exist.

There is another list of shields on the playground (playground.arduino.cc) under "Related Hardware and Initiatives." Under "Navigation" is a link to "Shields."

Shopping for a shield on a distributor's website is more rewarding. You won't identify a shield that seems to be perfect only to discover that you can't actually buy it. No one distributor stocks everything, so you need to visit a few.

Distributors such as Sparkfun, Adafruit, Rugged Circuits, and (of course) Arduino stock shields that are currently purchasable. Even Radio Shack has gotten into the game.

COMPATIBILITY ISSUES

Even though shields are stackable, there is a limit to how many you can stack. The limit may be pin or address conflict or physical arrangement.

Because most shields are controlled via a serial port, like the SPI, you can control only one or two shields at a time. Pin conflicts for the SPI's device select pins, in many cases D4 or D10, prevent control of more than one or two shields.

Even when the SPI isn't involved, stacking of shields runs into other limits. Basic motor shields use dedicated pins, so stacking more than one does not allow independent motor control.

Conflicting (duplicate) 2-wire addresses can limit multiple shield use. Some of these addresses can be changed, and some can't.

Physical arrangement of components, cables, displays, or buttons sometimes prevents shield stacking. A display stacked under a keypad is useless.

The last limitation imposed on shield use may be your wallet. Shields are not the most economical way to provide hardware. The cost of the connectors for stacking and plug-in convenience adds a lot to the cost of the shield. To be stackable, every pin must be carried through the shield, not just the ones that are used.

BREAKOUT BOARDS

Breakout boards provide many of the same functions as shields, except they are wired rather than plugged. Because they don't need to plug into the headers, the physical sizes vary. Some are much smaller, like motor controllers, whereas others are larger, like relay boards.

Freedom to connect the breakout board's pins to any of the Arduino's pins allows the SPI to control more boards. Nearly any Arduino pin can be used as a device select, imposing fewer limitations.

Motor driver breakout boards require a Pulse Width Modulation (PWM) pin, so the limit is the number of PWM pins available. In general, the number of special pins (or total pins) limits the number of breakout boards that can be controlled at one time.

Breakout boards are cheaper than shields because they don't have the cost of the connectors. Being smaller also reduces the cost.

BEYOND SHIELDS

Breakout boards are not the only devices your Arduino can control. You can use any digitally controlled device from an MP3 player to a toaster to expand the Arduino's abilities. These pieces can be used like breakout boards to add whole functions at a time.

Some devices, like MP3 players, are intended to connect to your control signals. Other devices, like coffee makers and toasters, aren't. Modifying an existing thing to be controlled by your Arduino crosses the line into hacking. Anything without directions takes special knowledge and care to connect to without damage.

Use caution when taking anything electrical apart. Voltages that may damage *you* can be present. These voltages can persist for an astonishingly long time (days) after the power is removed. Approach any hacking activity with extreme caution.

Hacking is not for everyone. (I'm a designer, not a hacker. But I also have an MSEE degree.) If hacking is your thing, research what you plan to modify. Be alert for potential hazards, and keep yourself safe.

DESIGNING YOUR OWN

Your last option is to design your own breakout board or shield. You can convert into a shield any circuit you can wire up. Any shield you want to build should first be wired up to verify that the design works. (This is called *prototyping*.)

Many shields are open source. Their designs are available for you to examine, copy, and modify for your own use. Don't copy designs that aren't licensed to you.

Tools for schematic capture are available for free (small boards) or low cost (larger boards). Although CAD files are sometimes supplied for open-source designs, they don't work for you if you modify the design. You need to generate new CAD files. If you plan to plug your shield into the Arduino's headers, be sure you get the mechanical pieces right.

Like hacking, designing might not be right for you. You can't copy a shield for a lower cost than you can buy one.

CHAPTER 14

APPLICATION IDEAS

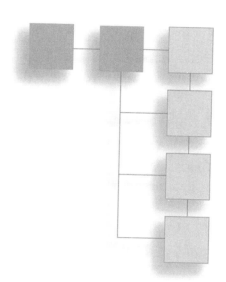

This chapter answers the following questions:

- What should I make with an Arduino?
- How do I impress my friends and family?
- What project will stay fun?

Now that you have a shiny new Arduino and know how to use it, you will want to show it off to friends and family. Don't be too disappointed if they are a little less enthusiastic than you are. Think of it as a challenge to engage them.

To engage any human, you need to appeal to the human senses. Adding smell and taste would give new meaning to a "vanilla" Arduino. But unless you want people to lick or smell your Arduino, you are limited to sight, hearing, and touch.

Let's look first at how you can appeal to your audience's senses and then at how to add these elements to a project.

LIGHTS AND SIGHTS

The biggest bang for your investment of hard work isn't a sound; it's a sight. Lights, especially ones that flash, grab people's attention. Every eye is drawn to a single flashing light. Add a string of lights and light them in sequence, and the eyes will follow.

People love patterns so much that they will see patterns where none exists. Even with a single light, various patterns or random flashes make people stare intently, trying to figure out the meaning.

Lights are one of those situations in which more is more. One light is good, but many lights are better. Arrays of lights allow you to add patterns, words, or pictures. Motion, another attention getter, can be implied by shifting light patterns.

Color works even better. Colored patterns may be one of the best attention grabbers invented. And moving color pictures? You could get people to pay to see that!

LIGHT PROJECTS

Lights are easy but impressive. This combination makes them an excellent choice as a first project. Of course, some projects are more complex than others. Save light projects with a mechanical element (laser writing) until you have more experience.

Code Flasher

In its simplest form, a *code flasher* is a single LED that flashes a message. Morse code provides a way to spell out any message you care to send. Your message can be permanent, entered through the console port, or tapped out with a telegraph key.

Other, less famous, codes exist, but because we're showing off here, stick with the famous one. Keep your message polite; you may be surprised by how many people know Morse code.

If your goal is to learn Morse code, you can use your Arduino as a training tool. It can translate a character, a word, or a phrase entered via the console port to light flashes. The inverse translation, flashes to characters, is also possible but will take much more sophisticated hardware and software.

Infrared Remote

The *infrared remote* is just like the visible light code flasher except the light isn't in the visible range. Codes to control TVs, DVRs, DVDs, and other electronics are specific to make and model but can generally be found on the Internet.

Learning the codes provides an alternative to looking them up. A receiver circuit can capture the codes from the devices' original remote controls. Once all the necessary codes are recorded, the transmitter uses the codes to control your favorite devices.

This handy project replaces your remote control clutter with a single custom version. Configure all your electronics for movie viewing with the convenience of a single button. Change to TV viewing with another button.

The remote is obviously a cool project. But before deciding to show it off, consider your feelings about other people touching it. After playing with your remote, they will want their own.

Strobe Light

A *strobe light* has many uses but is often used to make repeated motion seem to stop. Strobe lights are used to adjust timing of car engines and turntables. They can be used to make interesting pictures or study fluid motion. Sometimes they are just entertainment.

The Arduino's timers provide precision control of a strobe light. The strobe light may be a single LED or a bank of high-power lights. The show-off potential is good but not great.

Light Cube

The *Light Cube* is a clear or translucent plastic cube that changes color. Single LEDs of various colors or a single tri-color LED provide illumination. Tissue paper, polished glass, marbles, or other translucent material fill the cube to diffuse the light.

You can change the colors randomly or allow the user to control them. Knobs, slider switches, and buttons can provide a means for user interaction. People love to push buttons and turn knobs.

This simple project has the "ooh" factor combined with the "Can I touch it?" factor. It's great for showing off and impressing your mother or your little sister. Your dad will likely see this as just a light switch. He might be impressed, but don't expect him to admit it. He would be just as impressed if you had wired a light switch instead.

Rabbit

If you have ever flown at night, you have seen rabbit lights. *Rabbits* are sequentially illuminated lights that appear to run along the ground, hence the name. This technique is a great way to add the illusion of motion without actual motion.

You're probably too young to remember the TV series *Knight Rider*, but those lights are a variation of rabbits. These lights move back and forth in a straight line. It was the '80s; it was exciting then.

Your rabbit isn't limited to a straight line. You can make your rabbit outline shapes, zigzag, double-back, or do loops. The motion of your rabbit is limited only by the placement of the lights. For more flexible motion, your rabbit could "run around" on an array of LEDs.

Build your rabbit with an eye toward future reuse. A straight-line rabbit can become a POV light bar with only a software change.

Persistence of Vision

Persistence of Vision (POV) relies on an artifact of the human eye to trick the brain into seeing pictures made by changing lights and motion. The lights usually come from a string of LEDs under processor control.

Both changing lights and motion are required, but you don't need to provide the motion. You can use the user's motion. One of the simplest POV displays relies on the user's walking motion to create the images. Once the user stops for a better look, the images disappear. Does this suggest a wicked Halloween idea to you, too?

If you prefer the user to remain still, you need to provide the motion. Motion can be created with a pendulum, rotating disc, spinning wheel, or anything that moves.

The rate at which the lights change has to be matched to the speed of motion, or the image appears distorted or stretched. Include a speed control for the lights, the motor, or both to allow the speeds to be matched.

Show-off potential is good, with a caveat. If you provide the motion, it's easier to view. Relying on the viewer's motion makes viewing less dependable.

Timer or Clock

With the addition of four 7-segment displays, your Arduino can become a clock. Although extremely useful, clocks are so common that this project probably won't impress anyone. It takes hard work, but the wow factor just isn't there.

Adding more displays and other functions like a stop watch, timer, temperature, day, and date makes it more impressive. Allowing the user to switch between the functions with buttons and knobs makes it more interesting. Variations include kitchen timer, chess clock, speech timer, alarm clock, score board, and countdown to graduation calendar.

The Arduino can keep track of relative time on its own. If you don't want to reset the time after every power glitch, provide a battery backup. Adding a Real-Time Clock (RTC) module or chip makes keeping track of day, date, and time easier. The RTC module provides its own backup battery. (With an RTC chip, you must provide the battery.) Refer to Chapter 13, "Expanding Your Horizons with Shields," for a discussion of RTC modules and chips.

Time-Based Controller

Although a time-based controller is a variation to the previous project, it deserves a category of its own. With the Arduino, adding control signals to the timer is easy and opens up a whole range of possibilities.

A time-based controller is the heart of most automated processes. Alarm clocks, coffee makers, and light controls are some of the simplest examples of time-based controllers. The traffic light and puppet show examples described in previous chapters are also examples of time-based controllers.

It's worth noting that time control is not the only way to automate processes. Sensor feedback can be used instead of, or in addition to, time. The puppet show could have used a limit switch to stop the curtain's motor instead of time. To control the light cycle, the traffic light could have used sensors to detect vehicles in addition to time.

You can automate any electrically controlled process. That's not to say that you should. Some processes require human intelligence for the times that something goes badly wrong.

Consider the consequences of control loss before trusting your programming, wiring, and components to work wholly on their own. And don't forget to consider the effects of power loss. Processes that might threaten lives (directly or indirectly) are obviously poor choices. For any process, thoroughly debug all logical paths, and provide an alarm indication for any unexpected conditions.

When using time to automate a process, keep the time display to provide an indication of exactly where in the process the Arduino is. In addition to providing vital debug information, displaying time remaining is an attractive feature. It can be one of the best features of your projects.

Display Boards

The display category includes a number of related items and uses. Electronic billboards, animated scoreboards, time and temperature bank displays, gas station sign boards, scrolling stock tickers and news feeds, and arrival/departure boards at the airport are examples of display boards.

Display boards can be static or provide eye-catching features like flashing, reverse-video, color changes, fading, scrolling, and animation. Many of these effects are not as hard to produce as you might imagine.

You can buy a display ready-made or build your own. Your display might include LCD displays, seven-segment displays, individual LEDs, LED matrixes, light bulbs, Cathode Ray Tubes (CRTs), or a combination of these and more.

LEDs (and LED matrixes) provide an excellent combination of low cost, color, flashiness, and easy control. Unless abused, they last a long time and consume less power than other types of displays. LEDs and LED matrixes can be monochromatic or tri-color devices that allow the blending of colors.

Seven-segment displays come in several types. Most are a variation of LEDs with built-in diffusers for wide-angle viewing. The diffusers allow for off-angle viewing by spreading out the light. As a side effect, this also makes them seem less bright than other LEDs when viewed straight on.

Seven-segment displays are not far behind LEDs on the usefulness curve with first-rate number presentation. If you need letters, too, these displays are less flexible. Some letters, like *X*, *Q*, and *W*, can't be represented with them.

Regardless of the display type you have chosen, you can build your own control circuit with shift registers or multiplexers, as discussed in Chapter 7, "Input and Output." Special-purpose control ICs, available for matrix and seven-segment displays, make your control task easier. Some ICs have built-in support for scrolling, brightness control, and reverse video.

Displays built from LEDs or LED matrixes are a great beginner project. The basic version is easy enough for a beginner to have great results. You can add special features and effects later without having to rebuild the circuit. If built with tri-color devices, color effects can also be added later. Displays have that wow factor, are great to play with, and can be usefully employed when you're done playing.

Sounds and Noises

Sound adds another dimension to your Arduino experience. Much like light draws the eye, sound draws the ear. Sound can draw attention from a broader area, around corners, and annoyingly through walls. Sound generation can be the focus of your project or be used to enhance a project with another focal point.

Most people focus on what they see first and then other senses. Unless sound is the purpose of your project, it will fade into the background. But just because it's in the background doesn't diminish its value. Scary movies aren't scary without the soundtrack.

The Arduino isn't wired for sound; it can't produce sounds directly. Amplified Pulse Width Modulation (PWM) signals can produce tones when they're connected to a speaker. Musical notes strung together produce rudimentary music.

For higher sound quality and efficient storage, music is encoded in digital form. MIDI and MP3 provide the most common digital formats. Although your Arduino doesn't understand MIDI or MP3, it doesn't need to. Your Arduino doesn't play or record directly in these formats; it needs an intermediary device. Yes, there's a shield for that, too.

Do you really need a shield? That depends on whether your focus is on data processing or getting on with the music. Because sound is the focus of this section, let's get on with the music. Using a shield provides data storage, encoding/decoding, stereo audio amplifiers (perhaps), and control features, allowing you to focus on the music.

SOUND PROJECTS

You can use sound to enhance other projects, but the focus of this section is sound as the point of the project. Let's divide sound projects into three broad categories: sound generation, sound recording, and sound playback.

Sound generation projects include doorbells, alarms, crickets, theremins, pocket pianos, light harps, and other musical instruments. All these projects need some form of control. Theremins use proximity to vary capacitance and change volume and frequency. Light harps employ light detectors. Pocket pianos use switches. Providing adequate user control and generating sound at the same time make these projects more challenging than other projects.

Sound recording with an Arduino involves changing signals from an analog form to a digital format. Your Arduino can't manipulate analog signals; it must convert them to numbers with an Analog Digital Converter (ADC). These numbers need additional manipulation to be transformed to a standard format like MP3.

Your Arduino doesn't have the horsepower to do MP3 conversions; it's just an 8-bit processor. MP3 encoding is best done on a shield or a serious computer. Transfer your samples via the serial port and have your computer do the heavy lifting. Remember, stereo recording doubles the amount of data.

Sound playback requires converting digital signals back to an analog format with a DAC. Your Arduino doesn't have a DAC, so you must supply one. It's possible to fake the functionality with a resistive ladder, but the quality will be poor. An external DAC provides better performance.

Before MP3 recordings can be fed to a DAC, you must decode them. Once again, a shield is a good investment.

Cricket

Like the annoying little bug, a cricket makes a short chirp at random intervals. The only purpose of a cricket is to irritate. Unless you want your roommate or your mother to trash your Arduino, use this judiciously.

Doorbell

The doorbell is a classic button-controlled sound maker. Every visitor provides an opportunity to show off and make some noise.

It can be the classic two-tone variety or a fancy wireless one that mimics church bells. It's not the button that's the interesting bit; it's how you choose to make the sound that's challenging.

You could use actual bells with a solenoid to strike them, like most hardware store models. You could use tones generated by the Arduino and played through a speaker. You could even play a short MP3 recording of bells.

There's no need to restrict your sounds to bells, though. Make a seasonal sound or join the noise of the month club. Tie in your RTC module and automatically update your tune based on season, day of the week, and time.

Piano

In its most basic form, the piano is a device that plays a note when a key is pressed. The mechanical nature of piano design causes waveform-shaping effects that are hard to mimic electronically. Although your Arduino will never be a full-fledged piano, it can be a keyboard-controlled music maker.

Each tone produced consumes the resources of one timer/counter. For monophonic sound, only one timer/counter is needed. Each key sets the timer's frequency to that of a particular note. That note is output as long as the key is held down or until another is pressed.

In theory, you can generate one simultaneous tone with each timer/counter available, raising the tantalizing possibility of a polyphonic keyboard. The tones produced then need to be mixed together before sending the resulting signal to your speaker. (Rather than building a mixing circuit, the mixing could be done with an external mixing board.) Before you decide to jump into a polyphonic piano project, consider sound quality.

There is more to music than just tones; sound quality matters, too. Pure tones are sine waves. The square waves the Arduino produces contain many *harmonics* (higher frequency components), which sound harsher than a sine wave. Using a low-pass filter reduces some of the harshness from the sound, but the musician inside you might not be satisfied.

Even so, a monophonic Arduino-based piano is easy enough for a beginner and would still be fun to play with. For attention, it's a good choice combining sound and touch. Sadly, even a battered iPod or antique Walkman outshines it for sound reproduction.

You may quickly become tired of this project because of its limitations. When you're bored with it, upgrade/modify it or reuse the pieces. Modify the control to change it into a theremin or light harp. Improve the sound quality by producing MIDI codes instead of PWM signals. (You also need a MIDI-controlled sound generator to make the sound.)

Memo Recorder or Parrot

For those interested in recording sound, a memo recorder is a good place to start. Function calls are fast enough to record telephone-like quality. Short recordings can be stored in native (uncompressed) format and played back through a Digital-to-Analog (DAC) without processing.

Getting sound to your Arduino pins and playing back through a DAC are necessary steps toward more serious sound recording. Making a memo recorder lets you play with sound sampling and playback without the added complexity of compression and encoding.

The real trick is data management. All those samples need to be written somewhere safe and retrieved as required. Keeping the recordings short and low-fidelity minimizes the data file sizes. Even so, your Arduino needs some help here.

Your Uno doesn't even have enough memory for ¼ second of recording time. Even the Mega has less than one second's worth of memory. Additional memory is needed for any type of audio recording. The quickest way to add memory to an Arduino is to use a memory shield of some kind; there are several types available.

A parrot records for a short time and immediately plays it back, continually alternating between recording and playback. For more control, you can trigger a recording with a button and have the recording play back over and over.

For added enjoyment, place the microphone and speaker near a fake parrot with the record switch near you. Amuse children and gullible adults with it. The parrot is more fun than a cricket but just as annoying in the wrong hands.

Light Harp

The light harp is a variation on the piano that uses light instead of buttons. A series of light sensors detects broken LED light beams to trigger a sound generation circuit. Like the piano, sound quality and other limitations will probably disappoint the serious musician.

The light harp does have the cool factor, but only if you can see the light. Light is only visible when it reaches your eyes. Something like mist or dust needs to scatter enough light so you can see the "strings," but not so much that it doesn't work. If you can't see the "strings," the harp just looks like an empty frame.

Unlike a real harp, there is no physical contact with the strings. Consider how you would hold and play it. How do you find the right string if you can't feel or see it?

Don't confuse light harps with laser harps. Laser harps are not suitable for a beginner project. In addition to being much more expensive and complex to build, laser harps are potentially hazardous to developers, users, and bystanders. Working with lasers requires protective equipment and extraordinary care. (Laser harps are discussed with combination projects in a later section.)

MP3 Player

Using an Arduino as an MP3 player has some problems. Decoding MP3 format, DAC sound generation, and song memory are the big three. Even if you overcome these issues, the show-off factor isn't there.

This trick has been done before and done well. Anything you do will be compared to existing players, including iPods. And you know how small and slick those are.

Controlling an MP3 player to provide the soundtrack for another project is flashier. Consider the famous "Wizards in Winter" YouTube video. Without the soundtrack, it would just be flashing lights. Your Arduino could control lights and sounds in a similar fashion. Ha! You can't do that with an iPod.

Alarm or Timer Notification

Not only can your Arduino keep track of time, it can do things. Who needs an annoying beep like a truck backing over your pillow? Your Arduino can turn on the heat, open the drapes, turn on the lights, and start the coffee.

Although you could keep track of time on your own, an RTC module provides more intelligence. The RTC module knows the year, month, day, and day of the week. Do you like to sleep in on holidays? No problem. Just tell your Arduino to check your list of holidays before waking you up.

Rather than being just an alarm clock, your Arduino can send you reminders at any time. You can add the ability to tweet or email to an Arduino. These protocols require Ethernet and access to a web server, making this aspect an intermediate-level project. You can find information on adding these protocols on the playground and other places.

REACH OUT AND TOUCH ME

Touch appeals to the kid inside all of us. Check out an infant's "busy box" if you need inspiration. Some have sounds and lights, but the biggest attraction is something to touch. There are buttons to push, knobs to turn, switches to flip, textures to feel, twirly things, things to pull on, and (vanilla?) things to chew on. What to do first?

Most touch in the adult world is used for control, but the appeal is still there. Control is part of the attraction. How the control feels is also important. Some knobs and switches have a soft feel, whereas others require firm contact. Some are "clicky" with definite discrete positions, and others are smooth.

Nearly every project you make will have some aspect of control. Often this control will be provided by something you touch. Because you need it anyway, flaunt it; make it fun.

TOUCH PROJECTS

Projects that are exclusively touch oriented are hard to imagine. Some projects, like converting text to Braille, are very touch focused. Most projects are more focused on using touch for control while still featuring it prominently.

Busy Box or Mystery Box

Build a box with lots of different switches, sliders, and knobs. It's really a way to experiment with using these devices for input, but it can easily become a toy. Make some controls change lights, make noises, or do nothing at all unless used in combination.

Call it a mystery box or black box and let the user figure out what it does. Use simple relationships to entertain children and more complex combinations for adults. If the relationships are obvious, it's not a mystery box; it's a "control box."

This project is attractive for button-pushers and people who can't keep their hands off. A box like this is something that's okay to touch and play with. When finished as a toy, this project gets a second life as a control panel.

Survey Box

Build a box with two buttons. Label one "Do not push this button." and the other "Push this button." and count which one is pushed more. Are there more rebels or conformists? Does providing feedback, like a buzz or ding, change the result?

Touch Screens

In addition to basic knobs and switches, touch control sensors provide a finger-friendly experience. A touch screen on a shield and its accompanying tutorial will have you finger writing in no time.

This project has the wow factor and ability to expand later. Discussions on touch screens and their uses can be found on the playground. There are many types of touch screens, so look for information that matches your model.

Move It Along

Motion projects include the usual range of vehicles. The Arduino accommodates remote-controlled or autonomous operation. Programming remote control operation is faster because the driver provides the intelligence. Autonomous operation requires you to teach your Arduino all it needs to know.

Beyond making motors turn, feedback keeps the motion under control. For the remote-controlled machine, the operator watches while driving. Autonomous vehicles need some other sort of feedback that can be as varied as the terrain.

Not all motion projects involve vehicles. A stroboscope, a solar panel tracking control, a robotic arm, and a speed-controlled fan are all projects involving motion but not travel. Combination projects often include an element of motion, like making curtains open or a POV wheel spin.

Motion Projects

Robots, blimps, airplanes, cars, vacuums, wheelchairs, and the like are motor-driven platforms. Their main purpose is to move through space, perhaps delivering or collecting a payload. All these projects have two basic issues to solve.

The first issue is locomotion and the power supply for it. Motors provide the driving force, and batteries supply the power. You must size both appropriately for the size and weight of the vehicle.

The second issue is navigation and finding a safe path for travel. Radio-controlled navigation relies on the driver to provide the intelligence. Autonomous vehicles require reference points for navigation and rely on marked paths for safety. They need a means to check their location and make adjustments if needed.

With any moving parts, safety is a consideration. The faster and heavier the vehicle, the greater the hazard becomes. Operate your vehicle in clear areas free from people, pets, livestock, and expensive property. Provide a kill switch for autonomous ones.

Robots and Other Vehicles

You can control anything that drives, flies, floats, and swims with an Arduino. All of these vehicles are motor driven in one way or another. Power to drive the motors is typically supplied by a battery.

Power cords hamper freedom but can supply greater power. You can accommodate limited-range motion requiring greater power with a cord. Temporary cord operation makes debugging easier.

Building the vehicle can be half the fun, or you can buy one ready-made. Search for "robot bases" instead of "Arduino robots" for more established robotic supply vendors.

Will your vehicle be radio controlled or autonomous? Autonomous vehicles need sensors to permit them to make decisions. They need to know where they are and where they are going. They need to avoid hazards and not become hazards themselves. Use a remote-control kill circuit to stop your machine if it behaves badly.

Remote control vehicles have a control range limit. Don't let your machine escape into the world uncontrolled. Consider using a kill circuit that safely brings it to a stop if the control signal is lost.

Stroboscopes and Phenakistoscopes

Phenakistoscopes provide primitive animation. A slotted cylinder or disc with a series of pictures on the inside creates animated images when spun. For the cylindrical version, the viewer watches the images inside the cylinder by looking through the slots. For the disc version, the viewer watches the images reflected in a mirror through the slots in the disc. As the cylinder or disc rotates, successive images appear, giving the illusion of motion. If you want to try making your own phenakistoscope, check out www.howcast .com/videos/148840-How-to-Create-a-Phenakistoscope.

You can draw images for your phenakistoscope by hand or copy them from old designs. You can find directions for drawing your own discs and pictures of classical designs on the web. Remember that reflected viewing reverses the image, whereas straight-on viewing does not.

Like their electrical cousins, mechanical stroboscopes provide a way to view repetitive motion as if it were stopped. The motion is viewed through slots in a spinning disc. Classical applications include turntable (record player) speed control, automotive timing adjustment, and water drop viewing.

Stroboscopes and phenakistoscopes provide fun and flashy ways to play with motor speed controls. The scope needs to turn slowly relative to motor speeds. PWM speed control may not be enough. You may also need to use gears or the like to make the scope turn slowly enough.

Solar Panel Tracking Controls

Solar panels provide the most efficient power generation when they're pointed directly at the sun. The sun takes a predictable path across the sky, and your Arduino can track it. You can use this tracking information to improve the efficiency of your solar system.

Tracking improves the efficiency of solar ovens, cell phone chargers, and any small solar-powered system. Start small and work your way up. Minimize control power so that adjustment power doesn't exceed the improved efficiency gain.

Robotic Arm

A robotic arm has to be one of the coolest projects. Picking things up and putting them down was never more fun. As enjoyable as driving a robotic arm is, automating one is even more exciting.

Like a vehicle, building the arm can be part of the challenge, or you can purchase one in kit form. A quick web search turns up dozens of examples.

This project has expansion possibilities. Use the arm to move chess pieces, conduct an orchestra, or build a car.

Speed-Controlled Fan

Like the stroboscope, the fan provides a way to experiment with motor speed control. Once the speed-control part is working, you can add other types of adjustment controls. Use a temperature sensor or humidity sensor to control the fan speed and provide environmental control. Greenhouses require this type of control to keep the plants healthy.

Snack Delivery System

Are you hungry and lazy? Build a snack delivery system that brings your snack to you! The irony here is that being lazy requires you to do the work of building and testing the delivery system.

Zip lines, electric trains, robots, conveyer belts, and soda launches are some of the delivery options. Service requests could come from a button or be sent via remote control, twitter, or Bluetooth.

This project does have the wow factor. Lifetime will vary. It could become addictive or too much bother, depending on reloading convenience and what you like to snack on.

Automated Model Train Controller

For the model railroad aficionado, the Arduino provides a way to automate control of trains, switches, special effects, accessories, and more. DCC (Digital Command Control) is a serial communication protocol that provides a modern automation approach.

In addition to power, DCC messages addressed to individual trains and components are sent over the rails. Each train decodes messages sent to it and adjusts its speed accordingly. Accessories also have individual addresses and can be controlled in the same way. An extension to DCC allows occupancy sensors to provide feedback to the controller.

You can find information on DCC on the web and in model railroading publications. The interface bits and pieces are discussed on the playground and on train enthusiast websites.

Automated Plant Watering System

An automated watering system forms a vital part of greenhouse control. Keeping a water-sensitive plant alive while on vacation demands an automatic control system. Or perhaps you just want to make watering a plant fun.

A plant watering system provides another example of motion without travel. This project does have moving parts—specifically, a pump and solenoid-controlled valves—but it doesn't go anywhere.

The watering system size can range anywhere from a single pot to a whole greenhouse. Individual hoses provide water where needed using solenoid-controlled valves. Pressure to move the water through the hoses comes from a water pump, turned on as needed, or water line pressure. Time or soil moisture sensors determine when it's time to water.

Caution

Water and electricity are a shock hazard. They can cause injury or death when mixed.

Use caution when using water and electrical components together. Water and electricity don't mix in happy ways. Keep yourself and your electronics dry. Don't touch electrical devices with wet hands.

Dancing Fountain

Fountains provide a flashier water delivery system. Create the illusion of water hopping between pools, imitate the Bellagio's fountains, or construct pictures with falling water drops. Whatever your tastes are, there are thousands of fountains to draw inspiration from.

Recirculated fountain water requires filtering and chemical treatment to keep it clean. The filter pump or a separate pump provides pressure to move the water. Solenoid control valves stream it where you want it.

Caution

Use caution when using water and electrical components together.

Water and electricity don't mix, so keep your electronics dry and happy. Keep your workbench and living room dry, too.

BRINGING IT ALL TOGETHER

Most intermediate and advanced Arduino projects require a combination of sights, sounds, motion, and control. Maybe that's a wee exaggeration, but the best projects involve at least a couple of elements together. Sights and sounds, motion and control, motion and sounds, and milk and cookies are all classic combinations. Each combination is better than a single component on its own.

You can enhance any basic project by adding another element to it. An alarm is good, but an alarm that tweets an intruder alert is better. A fountain is good, but a lighted fountain set to music is better.

COMBINATION PROJECTS

Many projects, especially more advanced ones, require a combination of elements. Each element adds to the complexity of building and controlling it. Where possible, divide the project into smaller, more manageable sections. Combine working sections, and adjust them as necessary to complete the project.

Some projects can't be divided into sections. The pieces must work at the same time, or nothing happens. This section contains some project ideas with integral elements that you can't separate.

Laser Writing

Laser writing combines light and motion to project a message onto a wall or other opaque surface. With a laser, enough light must be diffused by the target area for the message to be visible, but not so much as to blind the viewer. (Don't use a mirror or other highly reflective surfaces.)

Caution

Protect your eyes. When working with lasers, always wear protective goggles matching the laser's frequency.

Lasers are potentially hazardous to developers, users, and bystanders. Working with lasers requires protective goggles matching the laser's frequency.

This project is tough to make look good. The motion must be both smooth and accurate. Synchronize the light control with the motion to avoid gaps and unwanted tails. The message must be constantly rewritten or it will fade. Unless the repeat patterns are precise, the message will move around or be annoyingly jittery.

Laser Harp

Laser harps look fun to play and, well, awesome. They have to be the coolest instrument ever! But they may not be what you expect.

A laser harp is a misnomer; it isn't actually a harp. Instead, it uses laser beams and range-finding sensors to generate MIDI codes. These codes are fed to a separate MIDI-controlled sound-generation device. The laser harp by itself makes no noise. The noise you hear comes from a separate device and can sound like anything.

MIDI devices are capable of waveform-shaped, polyphonic sound generation, making them a big step up from PWM signals. MIDI signals contain both pitch and volume information, more satisfying to a musician.

The laser harp is an extremely challenging project that requires a mix of control types and programming to generate MIDI signals. Divide the harp into two big pieces: roughly input and output. The laser part of the harp is the input piece, giving the Arduino pitch and volume. The output piece is the serial stream of MIDI codes destined for your sound box.

Caution

Protect your eyes. When working with lasers, always wear protective goggles matching the laser's frequency.

The users of a laser harp must wear goggles that completely block the laser light. Failure to do so can result in permanent blindness. This also means that the laser harp player can't see the strings while playing it. Not quite what you expected?

Highly reflective surfaces, like mirrors, are also dangerous. Too much light can reflect toward bystanders' eyes. To be safe, bystanders should wear protective goggles, too.

Like the light harp, the laser harp's strings are visible only if some light is diffused and reaches the viewer. Smoke, fog, mist, or dust need to scatter enough light so the strings are visible, but not so much that the harp doesn't work.

Once again, laser harps are potentially hazardous to developers, users, and bystanders. Working with lasers requires protective goggles matching the laser's frequency. Be careful with them!

So if you're never supposed to look at a laser harp, how can you see one in action or play one? Video replay is the quick, cheap, and easy viewing option. A video isn't bright enough to cause eye damage even if the original source is.

Playing the harp requires listening to it. You can't see the strings, but you can hear the effect they have. Clearly, this takes practice. As an aid, you can use marker lights, like LEDs, with a different color (frequency).

Quadcopter Surveillance Drone

The age of the drone is here to stay. Build your own quadcopter (helicopter with four rotors), and get aerial views of your neighborhood. Connect infrared cameras and spy in the dark. Potentially anything light enough can be attached to your copter.

Some drones are flown by Remote Control (RC). Other drones are RC for takeoff and landing and are autonomous once at safe altitude. The navigational capabilities of an autonomous drone depend on its sensor package and its software.

Caution

Propellers are invisible hazards that spin fast enough to remove fingers and other soft body parts.

Debug your drone before attaching the propellers. Operate your drone only in areas free of people, pets, and livestock.

Research the laws governing Unmanned Aerial Vehicle (UAV) operation in your area before starting this project. You are always required to operate your drone in a safe manner. Consult FAA Advisory Circular 91-57 for information on the operation of model aircraft. Local or state regulations may also apply.

Caution

Comply with federal, state, and local laws while flying your drone.

Camera Trap or Security Camera

Who is raiding your bird feeder or candy stash? Build a camera trap and capture an image of your dining guest.

Use your Arduino to monitor motion, heat, or pressure sensors and trigger a camera for a candid photo. Illuminate the scene with infrared or visible light, if needed.

A camera trap also works as a security camera if your "wildlife" is human. For security, you might prefer notification of some kind in addition to the photo.

Greenhouse Controller

A greenhouse is only as good as its operator. Light intensity, temperature, humidity, soil moisture, and CO_2 and O_2 gas levels are all important for maximum plant growth. Each type of plant wants its favorite environment.

Automate this full-time control job with an Arduino. Combine your automated plant watering system and speed-controlled fan with light intensity control for a good start.

Be a Copycat

The Exhibition (http://playground.arduino.cc/projects/arduinoUsers) area of the Arduino playground contains many projects that you can copy. Some of the interesting projects include games, displays, automated devices, robots, environmental controllers, and many others. You'll find that certain projects include schematics and code, while others don't.

You can find additional projects with a quick web search. Before setting out to copy a project, make sure you can locate all the information you need. It's not necessary to copy a project exactly. Modify what you find to suit your own needs.

INDEX